Death of an Overseer

IN
memory
of
D.B. SKINNER,
Born
the 29th of
Jan. 1820.
Died
on the 14th
of May,
1857.
Be ye also ready,
for in such an hour,
as ye think not, the
son of man cometh.

DEATH

of an

OVERSEER

*Reopening a
Murder
Investigation
from the
Plantation South*

Michael Wayne

OXFORD

UNIVERSITY PRESS

2001

OXFORD
UNIVERSITY PRESS

Oxford   New York

Athens   Auckland   Bangkok   Bogotá   Buenos Aires   Calcutta
Cape Town   Chennai   Dar es Salaam   Delhi   Florence   Hong Kong   Istanbul
Karachi   Kuala Lumpur   Madrid   Melbourne   Mexico City   Mumbai
Nairobi   Paris   São Paulo   Shanghai   Singapore   Taipei   Tokyo   Toronto   Warsaw

and associated companies in
Berlin   Ibadan

Copyright © 2001 by Michael Wayne

Published by Oxford University Press, Inc.
198 Madison Avenue, New York, New York 10016

Oxford is a registered trademark of Oxford University Press

Illustrations and maps by Phil Richards.

Library of Congress Cataloging-in-Publication Data
Wayne, Michael.
Death of an overseer: reopening a murder investigation
from the Plantation South.
p. cm.
Includes Index.
ISBN 0-19-514003-6—ISBN 0-19-514004-4 (pbk.)
1. McCallin, John, b. 1812.   2. Murder—Mississippi—Adams
County—History—Case studies. 3. Murder—Mississippi—Adams County—Historiography.
4. Murder—Investigation—Mississippi—Adams County—History—Case studies.   5.
Murder—Investigation—Mississippi—Adams County—Historiography.   6. Adams County
(Miss.)—History.   7. Adams County (Miss.)—Race relations.   I. Title.
HV6534.A33 W38 2000
364.15'23'0976226—dc21   00-032416

1 3 5 7 9 8 6 4 2

Printed in the United States of America
on acid-free paper

*Dedicated
to my students
and to the
memory of
J. H. Hexter*

Contents

On History as Common Sense   3

1   Investigation and Verdict   9

2   The Evidence   39

3   The Evidence Reconsidered   61

4   Slavery   79

5   The Question of a Frame-Up   113

6   Black Images, White Minds   135

7   Democracy and Justice   157

8   In Search of John McCallin   179

An Epitaph for Duncan Skinner   193

APPENDIX I: First Draft and Fragment of a Second Draft of the Letter from Alexander Farrar to Henry Drake   197

APPENDIX II: Court Records from the Trial of Henderson, Reuben, and Anderson   207

APPENDIX III: Additional Materials in the Newspapers Relating to the Trial and Execution of Henderson, Reuben, and Anderson   211

APPENDIX IV: Additional Archival Material   217

Essay on Sources and Suggestions for Further Reading   221

Acknowledgments   243

Note to Readers   247

Index   249

Death of an Overseer

On History as Common Sense

History is the most democratic of subjects taught at a university. I first fully came to appreciate that when I was doing my doctorate at Yale and took a course called "Historiography" from the distinguished historian of early modern England, J. H. Hexter. Jack Hexter was a small—I'm tempted to say gnome-like—man who had a reputation among students as being kind of curmudgeonly. He was one of those professors you either loved or hated. Those students who hated him suspected he took secret delight in their suffering. Those of us who loved him—and I use the term "love" loosely here—thought pretty much the same thing. We just figured his seminars were uncommonly challenging and enlightening and imagined the suffering was good for us.

The title of the course seemed a misnomer to me, since, like most students, I understood historiography to be the study of how historical interpretations have changed over time, while what Hexter offered was an exercise in doing history. He came into the first day of class and dropped about sixty pages of Xeroxed material in front of each of us. You have two weeks to write the history of the event described in these documents, he said. Then he sent us on our way without further direction.

The topic we were assigned to investigate was a disputed election in England during the reign of James I. I suppose the main goal of the three of us taking the seminar was simply to avoid embarrassing ourselves. Not only was Hexter one of the leading scholars in his field, but none of us intended to specialize in either English history or the early modern period. I remember feeling a sense of relief when the assignment was done . . . and a sense of mortification the following week when Hexter returned our essays ripped to shreds. (I'm pretty sure I mean that figuratively, but it was a long time ago.) And then began the real work of the seminar. We spent the rest of the

3

term going over the records document by document, working through the problem of how to piece together the story and significance of the election from these surviving remnants of the past. We talked about how to reconcile apparent inconsistencies between sources, debated how and when speculation might legitimately be used to fill in gaps in the evidence, and examined other materials not specifically related to the election itself, both original sources and works by scholars, to help us unravel what had happened and why. It was like being a raw recruit in a police force doing detective work under the supervision of a grizzled veteran.

As it turned out, the main lesson I took from the seminar was the main lesson Hexter wanted us to take. (I say, "as it turned out," because in my experience, professors and students don't always arrive at the same conclusion from course material.) And that lesson was: interpreting the past is basically an exercise in common sense. Maybe I should put that in quotation marks since for Hexter it was the cardinal rule of doing history: "Interpreting the past is basically an exercise in common sense." In other words, the cardinal rule is that there are no rules. When you pick up a document, there is no handbook of established methods, no set of axioms, that instructs you how to extract its meaning or determine its significance. All you can fall back on is the common sense which presumably everyone has in greater or lesser degree. It is in that respect that I mean history is the most democratic of academic pursuits. Indeed, all of us do history from an early age: as young children drawing on things we've heard from others and our own recollections to piece together a mental image of our last birthday party or a holiday at the beach, as adults listening to the news on the radio, watching TV documentaries and movies, reading newspapers, magazine articles, and books to understand what happened in the Balkans last week, in Vietnam a generation ago, at Gettysburg July 3, 1863.

Of course, what is common sense to you may seem nonsense to me. We all view the past through the lens of our own experiences, our own personal histories. That explains, I suppose, why some people are determined to assert proprietary claims over the lives of those with whom they share race, religion, gender, nationality, sexual orientation, whatever: "Only a black person can teach African history." "Only a Jew can grasp the meaning of the Holocaust." In William Faulkner's *Absalom, Absalom*, Quentin Compson says to his Harvard roommate, Shreve McCannon, "You cant understand it. You would have to be born there," meaning Shreve could never understand the history of the South, because he was a Canadian.

If I get less outraged than some of my colleagues when I hear comments like that, perhaps it's because I'm more mindful of the time when opportunities to teach history at the college level (and here I mean everybody's history) were effectively limited to white males with a proper Christian upbringing. Today few thoughtful people would disagree that there are many windows onto the past. The eminent historian John Hope Franklin, black and raised in Oklahoma, has significantly advanced our knowledge of American race relations through more than a half century of scholarly writings. Gunnar Myrdal, Swedish and white, made a seminal contribution to the same field with the publication in 1944 of his monumental *An American Dilemma*. Indeed, what makes historical understanding possible at all is the ability of men and women of different personal histories to learn from each other. The more perspectives, the more there is to think about, and potentially the more fruitful the dialogue. As William H. McNeill, himself the author of books on a wide range of topics covering a great many societies, has observed, "There is nothing like a radically new angle of vision for bringing out unsuspected dimensions of a subject." The process of historical reinterpretation is never ending. Old questions are constantly being reexamined, new questions are raised. It is history that has the last word, not any individual historian. But over time our knowledge of the past has broadened and deepened. It is scarcely possible to ask for more than that.

⊨ ✠ ⊨

The following pages deal with the death of a plantation overseer in Adams County, Mississippi, a few years before the Civil War. A group of men acting on behalf of the community took on responsibility for investigating how he died. Our task—yours and mine—will be to determine whether they reached the right verdict. It might seem impossibly difficult to reconstruct the circumstances surrounding a death a century and a half ago. After all, no witnesses are around to interview; much of the evidence that once existed has disappeared. However, the passage of time has provided us with certain compensations. We possess a measure of dispassion lacked by men and women at the time. More than that, we have a wealth of knowledge about antebellum southern society, the result of research by several generations of historians. In many respects we understand the people of the Old South better than they understood themselves. We can use that understanding to reach an independent verdict in the case—or a diversity of independent verdicts, since there is no guarantee your interpretation will agree with mine.

But here I'm getting ahead of myself. There are complications. The findings of historians are less definitive, more provisional, than my remarks to this point might suggest. Scholars often agree on facts while disagreeing on their meaning. To be able to make a judgment of your own, you will have to give some consideration to the nature of historical inquiry and weigh competing interpretations of the antebellum southern experience. At times, the following pages will take on the character of a seminar on the history of the Old South. As in any seminar, you should come prepared to challenge the views of your instructor. It will help if you have a taste for irony and a

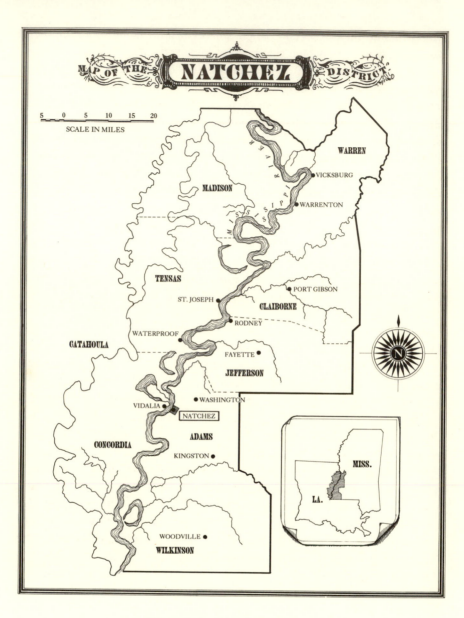

Map of the Natchez District

good (though not overactive) imagination. I take it for granted you have common sense.

One warning, however. In the years before the Civil War the great majority of white Americans held racial beliefs that would be viewed as abhorrent by all but a small proportion of the population today. Those beliefs are an important part of the evidence I want you to consider, and it has been necessary for me to quote at length from contemporary writings. You may well find some of the language used and views expressed deeply disturbing. I am genuinely sorry about that. It is a sad truth that historical understanding often brings pain along with enlightenment.

⚐ 1 ⚐

Investigation and Verdict

It was just after breakfast when the slaves first reported that Duncan Skinner was missing. He had gone off at daybreak to do some hunting and that was the last they had seen of him. So they said, anyway. By late afternoon some of his friends became alarmed and organized a search. A little while later they came upon his horse wandering along the road, riderless, its saddle pulled loose. But it was past midnight when, guided by torchlight, they finally found the body of the overseer. It lay sprawled across the exposed roots of a beech tree, no more than a half-mile from his cabin, in a strip of woods running along the edge of the plantation.

The following morning a coroner's jury convened on the site. Their examination determined that Skinner's neck had been dislocated and he had a wound on his temple. Near his body lay his gun and, a little farther off, his game bag, cap, and whip. His death had been accidental, they concluded, caused by a fall from his horse while hunting. If any of the men thought that foul play might have been involved, they kept it to themselves.

Duncan Skinner was thirty-seven years old when he died on Thursday, May 14, 1857. Born in South Carolina, he had come to Adams County, Mississippi, in the 1840s with his brother Jesse, ten years older, as part of the great westward migration that took place in the United States during the first half of the nineteenth century. A younger brother, Benjamin, had followed them a decade later. At the time of his death, Duncan was employed as an overseer on Cedar Grove, a 900-acre plantation with more than 80 slaves, 13 miles southeast of Natchez along the road to the small village of Kingston.

Overseeing was a demanding job. It involved supervising the work of slaves, monitoring what they did in their spare time, and, in many instances, taking part in the financial operations of the plantation. A man hired to the

9

position had to produce enough cotton to satisfy his employer while keep-ing at least a semblance of harmony and order among the slaves. The high turnover rate for overseers on most plantations proves that this was an al-most impossible task for any length of time. But despite the difficulties he must have faced, Duncan Skinner appears to have been well regarded by Clarissa Sharpe, the fifty-five-year-old widow who owned Cedar Grove. She evidently consulted him not only on business matters but about her per-sonal affairs as well.

It was Jesse Skinner, working as overseer on nearby Smithland planta-tion, who first raised questions about the verdict of accidental death. Sus-pecting that the coroner's jury had done a careless job, he prevailed upon some local planters to reexamine the site where the body had been found. What they discovered lent substance to his concerns. Ordinarily when he went hunting, Duncan Skinner would use a Spanish saddle and hang his game bag on the horn. However, his Spanish saddle remained on the wall of his cabin; it was an English saddle, without a horn, that was found on his horse. Furthermore, the game bag on the ground near the body was an old one, full of holes, not the newer one he normally carried. And there was no sign of the powder flask and shot pouch he undoubtedly would have taken had he planned on doing some hunting. The body itself lay upon the roots of the beech tree in what appeared to be an unnatural suspension above the ground, almost as if it had been placed there. And the wound to the head was on the left temple, while it was the right temple that rested against the tree. Finally, a search of Skinner's cabin revealed that his money was missing.

For several weeks no one involved in the investigation spoke publicly about the case. Then one morning in late June, in unusually cool weather for the early summer, eighteen men, including three who had served on the coroner's jury and Jesse and Benjamin Skinner, descended on Cedar Grove. They were led by Alexander K. Farrar and David P. Williams, planters in their forties who, between them, owned almost 500 slaves. Farrar, the prin-cipal figure involved, was a man of considerable standing in Mississippi, holding at one time or another various public offices, serving in the state legislature and senate, and sitting on the boards of numerous charitable organizations and educational institutions. Although in 1861, as a represen-tative from Adams County to the Mississippi secession convention, he would oppose breaking up the Union, he went along with the decision of the majority and was the first delegate to sign the state secession ordinance.

The investigators rounded up most of the domestic servants and sent the new overseer to get the field hands and bring them to the plantation house. They handcuffed several of the male slaves to trees some distance away to prevent them overhearing what was being said and ordered the rest of the slave force, both men and women, to stand in a line and re-

Alexander Farrar

main silent. Then they took aside Jane, the cook, and told her that they knew a serious crime had taken place on the plantation and she had better tell them all about it. According to Alexander Farrar, she proceeded with no further encouragement to disclose that Henderson, the carriage driver on Cedar Grove, Reuben, a carpenter, and Anderson, one of the field hands, had murdered Skinner and then attempted to cover up the crime by making his death appear accidental. She also reported that, after killing the overseer, the three men stole Skinner's money and divided it up with the other slaves, several of whom decided to hide their share in a trunk belonging to John McCallin. This was the first mention of the Irish-born carpenter and ginwright who would come to be the central focus of the investigation.

After finishing with Jane the investigators turned their attention to Reuben. He corroborated her testimony, presenting in some detail the manner in which he, Henderson, and Anderson had murdered Skinner. As Reuben described it, before daybreak on May 14 the three of them stole into the overseer's cabin while he was still in bed and attacked him in his night clothes with a club. Skinner managed to tear himself free and run into an adjoining room, but they chased after him, wrestled him to the ground, and bludgeoned him into unconsciousness. They then carried him off into a wooded area where, when he gave occasional signs of life, moaning and twitching, Reuben grabbed his head and twisted it violently, snapping his neck. Anderson returned to Skinner's cabin and gathered up his watch, gun, riding whip, one of his game bags, and a change of clothes, and brought them, along with the overseer's horse, to the spot where the body lay. The three slaves dressed Skinner in the clothes that Anderson had retrieved and took the bloodied nightshirt along with the club used in the killing to Jane, who burned them both and then went to Skinner's cabin where she attempted to scrub the bloodstains from the floor.

Henderson now left to attend to his regular duties in the stables and garden and about the house. Meanwhile, Anderson and Reuben lifted Skinner up on the horse and then Anderson rode some distance into the woods until he came to the beech tree where the body was later found. He trampled the exposed roots of the tree and dumped the corpse on top of them. Then he loosened the saddle and released the horse. After firing off one barrel from the gun, Reuben dropped the weapon a short distance from the body and placed the whip, game bag, and Skinner's cap nearby, trying to make it appear as if something had frightened the horse, which had then reared, throwing the overseer to the ground. Returning to his cabin, they helped themselves to his money, then went back to where they had left the body and put the key to Skinner's trunk in his pocket. Finally, they returned to the slave quarters and got the drivers to hurry the field hands out to work, hoping to create the impression that everything was normal on the plantation.

Following their questioning of Reuben, the investigators went to examine the overseer's cabin. There, on the floor in the corner of the room where, according to Reuben, he, Anderson, and Henderson had clubbed Skinner unconscious, they found what looked like bloodstains. Then they interrogated several more slaves, all of whom corroborated the testimony of Jane and Reuben. Anderson had fled from Cedar Grove after the murder. However, Henderson was inside the plantation house and they had him brought out to the yard and tied up for questioning. He denied being involved in any killing, but the men in the investigating party concluded that his "conversation and looks . . . clearly indicated his guilt." After finding scars on his neck—received, Reuben said, in the struggle with Skinner—they unanimously concluded that the three slaves had murdered their overseer and, furthermore, that every slave on the plantation knew something about it. At this point, seemingly all that remained to be learned was what had happened to the money that Anderson and Reuben had taken from the overseer's cabin.

The search for the missing money began with Jane. She and her husband, Burrell, led the men to their hen house, where they dug up a tin box containing $18, their share of the stolen cash. Reuben confessed he had kept a $20 gold piece for himself but claimed that he had given it to Dorcas, a house servant, to hide for him. The investigators then tracked down Dorcas in the plantation house and demanded that she turn over all the money she had received from the other slaves. She led them to a room over the infirmary and recovered a $20 gold piece, which she admitted Reuben had given to her. However, she denied knowing of any other money.

With a good deal of gold and silver still unaccounted for, the investigators decided to question Henderson once again. When he continued to protest his innocence, they turned their attention to his brother Lem. According to at least some slaves, Lem had originally been part of the conspiracy. He had supposedly gone along with the others on the morning of the murder but had lost his nerve at the door of Skinner's cabin and run away. Lem, too, however, professed ignorance of any crime. Exasperated and impatient to find the missing money, the investigators got permission from Clarissa Sharpe to whip the brothers. They divided into two companies, one to deal with Lem, the other with Henderson. According to Alexander Farrar, once Henderson was beaten he quickly made a full confession, his testimony filling in some minor details of the crime. The reason there had been no shot pouch or powder flask found near the body was because Anderson had inadvertently left them behind when he retrieved Skinner's clothes. Henderson himself had removed the pouch and flask later and thrown them into a small horse pond on the plantation. As for his portion of the money, he had given it to Dorcas to put in John McCallin's trunk. This led the investigators back to Dorcas, who admitted having received gold from

Henderson but said she had concealed it in the loft above the ironing room. Taking them there—the ironing room was in an L-shaped building next to the main residence—she produced one $5 and four $10 pieces, the exact quantity and value of coins Henderson said he had left with her.

By now it was late afternoon. In the course of their investigations the men had learned that Anderson was hiding out on Magnolia, a neighboring plantation. He was said to be waiting for Reuben and supposedly knew a place where the two of them would be safe. The investigating party placed Reuben, Henderson, and Lem, as well as a few other slaves on Cedar Grove, under guard. Then, while some members went home, the rest went after Anderson. He was captured without difficulty and when interrogated apparently told a story that confirmed what they had already learned.

⊭✢⊭

The following day the investigators returned to Cedar Grove. They wielded the lash more freely now, to punish the men and women involved in concealing the crime and to learn more about the stolen money. Under the whip, several slaves admitted to receiving gold or silver. They all swore that they had turned it over to Dorcas for safekeeping, however, and that she had concealed it among John McCallin's belongings. Concluding that Dorcas had lied earlier, the investigators ordered her to take them to McCallin's trunk. Inside, they found several pairs of women's slippers, other articles that Dorcas claimed were her own, a daguerreotype of McCallin, some of his clothing, and three purses with gold and silver amounting to more than $60.

Although a portion of the money still lay unrecovered, the investigators now turned their attention to what was for them a far more troubling issue. Why had Dorcas used McCallin's trunk as a hiding place? Dorcas herself refused to tell them, but under the lash some of the field hands offered an explanation, implausible as it may at first have sounded: Dorcas had been McCallin's mistress for fifteen years or more. McCallin was pressing his attention on her owner, hoping to marry his way into a fortune. However, Clarissa Sharpe went by everything Duncan Skinner said, and Skinner disliked and distrusted McCallin. McCallin told Dorcas that, if the slaves did away with their overseer, he was confident Clarissa Sharpe would accept his proposal. Then he'd acquire title to the plantation and ensure that all the slaves had comfortable lives. According to Alexander Farrar, the field hands also revealed that shortly after the murder McCallin appeared at the plantation, warned the slaves that there was going to be an investigation, and advised them not to admit to anything.

The investigating party now called for Henderson again, this time to question him about McCallin. Henderson corroborated what the field hands had said and recounted the following story: On McCallin's last visit to Cedar

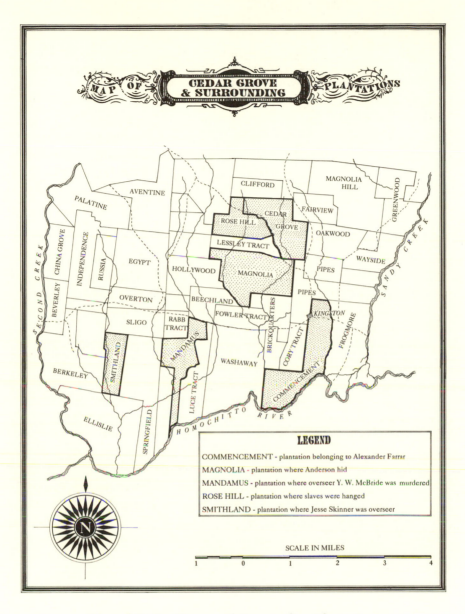

Map of Cedar Grove and Surrounding Plantations

Legend:

LEGEND

COMMENCEMENT - plantation belonging to Alexander Farrar

MAGNOLIA - plantation where Anderson hid

MANDAMUS - plantation where overseer Y. W. McBride was murdered

ROSE HILL - plantation where slaves were hanged

SMITHLAND - plantation where Jesse Skinner was overseer

SCALE IN MILES

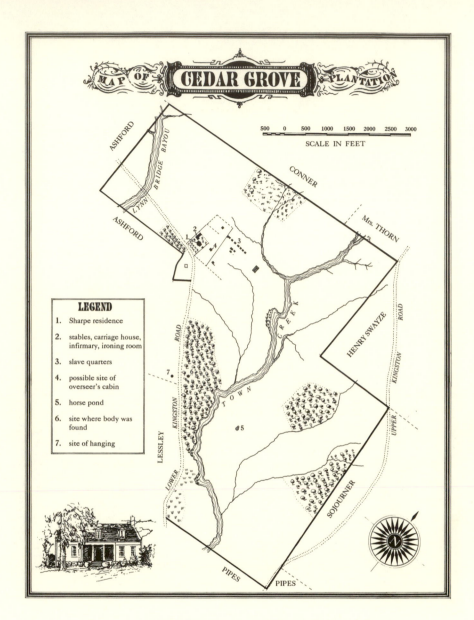

LEGEND

1. Sharpe residence
2. stables, carriage house, infirmary, ironing room
3. slave quarters
4. possible site of overseer's cabin
5. horse pond
6. site where body was found
7. site of hanging

SCALE IN FEET

500 0 500 1000 1500 2000 2500 3000

Map of Cedar Grove Plantation

Grove before the murder, he—Henderson—went to the carpenter's room one evening to collect his boots for cleaning. McCallin was standing by a window looking out into the quarter where Skinner was whipping some slaves. "Hen', there is quite a fuss in the quarter tonight," McCallin said. Henderson agreed, but added, "it is no uncommon thing here." McCallin then suggested, "Well if I was you boys, I would get rid of that man. I would put him out of the way." The following morning, when Henderson returned with the boots, McCallin asked him how long the whippings had continued the previous night. Henderson replied that he didn't know, that scenes like that were so common he didn't pay much attention to them any more. "You boys are a cowardly, chicken hearted set," McCallin shot back, "or you would not stand that man's whipping and beating you so—you would put him out of the way. If you were to do so, then I could marry the widow, and there would be no overseer, and you would all have better times."

Henderson told the investigators that it was after these exchanges with McCallin that he came up with the idea of killing Skinner. He also confirmed the testimony of the field hands that McCallin returned to Cedar Grove after the murder to put the slaves on their guard. The plough driver provided further evidence on this point, claiming that McCallin said to him, "I don't know whether you boys killed Mr. Skinner or not, but if you did you had better keep your mouths shut."

Several days after completing their investigation at Cedar Grove, a few of the whites met at Mandamus, a nearby plantation belonging to William B. Foules. On June 7, a few weeks after the body of Duncan Skinner was found and when the official verdict in the case was still death by accident, some of the Foules slaves had killed their own overseer, a Louisiana native named Y. W. McBride. The men responsible claimed they had been encouraged by the seeming success of Henderson, Reuben, and Anderson in concealing their crime. Later that week the investigators went to Magnolia, the plantation where Anderson had been hiding at the time of his capture. Once again, as during the original investigation at Cedar Grove, they formed the slaves in a line and prohibited them from speaking to each other. Then they took them off one at a time for questioning. The Magnolia slaves confessed to having helped Anderson and related that he had said he didn't care if he was found out, "he had no peace of mind since Skinner was killed." They also admitted having heard about the murder from Henderson and reported he had left a pistol with them and had confided in them about McCallin's part in the crime. According to what Henderson told them, McCallin had advised Dorcas not to feel hurt if he married her owner and to act as if there had never been anything between them. He would be able to do more for her if he became the owner of the plantation, he assured her, than he could in his present circumstances. Alexander Farrar was of the opinion that Dorcas was in fact quite pleased by the idea of the proposed match. Some slaves claimed that she would point to McCallin while he was out walking with Clarissa Sharpe and say, "you see that man yonder, he will be your <u>master</u> yet."

A few days later the investigating party interrogated Henderson for the fourth time. By now he, Reuben, and Anderson were in the county jail in Natchez. He admitted giving the gun to the slaves on Magnolia. And was it true, the whites asked, what the Magnolia slaves said about McCallin and Dorcas? He paused for a moment, then broke into a laugh. "Oh! I'll tell you," he replied, and then described their relationship in exactly the terms the Magnolia slaves had used.

⊶✞⊷

By the time the eighteen men involved in the investigation had completed their work, they were satisfied that they had a clear picture of how Duncan Skinner had come to his death: The three slaves, Henderson, Reuben, and Anderson, had murdered him, surprising him in his sleep, beating him with a club, and breaking his neck. Although Anderson and Reuben had then stolen his money, theft was not the motive for the crime. The slaves were in effect agents for the white carpenter, John McCallin, acting in the expectation that later he would reward them with "better times." For his part, McCallin assumed that, once Skinner had been removed, he would be free to marry Clarissa Sharpe and acquire title to Cedar Grove.

The investigators left Henderson, Reuben, and Anderson with the sheriff, to be dealt with by the legal system. But bringing John McCallin to justice was more complicated. According to the laws of Mississippi, as well as the laws of other southern states, testimony by blacks against whites was inadmissible in court. Since the case against McCallin was based entirely on evidence provided by slaves, there were no grounds for indicting him. As a result, the investigators decided to take matters into their own hands. And so they published the following notice in local newspapers in late July:

> WE, THE UNDERSIGNED, having examined the negroes on Mrs. Clarissa Sharp's plantation, in reference to the murder of Mr. Duncan B. Skinner, find, upon examination, that he was without the least shadow of doubt murdered; and from the confessions of the negroes, made separately and apart from each other, without their having any possible chance of knowing what each had confessed, that the conduct of MR. JOHN McCALLIN has been such, that we hereby warn him not again to make his appearance among us; and we, the undersigned do hereby pledge ourselves to enforce the warning herein given:

To give added weight to their warning, they appended a declaration of support signed by seventeen of the most prominent men in the community:

We, the undersigned, believe the foregoing statement, and hereby pledge ourselves to co operate in any course that the foregoing signers may deem necessary.

These initial efforts at intimidation proved unsuccessful, however. A week after the notice was first printed, McCallin issued a defiant response in the same newspapers:

> I HAVE A LATELY SEEN A NOTICE in the Natchez Courier, signed by A. K. Farrar, David P. Williams, and numerous others, the tendency of which is to charge me, upon the statements of negroes, with being implicated in the murder of my *friend* Mr. Duncan B. Skinner, and which also threatens me with personal violence. The charge so contained is utterly false, and as I believe maliciously prompted by the negroes, as in due time will be made to appear. As to the threats against me, although I also may be murdered, I shall entirely disregard them.

To working-class acquaintances in Natchez, McCallin charged that Alexander Farrar was trying to frame him. Farrar, he suggested darkly, had swindled Clarissa Sharpe out of some land. Both he and Skinner knew what had happened and so Farrar arranged to get rid of both of them.

John McCallin was forty-five years old in 1857. A native of County Derry in northern Ireland, he had immigrated to the United States in 1831, an early participant in the massive transplanting of Irish Catholics to America that took place in the decades before the Civil War. He first went to Albany, then moved on to Philadelphia, apparently with the intention of settling there. However, sometime in 1836 or 1837 he decided to head south to Natchez, probably because he heard the town was experiencing a building boom. Not long after his arrival he filed an application for naturalization and in 1840 became an American citizen.

One of the attractions of Natchez for him was undoubtedly its cosmopolitan character. During the 1850s the population of the town was over 6,000, with about one-third of its residents foreign born. Of the roughly 2,000 immigrants, perhaps 700 came from Ireland and there was an active Hibernian Society. Some years earlier a British visitor had reported favorably on the Irish men in the community, most of whom were common laborers, describing them as "good fathers, good husbands, good children, and good friends." But popular opinion was less favorable, better captured in a joke that ran in a local newspaper: "An Irishman coming from the Fourth of July considerably bewildered, and seeing the houses and everything else going round in a queer manner, concluded that the easiest way to get home was 'to stand still till his own door passed him, and then make a dive for it.'"

John McCallin first came to work at Cedar Grove in 1838, almost certainly under contract to a Natchez builder who had been hired by Clarissa

Artist's Conception of John McCallin Based on a
Photograph of His Grandson

Sharpe's husband, Absalom, to construct a new residence on the plantation. He apparently acquired a good reputation as a carpenter and ginwright
and over the next few years found other opportunities for employment in
the neighborhood. However, sometime after Absalom Sharpe died in early
1851, he decided to move to Tensas Parish, Louisiana, settling in Waterproof, a town on the Mississippi River fifteen miles or so above Natchez.
He managed to accumulate enough money to buy a modest home and a
part interest in a small store. But he continued to drop in at Cedar Grove

from time to time, generally staying for only a week or two but remaining for much of the summer of 1853 to escape a yellow fever epidemic—"yellow jack," they called it—that took 750 lives in Natchez. Although he was taciturn and would usually keep a low profile, those who were familiar with him commented on his attention to Clarissa Sharpe and how he had begun to dress more fashionably in an attempt to impress her. Rumor was he had bragged to acquaintances back in Louisiana that he was going to marry a rich widow in Mississippi. There was also talk he had complained that the local planters looked down on him because of his modest station in life and wanted to prevent him from marrying into their exclusive social circle.

In response to the printing of the two notices in the newspapers, a public meeting was called for Saturday, August 8, in the town of Kingston, about a mile down the road from Cedar Grove. Kingston traced its origins back to the years just before the American Revolution when a handful of New Jersey Congregationalists, including Alexander Farrar's grandfather, Caleb King, for whom the town was named (or, more accurate, renamed, since it was originally called "Jersey Town"), secured a grant of 25,000 acres from the British government. The town was held by the Spanish from 1779 until the United States took over at the end of the century, becoming for a time a thriving trading center. Its distance from the Mississippi River and the poor quality of roads in Adams County, however, hindered commercial development, and after a tornado in 1840 left most stores in ruins, prospective merchants turned their attention elsewhere. By 1857 the town was scarcely more than a convenient gathering place for planters and farmers from the vicinity.

It was a typical summer day for southern Mississippi, brutally hot, with heavy clouds, when the meeting convened under the chairmanship of Dempsey P. Jackson. Jackson, 61 years old and a cousin of the ill-starred Civil War general George Pickett, was a very wealthy planter and a former state legislator. Though crippled in his right arm and left hand by an accident in childhood, he had led a hard-driving life, almost as if to prove to himself that, in this society that put a premium on acts of physical courage by white males, he was no less a man for his infirmity. Coarse in manner, he drank too much and at times could be unbending. "Stern and inflexible as a Covenanter in the earnestness of his convictions" was the way a local historian put it. But he was also plain-speaking and his honesty was unquestioned.

What, if anything, John McCallin expected from the meeting is unclear. He may well not even have been there. Jackson opened the proceedings by mentioning his long acquaintance with the carpenter and stating that, so far as he knew, McCallin had always "sustained a good character." He also urged those in attendance to consider the evidence in a calm and thought-

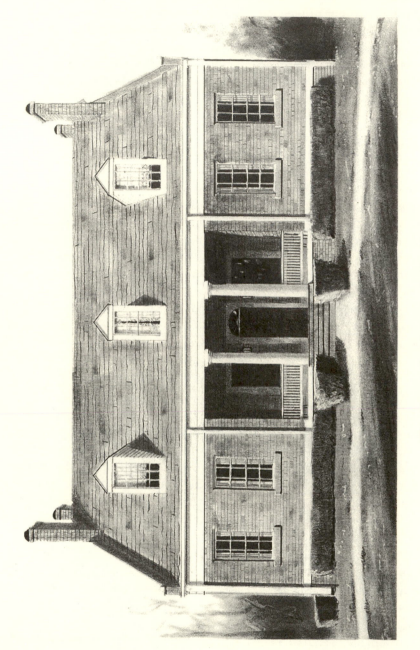

The Sharpe Residence at Cedar Grove

ful manner. No record exists of who spoke or what they said, but when the discussion was over and Jackson asked if there was anyone who doubted that McCallin was guilty, no one responded. He then appointed a committee to draft a series of resolutions expressing the views of those present. The five men selected produced the following document:

WHEREAS, Many prominent, well known citizens of this county, upon full investigation, published a card, warning the public against one John McCallin, and notifying him not to make his appearance again among them, because of his complicity in the murder of the late Duncan B. Skinner; and, whereas, the said McCallin has since made a publication, reflecting upon the motives and conduct of the authors of the first mentioned card: now, we citizens of the county of Adams, in public meeting assembled, having investigated the facts upon which the original card was based, and entirely approving the course pursued by our fellow citizens, do, therefore, *resolve,*

1st. That the thanks of this community are due to Messrs. Farrar and Williams, and the other gentlemen who aided them, for their efforts and success in the discovery of the murderers of Mr. Duncan B. Skinner, and of the tampering of said McCallin with the slaves upon the Sharp Plantation, and his suggestions to said slaves, which, if not the prime cause of said murder, were instrumental in producing it.

2nd. From the evidence before us, we are satisfied that said McCallin, in his card, has falsely styled himself the friend of Mr. Skinner. That on the contrary, Skinner distrusted him—and said McCallin, though cognizant of the murder, and knowing those who perpetrated it, concealed the facts from the public, and advised the murderers of the efforts making to discover them.

3rd. That the intimation of said McCallin, that the negroes were prompted to accuse him, is wholly false; and that the slaves, on the Sharp and Smith estates, under circumstances which precluded any concert between them, when examined separately, and apart, without suggestion or prompting, established a clear, consistent and convincing case of guilt against said McCallin; and that there is no reasonable ground to doubt that said McCallin did suggest to the slaves, upon the former estate, the possibility, and propriety of their "putting Skinner out of the way," to use McCallin's own language, or more plainly, advised them to murder their overseer, and that this crime led to the subsequent murder of McBride, on a neighboring place, and the general restless state of the slaves in that vicinity.

4th. That said McCallin's presence in a slave community, is alike detrimental to the slave, and dangerous to the master.

5th. That we esteem it the duty of all good citizens to aid in ridding the country of such characters.

6th. That the warning heretofore given to said McCallin, is now here repeated, let the consequences be what they may.

Two weeks later, perhaps influenced by the recent events, Clarissa Sharpe made out a will for the first time. Born in Tennessee, the oldest of twelve children, Clara, as she was known to those close to her, had found tragedy among the comforts of Mississippi plantation life. She had given birth to three children, all boys, all of whom had died at an early age. Thomas Morgan, born in 1821, had survived barely two and a half years. Edward, born in 1830, and Levy, in 1832, had lived only five months. Their graves lay in the family cemetery just a short walk from the plantation house. Her father, Joseph Thomas, was buried there, too, as was her husband, Absalom, the two men who had plotted the course of her life. Some women were able to develop an independent cast of mind in this patriarchal society, but there is no evidence to suggest that Clarissa Sharpe was one of them. After Absalom died, she depended heavily on Alexander Farrar for management of her finances and left Duncan Skinner largely free to run Cedar Grove as he chose. Writing a will may well have represented one of the rare occasions on which she found the resolve to take responsibility for her own affairs. In it she made no mention of John McCallin or anyone else involved in the recent events. She left separate allotments of several thousand dollars each to a sister, a niece, and two friends. Cedar Grove was to be operated by a panel of trustees for twenty-one years after her death. She directed that money earned from the plantation be used to fund a school for indigent girls in Natchez. The trustees were enjoined from selling any slaves during that time and instructed that, in any sales that took place afterward, family groups be kept together.

⊯✠⊮

The town of Waterproof, Louisiana, was first settled around 1830. According to an apocryphal story, it got its name during one of the frequent floodings along that stretch of the Mississippi, when a steamboat captain came upon a resident stranded on a strip of land and said, "Well, Abner, I see you are waterproof." It was Waterproof where McCallin lived at the time of the murder and Waterproof where he fled after the decision was handed down against him in Kingston. He must have convinced at least someone of influence that there was reason to believe he was being framed because, at a public forum late in August, a committee of three slaveholders—Henry W. Drake, Zenas Preston, and Robert Bowman—was appointed to look into his allegations and make a report.

On August 27 Drake sent Alexander Farrar the following letter:

> The citizens of this place & vicinity this day held in meeting, to take into consideration certain cards published by yourself & others relative to John McAllain. The only action taken by the meeting was to appoint a committee of three to investigate the charge against McAllain & report

Clarissa Sharpe

to a subsequent meeting. As one of that committee I am directed to address you, requesting you to forward to us a statement of the grounds upon which you have acted in this matter—in short a full history of the case.

It has been reported here, that Mrs. Sharp's negroes were examined under the lash, & that they were prompted to accuse McAllain. It has also been reported, that the meeting, at which Mr. Jackson presided, was a meeting of the American party, for the purpose of making nominations, & that after that business was attended they took up McA.'s case, as a kindred subject. McAllain's friends are trying to make the impression, that the whole thing is a mere <u>political</u> persecution. Please inform us explicitly on these points.

Excuse me for troubling you. I would not have done so, except under a sense of duty.

Farrar took great pains with his reply, working his way through several drafts. He devoted most of his attention to describing the particulars of the investigation, reporting how the slaves had been interrogated and what they had said. But he also answered the charges that Drake had alluded to in his letter, responded to some other allegations that apparently were making the rounds, and presented what he saw as the major pieces of evidence in the case against McCallin.

He denied that the slaves were beaten to coerce them into implicating the carpenter. It was Jane the cook who first mentioned McCallin's name, Farrar pointed out, and she did so without any prompting from the whites and without ever feeling the whip. In fact, stated Farrar, many of the men in the investigating party had never heard of McCallin before they came to Cedar Grove to interrogate the slaves, and those who knew him never would have imagined that he had played a role in the killing.

As for the claim that the accusations against McCallin were part of a political vendetta, that was based on a misrepresentation. The hearing at Kingston was not, as McCallin, a Democrat, alleged, a meeting of the American Party to make nominations, but a forum open to the public and held for the single and express purpose of taking up the two notices printed in the newspapers. There were many Democrats in attendance, more than usually voted at the Kingston precinct, a stronghold of American Party support. Among them was Alex Boyd, a brother-in-law of Clarissa Sharpe and one of the oldest and most esteemed citizens in the community. Boyd had been satisfied from the beginning that McCallin was guilty but had refused to endorse the declaration of support for the investigating party that appeared in the papers because "he was an old man and did not want to pledge himself to any course that might lead to violence." At the meeting at Kingston, however, he made his feelings public and joined with forty or so other men in signing a document approving the resolutions brought forward.

Farrar also challenged McCallin's claim that he and Skinner were close friends. According to the slaves, Skinner had threatened to whip them if they ever talked to McCallin. Clarissa Sharpe told the investigators that whenever McCallin visited Cedar Grove he would stay mostly around the house and yard and avoid the overseer.

Then there was the evidence implicating McCallin in the murder. The main point, said Farrar, was the close agreement in the testimony of the slaves. "[W]e cannot conceive how nearly all the leading negroes on a plantation when arraigned and taken off from each other so they could not hear the statements of each other could tell a story agreeing so precisely with each other and a portion of it, be true, and the rest false." He also made much of McCallin's movements following the murder. Evidently McCallin arrived at Cedar Grove within a day or two of discovery of the body and stayed for more than a week. He then left for Waterproof, only to reappear without explanation the next day. According to the plough driver and Henderson, he came back because he had learned in Natchez it was suspected Skinner had been murdered and he wanted to warn the slaves.

McCallin was a quiet individual, Farrar observed, a man few people in the community seemed to know very well. It was widely believed that since his arrival in the area he had kept Dorcas as his mistress. Dorcas was "a smart, sensible woman," Farrar added, who doubtless believed that McCallin would be able to take better care of her if he married Clarissa Sharpe.

He concluded the letter by taking up the accusation that was obviously most painful for him: that he himself was responsible for the murder or, if not for the murder, for the effort to place blame on McCallin. There were evidently two allegations making the rounds. The first was that Skinner and McCallin had together foiled an attempt by Farrar to swindle Clarissa Sharpe out of some land and, in revenge, Farrar had ordered Henderson, Reuben, and Anderson to do away with both men, getting messages to them through one of his own slaves who regularly traveled between Farrar's plantation, Commencement, and Cedar Grove. The second was that Farrar was trying to frame McCallin for the murder because McCallin knew that he had cheated Clarissa Sharpe out of some property. It was obviously with heart-felt indignation that Farrar commented: "I have lived to but very little purpose, in this life if in the community in which I am known, it is even rendered necessary for me to deny such vile and infamous charges."

The meeting at Waterproof took place on Saturday, September 19, a rainy day, under the chairmanship of Ham McCullough, a 40-year-old planter. The committee of Drake, Bowman, and Preston presented the evidence they had gathered, most of which probably came from the pen of Alexander Farrar. Whatever McCallin said in response, he failed to persuade those in attendance of his innocence. It seems that he accused Farrar of deliberately attempting to frame him, and that at least Bowman and likely other members of the committee responded angrily. The one charge the meeting did credit was that he had been prevented by threats against his life from obtaining certain evidence, not specified in the records, that he believed would exonerate him. And in response he was given a bodyguard and a guarantee of personal safety. But he was also told that at the moment there was no reason to believe the investigating party had been mistaken and warned that if he was not able to come up with any new evidence in the next two weeks, "the citizens of Tensas parish . . . will regard it as conclusive against his innocence, and regard him as he is regarded by the citizens of Adams county, as dangerous and unworthy to remain in any community, and advise him to leave forthwith."

On Thursday, October 1, Alexander Farrar appeared at Cedar Grove with William B. Foules of Mandamus Plantation and a planter named Alfred Swayze to take testimony from Clarissa Sharpe. The three men asked her specifically about McCallin's movements in the days following the murder. She informed them that he had appeared at Cedar Grove not long after the discovery of the body and stayed for eight to ten days. When he left to return to his home in Waterproof, she asked him to check at the jails in Natchez and across the river in Vidalia, Louisiana, for Anderson, who had run away. She added that she was surprised when he reappeared at the plantation the following day, that he never told her why he came back, and that she could only assume it was because he wanted to warn the slaves, as Henderson and the plough driver had testified. The deadline the committee in Waterproof had set for McCallin was almost up when the three men arrived to interview Clarissa Sharpe. What use, if any, they made of her statement is not reported in the historical record. Indeed, no evidence exists that any further public consideration was given to McCallin's role in the murder.

⌖

The town of Natchez lies on the Mississippi River, 200 winding miles above New Orleans. In the early days of the nineteenth century it was best known for the saloons, brothels, and gambling dens that crowded the landing where the flatboats docked. A haven for outlaws and fugitive slaves, the landing—Natchez-under-the-hill it was called, since it sat beneath a 175-foot-high bluff—carried a reputation as "the most abandoned sink of iniquity in the whole Western country." A visitor in 1808 described it this way:

> [I]t is well known to be the resort of dissipation. Here is the bold-faced strumpet, full of blasphemies, who looks upon the virtuous part of her sex with contempt and hatred; every house is a grocery, containing gambling, music, and dancing, fornicators, &c. This is the stopping place for all boatmen from Kentucky, Tennessee, &c.; yes, I have in that place seen 150 boats, loaded with produce, bound to New Orleans, delaying their time, and spending days in the lowest orders of dissipation.

By about 1830, however, warehouses had begun to replace brothels, and order, if not orderliness, had come to the community. The lower Mississippi Valley had emerged as the richest cotton-producing region in the United States, and Natchez, next to New Orleans, was its most important trading center. Indeed, the stretch of counties and parishes extending above and below the town—counties on the east bank of the Mississippi, parishes on the west, the Louisiana, bank—was known as "the Natchez district."

On the top of the bluff, buildings went up rapidly, filling in streets laid out in a grid pattern back toward a ravine, spanned by bridges, that effectively marked the eastern boundary of the town. Much of the land in the immediate vicinity of Natchez had been exhausted by intensive cultivation, giving something of a desolate appearance to the surrounding countryside. And in 1840 a catastrophic tornado—the same tornado that devastated Kingston—claimed more than 300 lives in the town, caused an estimated $5 million in property damage, and laid waste to Natchez-under-the-hill. But the depth of the alluvial soil across the river in Louisiana ensured the continued profitability of planting in the region, and though a nationwide depression beginning in 1837 and lasting for six years made recovery difficult, by the 1850s Natchez was booming.

Signs of prosperity were everywhere: in paved streets and sidewalks, in gas lighting, in the appearance of small manufacturing enterprises, but above all in the proliferation of general and specialty stores, many of them run by European immigrants. Some of these shops were intended to provide for the needs of the townspeople, but others catered to wealthy planting families, with their increasingly discriminating tastes. "Just received 50,000 of the best Havana Segars," ran an advertisement by the Italian merchant John Botto: "Cervantes, El Congresso, Meridiana, San Roman, Valor de la Rama, Sultana, Louisa Miller, Odelina, Washington, Clay, Calhoun, Webster, Flor de Peyadas and many more too numerous to mention." He offered liquor as well: "Heidsick, Champagne, Porte, Madeira, and Claret Wine." And, for women, "ice cream saloons," where he promised to "keep on hand at all times Ice Cream, Sherbets, etc. which he guarantees to be the best. He assures those ladies who patronize him that they shall have a private and quiet entertainment."

Prosperity was also reflected in the town's rapidly growing cultural life. By the 1830s stage companies from New York and New Orleans were making regular appearances at the local theater. Edwin Forrest played Hamlet there in 1829 and in 1851 Jenny Lind, "the Swedish nightingale," gave a recital at the Methodist church. Touring art exhibits also stopped in Natchez, including a selection of works by the celebrated painter Benjamin West. For those with less refined tastes, there were engagements by the Rockwell circus, trained animal acts, and quarterhorse races down by the landing. Tom Thumb, the famous 25-inch dwarf, made three visits to the town before the Civil War.

Still, for all its economic development and improved social climate, Natchez remained a frontier town in many respects. The journalist Frederick Olmsted, who after the war went on to become America's most acclaimed landscape architect, reported in the 1850s that pigs roamed freely around the public gardens at the top of the bluff. Visitors to the square across from the courthouse now and then had to step over dead horses or dogs, and whenever flooding threatened at the landing, cattle were set loose to run up through the narrow streets of the town. Furthermore, despite persistent efforts to clean up Natchez-under-the-hill, prostitution still flourished and gambling was so popular that the authorities made little attempt to suppress it. Or to control the brawling that was common among all classes of whites. On October 5, 1857, for instance, an unruly group consisting of four white men and two slaves—one of the whites was James Jackson, son of Dempsey Jackson, who had chaired the meeting at Kingston—went on a drunken spree through town, hurling bricks at a hotel and clothing store, assaulting a carpenter, and firing off a pistol. The event was unusual only in that it united rioters across racial lines.

As Natchez developed, so did evidence of disparities in wealth among its white inhabitants. During the first half of the nineteenth century, quite a few large slaveholders from the nearby Louisiana and Mississippi countryside took up residence in the town, erecting imposing mansions in Federal and Greek Revival style. The homes of the growing number of merchants, professionals, and skilled craftsmen were much more modest as a rule, although often made of brick and neatly furnished. As for ordinary laborers, they rented rooms in boarding houses or cheap hotels or made do with small wooden cottages. Except in the alleyways under-the-hill, however, where the only dwellings to be seen were dilapidated shacks, the pattern of residence was not segregated along class lines. Rich, middling, and poor lived close to each other, often shared the same block. If they encountered one another as neighbors, however, it was rarely as friends and never as equals. The large slaveholders—the planting elite—saw laborers and common tradesmen as ignorant rabble—"the vulgar herd," to borrow a term sometimes heard. Meanwhile, except, perhaps, for the small number of established professionals and the handful of merchants who had legitimate aspirations to become large slaveholders themselves, the planters were "aristocrats" in a society where that term was generally used in a pejorative sense. For all the assumed airs and resentments, however, whites of all ranks remained united in one critical regard. They all believed in slavery for blacks.

The great majority of slaves in the district lived on plantations. However, more than 2,000 could be found in Natchez, representing about one-third of the town's population. Many were domestic servants in the mansions of the planters or the homes of successful merchants and professionals. Others served as common laborers or drayers or worked down at the docks or in one of the small factories around town. A few may have been owned by the municipality itself and employed in public works. It was a fairly common practice in town, although far less so on the plantations, for a slaveholder to hire out a slave, the length of time ranging anywhere from a day up to a year or more. Some slaves were even allowed to "hire-their-own-time," making arrangements for employment themselves and turning over a share of their earnings to their owners. And although technically it was against the law, an increasingly large number were also allowed to "live out," renting rooms in cheap boarding houses or, to save the money, bedding down in abandoned warehouses or in alleyways or in some brothel under-the-hill, where they joked, fought, drank, gambled, and slept with the poorest of the town's whites.

There were free blacks in Natchez as well, more than 200 of them. Most lived a meager existence as woodchoppers, fishermen, prostitutes, or un-skilled laborers, doing work often assigned to slaves and living, as slaves lived, in the neglected corners of the town. "Slaves without masters" is the term applied to them by one historian. But a small minority managed to find work as craftsmen and a handful even accumulated substantial wealth. The best known of this privileged elite was William Johnson, who was murdered by a white neighbor in a property dispute in 1851. A barber by trade, his home was furnished with handsome carpets and furniture, his liquor cabinet con-tained a wide selection of imported whiskeys and wines, he subscribed to the *New Yorker* and the *Saturday Evening Post*, he owned the collected works of Shakespeare, and he socialized, if never on equal terms, with many of the most respected planters in the town. He also owned fifteen slaves. His life represented one of the many contradictions in the community where the fate of the slaves charged with murdering Duncan Skinner was now, in November, 1857, to be decided.

❧✞❧

The Adams County courthouse stood on the public square two short blocks from the bluff. Made of brick and topped by a cupola, it faced lawyers' offices on three sides. Across the street and to the south, was the county jail, a stately building designed to resemble a gentleman's residence. Henderson, Reuben, and Anderson were confined in the jail when they were first taken into custody in June. And they were still there during the second week of November when the grand jury, after taking testimony from Jane, Dorcas, and two members of the investigating committee, brought down an indict-ment against them for the murder of Duncan Skinner.

The trial was held in the courthouse on Tuesday, November 17. The temperature had dipped to the freezing point the night before, and the day was cool though sunny. Among those in attendance was Giles Hillyer, the 38-year-old editor of the Natchez *Courier*, one of the most highly regarded small newspapers in the old Southwest. Hillyer had served a term in the state legislature as a representative of the American Party, but had lost to the popular Democratic "fire-eater" John Quitman in a bid to gain a seat in Congress. During his ten years or so as editor of the *Courier*, he had turned the newspaper into a profitable enterprise. The official organ of

The Adams County Courthouse

the American Party in Adams County, it had a circulation of approximately 1,300 and catered to local planters as well as the large merchants, bankers, and professional men of the town. But in his desire to increase his small slaveholding, Hillyer's financial reach routinely exceeded his grasp and he was constantly under pressure from creditors, including Alexander Farrar, who had advanced him almost $4,000. "Everything he has [is] encumbered by mortgage & Deed of Trust, beyond its value," complained the local representative of the R. G. Dun & Co. Agency, forerunner of Dun & Bradstreet.

It was rare for the *Courier* or its rival paper, the *Mississippi Free Trader*, to devote more than a paragraph or two to local stories. But the sensationalism of the case had obvious popular appeal, and although Hillyer denied being influenced by the prospect of increased sales—a motivating factor for editors in "large cities," he scoffed, but hardly Natchez—he elected to give the trial front-page coverage. Copies of the paper quickly sold out and two days later he used the public's fascination with the murder as an excuse to run the story again.

In his commentary on the proceedings, Hillyer played upon the sectional passions of the time. The case, he stated, proved above all the justice of slavery and the southern social order. "It would have been a goodly sight," he wrote, "could abolition Massachusetts or Rhode Island have seen with a collective eye, the proceedings of yesterday and the day before; with what scrupulous exactitude the rights of the prisoners—the same in these respects as those of the white race—were observed by the prosecution, were exacted by the defence, and were maintained by the Court. The same arraignment, the same venire, the same challenges, the same employment of counsel, the same rules of evidence, the same enlistment of eloquence and talent, the same charges from the bench, the same solemnities of the verdict, that would have marked the trial of the free white man on a similar charge, were all here exhibited."

The jury constituted a fairly representative cross-section of middle-class Natchez. It was dominated by merchants and craftsmen in their thirties and forties and included six men of foreign birth, among them John Botto of the "ice cream saloons" for ladies. The judge, Stanhope Posey, was a planter, 43 years old, whose considerable wealth included about sixty slaves on his estate in Wilkinson County, to the south of Natchez. Officially the prosecution was in the hands of the district attorney, Henry S. Van Eaton, 30, a former schoolteacher and, more recently, mayor of the town of Woodville. However, he turned over responsibility for the case to 34-year-old William T. Martin. Martin, who would rise to the rank of general in the Confederate army, had come to Natchez from his native Kentucky in 1842, finding work as a tutor in the household of John P. Walworth, a merchant and planter with vast slaveholdings in Mississippi, Louisiana, and Arkansas. He also received instruction from Walworth in the law, later entering into practice on his own and quickly gaining a reputation as the most able attorney in the community. Professional success had translated into social standing, allowing him to marry the daughter of a wealthy planter. In the opinion of the representative of the R. G. Dun & Co. Agency, writing in 1856, he had "the best prospects before him of any in the City." He is, the agent added, "an excellent man standing high as to integrity & honor."

By law a slave charged with a criminal offense was entitled to legal representation, with all costs to be paid by his or her owner. For whatever reason, Clarissa Sharpe chose not to provide counsel for Henderson, Reuben, and Anderson, and so the court stepped in, selecting Joseph D. Shields and Douglas Walworth. Shields, the leader of the team, partner in the successful firm of Carson & Shields, was a diminutive man of enormous energy, 37 years old, who had received a law degree at the University of Virginia. His father, William Bayard Shields, had been a member of the first Supreme Court of

Mississippi. Walworth, only 24 at the time of the trial, was son of the planter who had originally given William T. Martin his start. Educated at Harvard and Princeton, he had received training in the law at Jackson, the state capital, and then from Martin himself, before opening up an office of his own.

The trial lasted through the day and into the night. The chief witness for the prosecution was Alexander Farrar, who described in some detail the evidence uncovered by the investigating party. Martin also called eight slaves from Cedar Grove as witnesses, including Jane, her husband Burrell, Dorcas, and Lem. It appears that they repeated the statements they had given to the investigators, placing blame for the murder on Henderson, Reuben, and Anderson. Two slaves from Magnolia provided additional evidence, confiding that Anderson had admitted to feelings of remorse and that Henderson had told them of being plagued by nightmares.

Shields and Walworth, who received $300 for their services, adopted two separate but related tactics in mounting the case for the defense. On the one hand they attempted to discredit the testimony collected by the investigating party, arguing that it had been secured through bribery and coercion. On the other, they presented what they claimed were plausible alternative explanations for Skinner's death. It was quite possible, they suggested, that the black witnesses who gave evidence against Henderson, Reuben, and Anderson had committed the murder themselves and were lying to conceal their own guilt. Or, more likely, Skinner had died as a result of a heart attack or a fall from his horse. But here Martin had evidently anticipated them. He called members of the coroner's jury, most if not all of whom now repudiated their original finding of accidental death. Conspicuous by its absence from the trial is any reference to John McCallin. The grand jury did not cite him in the indictment, he was not called as a witness, there is no suggestion that Farrar or any of the slaves referred to him in their testimony, and Shields and Walworth did not mention him.

In his closing statement, Martin made a point of thanking the members of the investigating party for their role in solving the crime. He then, in the words of the *Courier*, "marked out the path of duty which that Court and Jury had to perform in justice to outraged laws and to the social institutions under which we live":

> Slaves had plotted an assassination; they had united rebellion to murder; had lifted their hand not against a comrade, but against their lawful commander. It was a social treason, as well as a horrid killing. They had placed themselves beyond the reach of human forgiveness, and had to suffer themselves the penalty of death, as wretches unfit for life, and as a warning spectacle to others of their class.

The members of the jury obviously agreed. It took them less than five minutes to deliver a verdict of guilty.

Four days later, on Saturday, November 21, Henderson, Reuben, and Anderson appeared before Judge Posey for sentencing. The *Courier* summarized his remarks to them in the following way:

> The prisoners had had a fair and impartial trial. The Court had employed able counsel for them, who gave them every opportunity to free themselves of the charge. But there had been no possibility of an acquittal. They were clearly guilty, having taken human life with premeditation and malice. There had been no excuse, no palliation in the circumstances attending the commission of the crime. It was proved beyond all question to have been a cold-blooded, deliberate and ferocious murder. There was no possibility of a pardon. No human mercy could be now shown them. Their death was inevitable; and their only business in this life, was to look to God for mercy in the next.

Posey then ordered that they be hanged, setting Friday, December 11, as the date for the execution.

Following the sentencing, a panel of five slaveholders appeared before the court. They had been selected by the sheriff, Oren Metcalfe, to determine the value of the convicted slaves. According to the law of Mississippi, a slaveowner was entitled to half the replacement cost of any laborer executed by the state. The men charged with making the appraisal placed a figure of $2,000 on Reuben, $1,500 on Henderson, and $1,400 on Anderson. For the loss of property she was to suffer, Clarissa Sharpe would receive the sum of $2,450.

᪥ ✝ ᪥

Responsibility for seeing that the execution was carried out was in the hands of the Adams County Board of Police, an elected body whose various responsibilities, ranging from tax assessment to overseeing road repairs, made it the most powerful branch of government at the local level. Among the members of the board at the time of the sentencing was William B. Foules, a friend of Alexander Farrar whose son had been one of the men involved in the original interrogation of the slaves. It was Foules' overseer, Y. W. McBride, who had been murdered a few weeks after the killing of Duncan Skinner. Farrar wrote a letter to Foules on December 6 to offer his advice on the impending hangings:

> Dear Sir: I intended to ride down to see you to day but have not had time. I have now to start down to Woodville. I wanted to talk with you about the hanging of the negroes. I think all that is necessary, is to show the negroes that there is no doubt about the hanging, in order to do away with any impression that may prevail among them that the "white folks send them off and don't hang them & c & c." If the negroes are brought out in public to be hung and they get up and talk out that they are prepared to die—that they have got religion, and are ready to go

home to heaven & c & c—it will have a bad effect upon the other negroes, hence I think to prevent unfavorable impressions that the best plan would be to hang them all privately and have them brought out in the country and buried by the negroes upon the spot where the murders were committed. If they could be hung publickly and not allowed to talk any, it would make no difference, but I am satisfied that impressions would be made of a bad tendency by their being allowed to talk. I have no particular wish about the matter, only that the negroes in our country may not be impressed with the belief that hanging is not such a dreadful thing, inasmuch as they see those who are about to be hung, undergo hanging calmly, and with evidence of their preparation of going home to heaven & c & c.

Despite Farrar's recommendation, the board ruled on December 7 that the interests of the community would be most effectively served if the execution took place in public. They selected as the site for the hanging a corner of Rose Hill plantation just across the Natchez-Kingston road from where Reuben and Anderson had dumped Skinner's body. According to the *Mississippi Free Trader*, that spot was determined to be "the most proper, where the slaves on all the neighboring plantations can witness the certain vengeance of the law."

The following day, Tuesday, December 8, three days before the execution, Reverend Joseph Stratton made his way to the jail. There had been heavy showers all morning and it would rain again that night. Stratton was minister of the First Presbyterian Church of Natchez, one of the richest and most elite congregations in the lower Mississippi Valley. Forty-one years old, he had been born into a wealthy New Jersey family and educated at Princeton, first in law and then, after he was admitted to the bar, in theology. He came to Natchez in 1843 as pastor of the First Presbyterian and immediately settled into a comfortable relationship with the large slaveowners, several years later marrying into a planting family and acquiring a few slaves of his own. In 1845 Stratton began preaching on the Sabbath to the slaves owned by members of his congregation, a practice he continued up to the Civil War. On this particular day in 1857 he presumably came to the jail at the request of someone connected to the case, Clarissa Sharpe perhaps, since she was a Presbyterian. He talked with Henderson, Reuben, and Anderson, and prayed with them, although what solace they may have taken from his words went unrecorded.

᭜✧᭜

It was cold and clear in Adams County on the morning of Friday, December 11, and there was frost on the ground. The sheriff, Oren Metcalfe, 46, member of a prominent slaveholding family, along with his deputy, Richard Samuel, 56, a farmer, took Reuben, Henderson, and Anderson from their jail cells and drove them the thirteen miles from Natchez to the site just off the Kingston road selected for their hanging. They arrived only minutes before the execution was scheduled to take place. About 250 people were on hand, slaves brought from neighboring plantations and interested whites, Giles Hillyer and Alexander Farrar among them. Also in attendance was the Adams County Light Guard, a volunteer marching unit of 30 men with muskets.

Metcalfe and the three slaves climbed the steps to the gallows. He asked them if they wanted to speak to the crowd, but they declined. Then he placed a noose around the neck of each slave and stepped aside. At the appointed moment he gave the signal, and the trap door swung open. And so, reported the *Courier*, "the curtain dropped on the awful drama of social treason and of murder."

◄ 2 ►

The Evidence

I first came across the murder of Duncan Skinner—stumbled across it, would be more accurate—more than twenty years ago. It was on a trip south to collect evidence for my doctoral dissertation, a study of how life changed on the plantations of the Natchez district after the Civil War. While searching through the papers of Alexander Farrar in the archives at Louisiana State University, I found a draft of the letter he wrote to Henry Drake in response to the questions raised at the hearing in Waterproof. Not that I understood what it was at the time or even gave it much notice; it was just one of hundreds of documents I photocopied back then, trying to gather as much information as I could before my grant money ran out and I had to head back north. As I discovered later, however, this particular letter was hardly typical of the mundane material I usually find myself reading. With its elements of class privilege, social striving, interracial sex, and violent death, it brought to mind a novel by William Faulkner or perhaps one of those overblown movies about the Old South that appear on TV from time to time.

As it happened, I never found a use for the letter in my dissertation. But when I began teaching, I realized it offered an entertaining way of introducing undergraduates to the problems historians typically face in interpreting evidence. I would give the document to students and ask them to tell me who they thought killed Duncan Skinner and why. Usually they would repeat the explanation offered by Alexander Farrar: The slaves Reuben, Henderson, and Anderson committed the murder on orders from the white carpenter John McCallin. I would then draw their attention to inconsistencies in Farrar's evidence and raise questions, suggested by his own testimony, about his impartiality.

After having the students speculate for a while about how Farrar's evident bias may have affected his interpretation of events, I would ask where they thought we might find additional evidence. Typically one or two students would suggest we locate Duncan Skinner's diary or perhaps letters from John McCallin to Clarissa Sharpe—sources that may never have existed, or, if they did exist, are unlikely to have survived. But eventually someone would propose that we look at local newspapers. And that, I would point out, was a good idea. Many newspapers from the nineteenth century have been preserved and, furthermore, quite a few have been copied onto microfilm. That was as far as I would let the discussion go, however. I wanted the students to learn something about the fragmentary nature of the historical record and the need to be analytical when reading documents, but I wasn't especially interested in getting them wrapped up in the details of any particular incident, even something as intriguing as a lurid murder. Besides, experience suggested that there was unlikely to be much more evidence on the crime in local papers; the southern press rarely devoted more than a paragraph or two to the killing of an overseer.

But one semester I decided to have the student who suggested we look at newspapers order whatever was available through interlibrary loan. Several weeks passed and, frankly, I had pretty much forgotten about the assignment when he showed up in my office one afternoon, very excited, and reported that microfilm copies of the two Natchez papers of the day, the *Courier* and the *Mississippi Free Trader*, had arrived, and they contained several articles on the case, including, in the *Courier*, a lengthy account of the trial of Henderson, Reuben, and Anderson. Now, that was hardly what I had expected. But the windfall turned out to be even greater than the student realized. Because, as I discovered when I examined the microfilm myself, buried away in the public announcement sections of the two papers were a notice from the men who investigated the crime warning John McCallin to leave the community; a reply from McCallin insisting that he was innocent; and reports of two meetings, one in Mississippi, a second in Louisiana, to consider the evidence against him.

By now I was very curious to see if I could figure out what had actually happened. I mean, doing history is really just solving mysteries of one sort or another, and this was a particularly fascinating one. So I decided to take a trip back south to see if I could track down more evidence. In Natchez I learned to my disappointment that the records of the circuit court had been abandoned years before to gather dust and mold in some dank corner of the courthouse basement and were unavailable for use, might well never be available for use. (Abandonment is not an uncommon fate for county records, but the consequences for recovery of the past can be tragic.) However, a tour of archives and libraries did lead me to some additional evidence, most of it located, ironically, in the same place where I found the original document, the papers of Alexander Farrar at Louisiana State University. I also collected a great deal of information on the individuals involved in the case as well as on the local community, and in 1990, drawing on the material I had uncovered, I began writing this book. At the time, I imagined my research was done.

Life should be so uncomplicated. In 1992 the Historic Natchez Foundation began the process of recovering and preserving the Circuit Court records. Documents from the trial were now available. That was the good news. The bad news was, I only learned about the good news as I was putting the finishing touches on what I thought would be my concluding chapter. You will understand when I say that my joy was something less than unbounded. Before long, however, the excitement of having access to more information overtook my disappointment at the prospect of additional research and writing, and in the end the further investment of time proved well worthwhile. My understanding of the murder is not dramatically different as a result of the evidence I found in the court records, but the reconstruction of events in the previous chapter is richer in detail.

Which brings us now to our central task: determining whether or not the investigation carried out in 1857 produced the right verdict. For that, however, you will need the surviving documents. You have already read the notice in the papers from the investigating committee; the response published by John McCallin; the resolutions passed by the meeting in Kingston; and the letter Henry Drake sent to Alexander Farrar requesting information for the hearing in Waterproof. To that must now be added the reply Farrar wrote to Drake; three articles printed in the *Courier*; the indictment handed down by the grand jury against Henderson, Reuben, and Anderson; and an affidavit signed by Farrar and two other planters. Read the documents with a critical eye. As you go through them, ask yourself the question I ask my students: "Who killed Duncan Skinner and why?"

⊷✧⊶

Let's take the evidence in chronological order, beginning with an article in the *Courier* on May 16:

> PROBABLE MURDER. Mr. Duncan Skinner, residing near Kingston, was killed on Thursday last. He left his home early in the morning to hunt turkeys. Towards night his horse and dogs returned, but without their owner. Search was made, and Mr. Skinner's body found in the woods. Several shot had entered various parts of his body, widely separated; his neck was broken and other injuries sustained.
>
> It is probable he was fired upon, and his horse taking fright, he was then thrown, the fall producing the injuries that killed him.

After the publication of this story there was no further mention of the crime in the press for more than a month. Then, on June 25, the *Courier* ran the following article under the heading "Arrest of Murderers":

Some few weeks since, the death of Mr. Duncan Skinner of this county was mentioned. He was overseer on the plantation of Mrs. Sharpe, about 14 miles south-east of Natchez. His body was found on May 14th, in the woods, about a quarter of a mile from the quarters, his neck being broken, and portions of his body greatly bruised. The first supposition was that he had been thrown from his horse and killed. A day or two since several of the neighbors, whose suspicions had been powerfully excited on the subject, collected, and determined to make a thorough examination into the matter. The result of the investigation was the discovery that Mr. Skinner had been brutally murdered by three or four of the slaves on the place.

The evidence collected, together with the corroborating circumstances, show that this was one of the most coolly planned and deliberate murders, ever accomplished. The negroes in the plot went to Mr. Skinner's house just before day, and aroused him on pretence of a child in the family being sick. He opened the door, while in his night clothes, and was knocked down by a blow on his breast from a heavy stick. Three stalwart negroes seized him, and after a severe struggle succeeded in choking him. While thus insensible, they carried him some few rods from the house, and there by main strength dislocated his neck. They then got out his clothes, dressed him, and to turn away suspicion, put his watch around his neck, and his purse with part of his money in his pocket; brought out his horse, saddled it; put the lifeless body on it, and led it to the woods, where the body was afterwards found. Here, after running the horse up and down, they took off the body, turned the saddle, and set the animal loose. The latter returned home a few hours after. The body of their victim, they placed in such a position, as would indicate the possibility of accidental death; they brought out his gun, cap, whip and game-bag; discharged one barrel, and placed the several articles in the tracks as if of a runaway horse.

So long a period had passed that the guilty assassins imagined the crime was unnoticed and would be forgotten. But a terrible and speedy retribution awaits them. The whole chain of evidence is complete as to the crime, its manner and circumstances. The three negroes were safely secured, and are now in jail in this city.

The letter Alexander Farrar wrote to Henry Drake exists in a first draft, dated September 4; an undated fragment of a second draft; and a third draft—the draft I photocopied as a graduate student—dated September 5. Although there are some noteworthy discrepancies between the three versions, by and large the letters are similar and for convenience I have chosen to place the first two drafts in an appendix. Here, then, is the third draft. In reproducing it I have indicated where revisions were made that I believe might be relevant for interpreting the case. Deleted passages have lines marked through them; passages that Farrar added in editing are enclosed in square brackets:

Dear Sir: Yours of the 27th August, relating to John McAllin, and requesting a full history of his case, came to hand by the last mail, and I now proceed to reply: The overseer of Mrs. Sharp, Duncan B. Skinner was found dead in the woods. A coroners inquest was held, and a verdict from the jury, that he came to his death by a fall from his horse. His brother Jesse Skinner was not satisfied with the verdict, and called upon the neighbors to assist him in an investigation. Caution was observed to prevent the design from becoming public. Mrs. Sharp was not apprised of the intention until the morning of the investigation. Her overseer went to the field, brought all the negroes to the house, and placed them upon a line before the company assembled. He permitted no conversation among them, nor was there any permitted during the investigation. Several of the men were handcuffed and tied to trees, sufficiently far apart to prevent the hearing of conversation. The cook of Mr. Skinner was taken aside and told that something badly had happened upon the place, that it could not happen without her knowing it, and that she had better tell all about it. She then disclosed the murder, those who participated in it, and the manner in which it was done.— [how they took a portion of Skinners money out of his trunk, and divided out among them—where her portion was hid, and that some of them had hid theirs in McAllins trunk. And how when her Misstress sent over word to Skinner that morning by Dorcas, she sent word back that Mr. Skinner had taken a cup of coffee before day light,—and, given out his breakfast—and said that he would be back to it—that he was going out to kill some squirrels.] But one of the murderers (Reuben) was then in custody, Anderson being runaway, and Henderson the carriage driver at Mrs. Sharp house. After getting through with Jane the Cook, we went to Reuben, making a similar statement to him, as was made to Jane, and he disclosed the whole transaction, agreeing precisely with Jane's statement. He told how they went into the house a little before day light, struck Skinner while in his bed with a club, how he jumped out of the bed on the opposite side to them, and ran into an adjoining room,—how they pursued him, got him down and killed him in the corner of the room,—then carried him off in his night clothes into the woods, and because of his occasionally manifesting symptoms of life, he took him by the head, and twisted it around, thereby breaking his neck,—how they laid him down, and Anderson returned to the house to get his clothes, watch, gun, riding whip and horse, how they dressed him, and took the bloody shirt to Jane, and she burned it and the club, and how she tried to wash the blood from the floor,— how Henderson left them and went to the stable to feed his horses, so as to be in time to attend to his duties in the garden and about the house and yard.—how Anderson got on the horse, and Reuben helped him up with Skinner, and he rode around through the woods, and around a beech tree, jumping the horse about the tree, skinning the roots, and throwing the body down upon them,—turning the horse loose, with the saddle turned upon his side,—how he fired off one barrel of his gun, and placed it within a few paces of the body, also his whip, and cap, arranging every thing so as to bear the appearance of the horse having been frightened and throwing his rider,—how they took his key to the house and unlocked his trunk and divided out a portion of his money, and then took the key back into the woods where he lay and put it in his pocket. [And how the plough driver, and the hoe driver, hurried the hands out of the quarter earlier than usual that morning & c & c & c—] We then went into the house and found the blood stains upon the floor, where they told us the murder was committed. We then examined a number of the other negroes, their confessions all agreed, and corroborated with each other, as well as the statements of Jane and Reuben. Henderson was sent for, and tied off from the others. At first he denied knowing any thing that had been done on the place that was wrong. His conversation and looks however clearly indicated his guilt. Reuben had previously told us that in the struggle Skinner had caught Henderson by the throat, and that the mark or print of his finger nails were still to be seen. We examined and the scars were plainly imprinted upon his throat. Several of those who composed the coroners jury were present, and they as well as the whole crowd assembled, expressed themselves as being fully satisfied that Reuben Henderson and Anderson had murdered Skinner, and that nearly every negro on the plantation knew something about it. Jane and her husband took us to their hen house, and dug up a tin box containing something over 18 dollars in gold and silver, which they said was Skinner's money. Reuben said that he had a 20 dollar gold piece belonging to Skinner and that he had given it to Dorcas to take care of. Dorcas being a house servant we went over to the house, and demanded her to give up the money Reuben had given her to keep. She took us up stairs, over the hospital, and got a 20 dollar gold piece, saying that it was the money Reuben gave her, and that she knew of no other money. Henderson still denied knowing of any thing wrong, or that he had any money belonging to any one. His brother Lem [who also at first, denied knowing any thing] was implicated by the negroes, as knowing all about the murder, and that he went to help,—got as far as the door,—his heart failed—and he fled. After some consultation, we concluded that both Henderson and Lem ought to be whipped for lying, consequently we formed a committee who waited upon Mrs. Sharp and obtained her consent. Up to this period, the lash had not been used. We formed two companies and took them out of the hearing of each other. Henderson received but a few stripes before he made a full confession, agreeing precisely with what the others had stated. He also told of his throwing the powder and shot flask of Skinner in the horse pond, and took us to the place, and after some searching we found them both. Upon being asked where his portion of the money was, he said that it was in Mr. McAllins trunk, that he had given it to Dorcas to put there and she said that she had done so. We then concluded to go over to the house and see Dorcas. While we were in the gallery talking to Mrs. Sharp, Dorcas walked up, and hearing us speak of Henderson that his money was in McAllins trunk, she spoke out and said, Henderson's money aint in Mr. McAllins trunk, its up stairs over the ironing room. We went with her and she produced four ten, and one five dollar gold pieces, such as Henderson told us of. By this time it was growing late in the day. We had found out from the negroes that Anderson was harbored by the negroes on the Magnolia plantation, the Estate of Stephen C. Smith, in the gin,—that he was there waiting for Reuben to go off with him,—that he had said, that he had, a good place, to go to. So we concluded to place the principal, and leading men, in confinement, with a guard over them, to prevent communication, until morning, which was done. Some went home, while others went in pursuit of Anderson, and were fortunate enough to capture him in the gin to which we had been directed. He immediately told the same story that the others had. Next morning we met again and concluded that in as much as there was a number of the negroes on the plantation who had participated in the murder, and could not be punished by law, that we would put them under the lash, and in the mean time we would find out more about the money, as there was much yet that could not be accounted for, we having a clue to the amount that had been taken. Companies formed of four or five to a negro, and took them out of the hearing of each other, and began whipping them. It was soon discovered that some two or three more spoke of money being in McAllins trunk, put there by Dorcas. She was sent for but denied putting any money in the trunk and at first of having the key. We took her to the house to her Misstress, who showed us up stairs, in her house and pointed out the trunk to us. We then ordered Dorcas to get the key and unlock it. She stepped to an armour, and pulled a small box from underneath which Mrs. Sharp says was Dorcas box, and took from it a key, and unlocked the trunk in the presence of her Misstress, and the crowd. In the trunk were several pair of womens slippers, and other articles which Dorcas claimed as being hers. There was also a lot of men's clothing which Mrs. Sharp and Dorcas stated were McAllins. His daguereotype was also in the trunk, and three purses with gold and silver in them amounting to something over 60 dollars. [In taking out the clothing Dorcas very adroitly undertook to conceal one of the purses by taking it up with a shirt.] We made a memorandum of the description of the purses, and also of their contents, signed our names to it and placed with the purses for safe keeping. [Mrs. Sharp not only informed us that this was McAllins trunk but has since informed us, that she immediately sent it from her house to Natches, to the care of P.H. McGraw, with instructions to deliver, to McAllin.] We then returned to the quarter to pursue our investigations for money, and like wise to scourge the negroes for committing and secreting the murder. We asked what made them think of hiding their money in McAllins trunk and why they called his name, which led to the following disclosure, to wit: Dorcas was, and had been the "<u>Sweet heart</u>" of McAllin, for some 15 years or more. That she told them, (the negroes), that McAllin said, he was trying to marry their Misstress, and that for some time past he had not been making such good headway, and it was on account of Skinner. That ~~if he was out of the way~~ it seemed like Mrs. Sharp had more confidence in Skinner than any body else, that she went by every thing he said, and the only chance he (McAllin) had, was for the negroes to put Skinner out of the way,—That if they would do that, he (McAllin) could then marry their Misstress, and then there should be no overseer, and they (the negroes) should have better times. Also that when McAllin returned to the place after Skinners death (which he did and remained 8 or 10 days) that Dorcas came out to them, and said, that McAllin said, that "now you have done got Skinner out of the way, and the white folks have been there and ~~could not~~ can't find it out, all you have got to do ~~was~~ is to keep your mouths shut." Also that he didn't know much about McBride, that he had seen him a few times, and knew his face, that he was a through going man, (meaning thorough we supposed) and take him up one side, and down the other, he was a full match for Skinner, and had got what he deserved. McBride was an overseer from near St. Joseph, who was murdered in the neighborhood a short time after Skinner, by Mr. Foules's negroes for whom he was overseeing. Henderson the carriage driver states that he went up stairs one night to get McAllin's boots to black, that McAllin, was standing by a window looking out towards the quarter listening to a noise there, occasioned by Skinner whipping some negroes,—that he said, Hen' there is quite a fuss in the quarter to night, and that he (Hen') replied yes, but it is no uncommon thing here. To which McAllin replied, Well if I was you boys, I would get rid of that man. How, asked Henderson? Why: I would put him out of the way. After some further talk Henderson went down stairs with the boots, and in the morning when he returned with them, McAllin rose up in his bed, and said, Hen' how long did that fuss last last night in the quarter? I don't know sir—it is such a common thing here, I didn't pay much attention to it. Well! says McAllin, You boys are a cowardly, chicken hearted set, or you would not stand that man's whipping and beating you so—you would put him out of the way. If you were to do so, then I could marry the widow, and there would be no overseer, and you would all have better times. [The Negroes on being asked if they understood what McCallin meant by putting out of the way, replied, why, killing him of course—] He further states that this conversation was held the last time McAllin was at the place before the death of Skinner. That he (Henderson) went out among the negroes and they formed the plan to kill Skinner. He further states that when McAllin returned after Skinners death, that Dorcas bore all the messages, which were as above stated. That after McAllin staid 8 or 10 days at his Misstress's he left to go up the river to where he lived, and on the next day returned,—that he McAllin came out to where he was engaged at the carriage house, cleaning his harness and rubbing the brasses and, said, Hen' do you know what Jesse Skinner is riding about here so much for. I don't know sir, says Hen. Well I can tell you, he is trying to find out who killed his brother, and if you boys dont mind and keep your mouths shut he will find out, for there is a great deal of talk that he was murdered. I have been up to Natches and hear a great deal said there about his being murdered. It is even in the newspaper that he was murdered. And I have come all the way back to put you boys on your guard. [The plough driver states that McCallin then came over to the horsepen where they were feeding and said to him I don't know whether you boys killed Mr. Skinner or not, but if you did you had better keep your mouths shut.] Now Jesse Skinner had been riding about the neighborhood, and staid all night at Mrs. Sharps a short time before then and also the night before McAllin left, and came back. There was a good deal of talk in Natches [as well as in the neighborhood] that Skinner was murdered. And it had been published in the Natches Courier that, Skinner was supposed to have been murdered. Mrs. Sharp says, that McAllin left her house for Waterproof, that she requested him, while on his way up, to examine the jails at Natches and Vidalia, and if Anderson the runaway was in either jail, for him to write her a letter and leave with Mrs. Holden in Natches, who as there was much passing would send it out to her,—that she did not know that McAllin was going to come back—that he never told her what he came back for,—and she did not know what he did come back for, unless, it was for what ~~Henderson said~~ [the negroes said]. McBride was an entire stranger in our community, no one knew him here before he came to oversee for Mr. Foules, and after that, he was not known off of the place by but few. McAllin <u>did know him</u>. And we think that he must have had some conversation with Dorcas concerning him. A few days after the investigation at Mrs. Sharps, a number of us met at Mr. Foules's. He had got the Sheriff to send his three men, who murdered McBride, out to his house, in order that they might produce something that would corroborate their confessions. They made full confessions, produced the watch, hat, shoes, clubs & & c. From their statements we learned that they knew that the Sharp negroes had murdered their overseer, and as the "white folks" couldn't find it out, they were induced to make a similar experiment.—A few days after this, we met at the Magnolia plantation, the Estate of Stephen C. Smith. The negroes had no knowledge of our coming. They were drawn up and put upon a line, and no conversation permitted among them. They were also examined seperate and apart from each other, and confessed to having harbored Anderson—how he had told them all about the murder of Skinner, and how he said he didn't care much if it was found out, that he had no peace of mind since Skinner was killed,—he "<u>harryragged him so</u>". [Anderson had previously made the same statement to us.] Reuben in his confession stated, that he, had made up his mind, that if the "white folks," ever got after him about the murder, that he intended to tell all about it, as he had no peace of mind, since it was done, and had not had any good sleep since. They confessed to having ~~visited Mrs. Sharps negores, and having~~ seen Henderson also, and that he had told them all about the murder. In short they confirmed every thing that Mrs. Sharps negroes had said about McAllins wanting to marry their Misstress, and his wanting the negroes to put Skinner out of the way—They told of _____ [brief missing passage] Mrs. Sharps negroes had told us. They said that Henderson told them, that Dorcas told him, that McAllin said to her, that when he married her Misstress, she (Dorcas), must not take it, too much to heart, and let it frustrate her feelings, and make her make a fuss,—but that she must behave herself, and act as if there never had been any thing between them,—that when he married her Misstress, he could do a great deal more for her (Dorcas), than he now could. A few days after this, some us went to the jail, to see Henderson, to know of him concerning a Pistol which one of the Magnolia negroes had given us, and said came from Henderson. He gave us a full account of the pistol agreeing with what we had already learned. We then asked him what it was, that he had told the Magnolia negroes, that Dorcas told him, that McAllin said she must do when he (McAllin) married her Misstress. He paused a moment, and then broke into a laugh, and said Oh! I'll tell you, and then repeated precisely what we had heard from the negroes at Magnolia. From what we could gather among the negroes, Dorcas was evidently well pleased at the idea of McAllins marrying her Misstress. She is a smart, sensible woman, and doubtless ~~was impressed with~~ entertained similar views with McAllin as related to his ability to do more for her, when he married her Misstress, than he could in his present condition. She would point to McAllin and Mrs. Sharp when they would be walking out to gether, and say, you see that man yonder, he will be your <u>master</u> yet. The negroes on the Sharp place say, that there was no good feeling existing between Skinner and McAllin—that McAllin knew that Skinner had ordered them, never to stop and talk with him, and that if they did, that he would whip them for it, and for that reason he never did stop, and talk with them, unless there was no chance for Skinner to see, or to hear of it. And that all the chance they had to communicate with McAllin, was through Henderson and Dorcas. Mrs. Sharp says that when McAllin visited her he confined himself mostly to the house, and yard,—that he would some times stay a week or two, and never go out about the place, and would often go away without seeing Skinner, to speak to him. There is no evidence here that McAllin and Skinner were friends. On the contrary, the proof is strong that they were not friends. McAllin has been known in this neighborhood ever since AD 1838. He then came here to work for Mr. Sharp, and it is believed that from that time until ~~the present~~ [he left here,] he kept Dorcas [as the negroes term it for a Sweet heart] ~~a misstress~~. The evidence of it is so plain, and palpable, that I presume he will not have the hardihood to deny it. He has been in the habit of visiting Mrs. Sharp and remaining with her a week or two at a time. During the epidemic of 1853 he remained with her all the time. He has always been a still quiet man here so much so that no one knows much about him. He would come and go, without its hardly being known that he had been in the neighborhood. His marked attention to Mrs. Sharp, as well as fine dressing has been the subject of remark, and a rumor has prevailed that he was trying to marry her. There is a report here that he has intimated at Waterproof or St. Joseph that he was going to marry her. We are satisfied, that Dorcas did tell the negroes what they report, and that such conversations between her and McAllin, did take place. Dorcas had no means of knowing any thing concerning McBride but through McAllin, who knew him in the neighborhood of St. Joseph. Her whole course indicates, McAllins guilt, and that the negroes have told the truth [about her]. They have made no statement in reference to her, but what she admits to be true, excepting the implication of McAllin. Jane told about telling Dorcas all about the murder when she came over early in the morning with the message from Mrs. Sharp to Skinner. Dorcas has confessed it all. And we cannot conceive of how nearly all the leading negroes on a plantation when arraigned and taken off from each other so they could not hear the statements of each other could tell a story agreeing so precisely with each other and a portion of it be true, and the rest false. No severe measure has been resorted to, in order to make Dorcas confess—McAllins leaving the place and starting home, and then returning the next day, after having been there 8 or 10 days, and the story of Henderson and the plough driver, in connexion with it, is with us irresistable. As regards the negroes being put under the lash, and prompted to say what they did concerning McAllin, it is wholly false. The confession in relation to him was made in part by Jane on the first day without her receiving a single lash (for we did not punish her at all during the whole investigation), or without our putting any questions in reference to McCallin. Many of the men who were present and took part in the investigation did not know who McAllin was, nor did those who know him, dream of his implication until criminated by the negroes. As regards the charge that the meeting at which Mr. Jackson presided was a Native American meeting for the purpose of making nominations and which after being made, McAllins case was taken up, is like wise false. The meeting was called for the purpose of examining the testimony upon which the first notice given to McAllin was based, and also to consider his card. The Chairman explained the object of the meeting, and spoke of his long acquaintance with McAllin—that he had always sustained a good character—and that the meeting ought to proceed with a great deal of calmness and consideration. The testimony was sifted closely, and not a man present would proclaim the innocence

of McAllin. [All were unanimous as to his guilt.] There were more democrats present than usually vote at the Kingston precinct. Mr. Alex Boyd
one of our oldest citizens, a brother in law of Mrs. Sharps and an old
democrat, attended both meetings. At the first one he did not sign the
notice to McAllin, because, as he stated publicly that he was an old
man and did not want to pledge himself to any course that might lead
to violence, but as to McAllins guilt he did not doubt it. He made the
same statement publickly at the last meeting, and then signed a paper
with some near 40 others, approving of the action of the meeting. The
reports which are in circulation, and which are well authenticated, are
in themselves sufficient to convict McAllin of lying, and of guilt as to
[complicity in the] murder. It is reported that he says that he was about
to marry Mrs. Sharp, and the community here being a rich, proud and
haughty one, they wanted to drive him off, because he was a poor mechanic and they did not want to see him elevated along side of them.
Another one is, that he and Skinner were friends, that the plot was to
kill him, as well as Skinner, that Aleck Farrar wanted them both out of
the way, because they prevented him from getting certain property from
Mrs. Sharp [leaving the inference that Aleck Farrar produced the murder and wanted to have him murdered also]. Again—that Aleck Farrar
wanted to drive him out of the country because he knew, that he
McAllin, knew that he (Farrar) cheated Mrs. Sharp out of some property. And also, that if the negroes were instigated to commit the murder, they were instigated to do it, by Aleck Farrar, through a negro of
his, who traveled back and forth between his places. And that the girl
Dorcas told him when he was there the last time that some one had
been trying to get into his room, and that they were after killing him
too. Here is an admission that he knew something of the murder, and
that too before it was found out.—I have lived to but very little purpose, in this life, if in the community in which I am known, it is even
rendered necessary for me to deny such vile and infamous charges—I
have now hurriedly sketched down the principal portion of the testimony in this case, there is however [much] more connected with it, if
I were to enter into the minitae, and detail of it all, quite a volume would
be required to contain it—

The next piece of evidence is an affidavit dated October 1 and signed
by Farrar and the planters William B. Foules and Alfred Swayze.

We the undersigned do certify that we called upon Mrs. Clarissa
Sharp and told her of the confession made by her negro man Henderson,
in reference to McCallin leaving her house to go up the river to where
he lived, and returning to put him on his guard about the finding out
about the murder—To which Mrs. Sharp replied that Mr. McCallin
left her house to go up to Waterproof, that she requested him, while
on his way up, to examine the jails at Natches and Vidalia and if Ander-

son the runaway was in either jail, for him to write her a letter and leave with Mrs. Holden in Natches, who as there was much passing would send it out to her—that she did not know that McCallin was going to come back—that he never told her what he came back for—and she did not know what he did come back for, unless it was for what the negroes said—

The indictment handed down against Henderson, Reuben, and Anderson by the grand jury can be found in the records of the Adams County Circuit Court, housed at the Historic Natchez Foundation:

In the Circuit Court of the said County of Adams at the November Term thereof, to wit at a term of said Circuit Court of the said County commencing & holden on the sixth Monday after the fourth Monday in September in the Year of our Lord one thousand eight hundred and fifty seven. The Grand Jurors of the State of Mississippi taken from the body of the good and lawful men of the County aforesaid elected empanelled sworn and charged to inquire in and for the County aforesaid, at the term aforesaid, of the Court aforesaid in the name and by authority of the State of Mississippi upon their oath present that Reuben a slave of Clarissa Sharpe, laborer late of said County, and Henderson a slave of said Clarissa Sharpe, late of said County, laborer, and Anderson a slave of said Clarissa Sharpe, late of said County, laborer not having the fear of God before their eyes but being moved and seduced by the instigation of the Devil on the fourteenth day of May in the Year of our Lord one thousand eight hundred and fifty seven in the County aforesaid in and upon one Duncan B. Skinner in the peace of God and of said State then and there being feloniously wilfully and of their malice aforethought did make an assault and that the said Reuben Henderson and Anderson with both their hands and feet the said Duncan B. Skinner to and against the ground then and there feloniously wilfully and of their malice aforethought did cast and throw and that the said Reuben, Henderson and Anderson with both the hands and feet of their the said Reuben, Henderson and Anderson then and there and whilst the said Duncan B. Skinner was so lying upon the Ground, the said Duncan B. Skinner in and upon the head, stomach, back, sides, and back part of the neck of him the said Duncan B. Skinner then and there feloniously, wilfully, and of their malice aforethought did strike, beat kick and wound giving to the said Duncan B. Skinner then and there, as well by the casting and throwing of him the said Duncan B. Skinner to the ground as aforesaid as also by the said striking, beating kicking and wounding the said Duncan B. Skinner in and upon the head, stomach, back, sides, and back part of the neck of him the said Duncan B. Skinner with both the hands and feet of their the said Reuben, Henderson and Anderson in manner aforesaid several mortal bruises in and upon the head, stomach, back, sides and back part of the neck of him the said

Duncan B. Skinner of which said several mortal bruises the said Duncan B. Skinner then and there instantly died. And so the jurors aforesaid upon their oath aforesaid do say that the said Reuben, Henderson and Anderson, the said Duncan B. Skinner in manner and form aforesaid feloniously, wilfully, and of their malice aforethought did kill and murder against the peace and dignity of the state of Mississippi.

And the jurors aforesaid upon their oath aforesaid do further present that the said Reuben a slave of Clarissa Sharpe late of said County, laborer, not having the fear of God before his eyes but being moved and seduced by the instigation of the Devil on the fourteenth day of May in the Year of our Lord Eighteen hundred and fifty seven with force and arms in the County aforesaid in and upon the said Duncan B. Skinner in the peace of God and of said State then and there being feloniously, wilfully, and of his malice aforethought did make an assault, and that the said Reuben with a certain club of no value which he the said Reuben in his right hand then and there had and held the said Duncan B. Skinner in and upon the right side of the head near the right temple of him the said Duncan B. Skinner then and there feloniously wilfully and of his malice aforethought did then and there strike and wound giving to the said Duncan B. Skinner then and there with the club aforesaid in and upon the right side of the head near the right temple of him the said Duncan B. Skinner one mortal wound of the depth of one inch and of the breadth of two inches of which said mortal wound the said Duncan B. Skinner then and there instantly died.

And the jurors aforesaid upon this oath aforesaid do further present that the said Henderson slave of Clarissa Sharpe late of said County laborer and the said Anderson slave of Clarissa Sharpe late of said County laborer on the day and Year aforesaid with force and arms in the County aforesaid feloniously wilfully and of their malice aforethought were then and there present aiding abetting and assisting the said Reuben the murder and felony aforesaid to do and commit and so the jurors aforesaid upon their oath aforesaid do say that the said Reuben, Henderson and Anderson the said Duncan B. Skinner in manner and form as charged alleged and set forth in this Court as aforesaid feloniously wilfully and of their malice aforethought did kill and murder against the peace and dignity of the state of Mississippi.

The *Courier* ran its account of the trial on November 19 under the title "AN EVENTFUL DRAMA":

> An unusual spectacle has been presented for the last two days in our Circuit Court. The first act of a drama has been performed, and we feel it not inappropriate to refer to the actors, the plot, and the denouement.
>
> On Tuesday last three intelligent-looking and valuable slaves stood their trial before a Jury of the country on a charge of murder, and yesterday three others were undergoing the same ordeal for a similar of-

fence, committed at a different time, and in a different locality. At the present time of writing, we can only refer to the trial of Tuesday. It is a humane provision of our Statutes that whenever a slave, degraded as he may be in social position, or in intellect, is charged with an offence involving life, the same aegis of protection is thrown around him, as around the white man. He is shielded by the same laws, tried by the same rules, entitled to the same guarantees, and favored by the same chances and presumptions, that protect his master and his superiors. Alike with the white man he must be indicted and arraigned, and then tried by an impartial jury of house-holders. The same rules of evidence, the same presumptions of innocence, apply. Nay more; under our Code, the Court appoints able counsel to defend the slave, to whom it awards a liberal fee to be paid by the owner; and we are confident that no exertion is unused, no legal learning unemployed, no appliance or ruling of the law omitted, in the case of the meanest slave, that would be resorted to, were the white man on trial for a similar offence. It would have been a goodly sight could abolition Massachusetts or Rhode Island have seen with a collective eye, the proceedings of yesterday and the day before; with what scrupulous exactitude the rights of the prisoners—the same in these respects as those of the white race—were observed by the prosecution, were exacted by the defence, and were maintained by the Court. The same arraignment, the same venire, the same challenges, the same employment of counsel, the same rules of evidence, the same enlistment of eloquence and talent, the same charges from the bench, the same solemnities of the verdict, that would have marked the trial of the free white man on a similar charge, were all here exhibited.

Without wishing to indulge in any of the claptrap of particularization which so constantly is employed in large cities, in spreading before the public every occurrence in a noted trial, and which panders to the love of the strange and eventful, for the sake of the return it will receive in the shape of larger sales or wider circulation, we yet think a more than passing notice is due to the trial of these cases, so timely and complete was the discovery of the crimes committed, and so important is it to our community that such crimes, when clearly established, should be speedily and promptly punished. At present we design only to speak of the trial on Tuesday of three negroes, *Reuben, Henderson and Anderson*, for the murder in May last of DUNCAN K. SKINNER, the overseer on Mrs. Clarissa Sharp's plantation, some twelve miles South-east of this city. The guilty plot was so ingenious, the concealment of the crime so complete for the time, and the final detection so triumphant, as to merit a notice in the criminal annals of the county.

Of a bright morning, in May last, Mr. Skinner did not return to his house at his usual hour for breakfast. The morning waxed on, and he still was absent; the noon came, and he had not returned. He went forth on horseback, the negroes say, at daybreak with his gun, and they have not seen him since. The day passed and there were no tidings of the missing man. Anxiety succeeded to surprise, and search was made by friends and neighbors. His horse was soon after found in the road, but with out a rider. The search was prosecuted into the night. When the moon goes down, the torch is lighted, and long after the noon of the night, by the roots of a beech tree, in a strip of woods upon the plantation hardly a quarter of a mile from his house, the cold and stiff body of the unfortunate man is found; his neck is dislocated; a wound appears upon the right temple; near his body is his gun; a little further on are his game bag and his cap, and in another place his whip. Friends watched the night out that lifeless corpse; a Coroner's jury is held the next day; the body is viewed; the jury is quickly satisfied, and a verdict entered that the deceased came to his death while out hunting, by a fall from his horse. But there was a terrible secret wrapped up in that gray May morning, and the verdict of the Coroner's Jury could not stifle inquiry. The dead man had brothers who loved, and friends who respected and esteemed him; and they were not satisfied. The lurking presentments that occasionally and so strangely surround crime, effected them, and they could not rest without thinking of the strange fate that had attended their brother and friend.

The saddle found on the horse was not Mr. Skinner's hunting saddle. When hunting he used a Spanish saddle, upon the horn of which he hung his game bag. That saddle was still in his room. 'Twas a new English saddle from which he fell at the roots of the old beech tree. The game bag found, too, was an old one, the holes of which incapacitated it from use. The good one he used, was not used that fatal morning. Powder-flask and shot-pouch were absent from his person. His money was gone from his room. The position of the body when found was a singular and unnatural one. But if there had been foul play, where was the clue to the mystery to be had? God had provided it in the infirmities of human nature itself. The debased negro, alike with the criminal white man, cannot keep a secret of the magnitude of murder. No one but those used to negro ways and conversation, can realize the full import of what was meant, when the testimony established on Tuesday how the ringleader in the murder first came to confess his guilt. It was to an acquaintance he told it; a slave on a neighboring plantation. He had had, he said, an "interesting dream," and he felt troubled about it, and wanted to tell some one. Another comrade in guilt had felt a pain in his side, "and was interested in mind," and he had something to communicate; and so they both told their tale of plot, and murder, and cruelty, and device, and deception, and falsehood; and the strange tale went round the plantation, until all knew it; and though they wondered the white folks never suspected the truth, still as weeks went on, they fancied the fatal secret was safe, even if buried in a hundred breasts. Continually before us, as we listened to the evidence on Tuesday last, rose up in memory the prophetic words of the great

Massachusetts lawyer and statesmen [Daniel Webster], uttered in the Salem murder trial:

"It is accomplished. The deed is done. He has done the murder— no eye has seen him; no ear has heard him. The secret is his own, and it is safe. Ah! that was a dreadful mistake. Such a secret can be safe nowhere. The whole creation of God has neither nook nor corner, where the guilty can bestow it, and say it is safe. Not to speak of that eye which glances through all disguises, and beholds everything, as in the splendor of noon,—such secrets of guilt are never safe from detection, even by men. True it is, generally speaking, that 'murder will out.' True it is, that Providence hath so ordained, and doth so govern things, that those who break the great law of Heaven, by shedding man's blood, seldom succeed in avoiding discovery. * * The guilty soul cannot keep its own secret. It is false to itself; or rather it feels an irresistible impulse of conscience to be true to itself. It labors under its guilty possession, and knows not what to do with it. The human heart was not made for the residence of such an inhabitant. It finds itself preyed on by a torment, which it dares not acknowledge to God nor man. A vulture is devouring it, and it can ask no sympathy or assistance, either from heaven or earth. The secret which the murderer possesses soon comes to possess him; and, like the evil spirits of which we read, it overcomes him, and leads him whithersoever it will. He feels it beating at his heart, rising to his throat, and demanding disclosure. He thinks the whole world sees it in his face, reads it in his eyes, and almost hears its workings in the very silence of his thoughts. It has become his master. It betrays his discretion, it breaks down his courage, it conquers his prudence. When suspicions, from without, begin to embarrass him, and the net of circumstance to entangle him, the fatal *secret* struggles with still greater violence to burst forth. It must be confessed, *it will be* confessed; there is no refuge from confession but suicide, and suicide is confession."

But while all this natural working of the conscience was going on, the relatives and friends of Mr. Skinner were not idle. It was a month or over before their plan of operations was formed, but when formed, it was executed with promptness, decision and success. And at the very first demonstration that an inquiry was to be made, the fatal secret reposed in fifty breasts came tumbling forth from every lip; was to be read in every countenance, and corroborated by an hundred circumstances. And what was the manner of that tragedy, and how was it performed?

Before day on the morning of the 14th of August [*sic*], as was the custom, the horse of the deceased was saddled and hitched behind the kitchen in its usual place, waiting for its owner's issuance from his house. The boy who hitched it, went into Mr. Skinner's room and informed him of the fact. He was in bed. Shortly after, the cook came to him for the kitchen keys, which it was her custom to bring to him each night. He gave them to her and she retired. The first grey streak of dawn was then heralding the break of day. As the cook went from the house to the kitchen, she met two of the conspirators going towards Mr. Skinner's room. She saw them enter, and she went on to the kitchen; a minute or two after, a scuffle ensued; she heard a tumbling over chairs, and then an agonizing cry of "Oh! Lord;" and a moment after there came forth from the room she had lately visited, three men bearing a lifeless body. Who were the three? She had seen and identified going and coming out, *Reuben* and *Anderson*. The third man was *Henderson*. The latter had tried the day before to get others into the plot, and that morning the three had coaxed a fellow servant to go as far even as the house gallery with them; but his heart failed, and luckily for himself he stopped, and when the agonizing cry of death came, he ran. The three entered. Mr. Skinner was in bed. *Henderson* struck him with a stick across his breast. He sprang up, and fled to the next room, where he grappled his assailant by the throat, leaving upon his fleshy neck the marks of his thumb and fingers so indelibly impressed in his death agonies, that they were visible upon the negro's neck for weeks after the occurrence, and were the mute witnesses of his guilt, and corroborators of the confessions made by the other conspirators. Against one, the hapless Skinner might have triumphed, but the other two came to the rescue, and they "down'd him" in the corner. They struck his head and gashed it and it bled profusely. They took the body, lifeless as it seemed, and carried it out in the grey dawn, which seemed to linger in its coming, as if in dread to look on a scene of so much horror; they carried it to a saw pit fifty yards off, and there, startled by a last groan from the swollen lips, and a last convulsive struggling of the limbs, the black fiends seized the inanimate form; one caught it by the body, another by the head, and then they deliberately twisted it until the neck was dislocated. The third, with a demoniac deviltry that a Nena Sahib might have envied, jumped upon the breast of the dead man, and danced and cut a pigeon-wing in triumph over his foe! The thunders of the Almighty have but slept, and the law's solemn vengeance, and the awful gallows scene, will yet be His instruments!

But the scene closed not here. Anderson returned to the room of the murder, took the dead man's clothes from his chair, his gun from the corner, his cap from the peg, a game bag from the gallery, and seizing the horse also by the rein, made straight for the saw pit. The body was in a night dress only. They took and deliberately dressed it, and put it across the horse. They led the animal to the woods; flung the body off against the roots of a tree; the gun they threw here, the cap there, the game bag in a third direction, and then trotted the horse up and down, right and left, and across the dead body which the hoofs trampled, and having thus made things appear as if accident, or a vicious animal, had been the cause, they turned the horse loose, went back and parcelled out the money of the deceased, and thought the secret safe! But 'twas not so. They had so done, and so left undone, that discovery was certain. The body lay unnaturally for the truth of the theory of accident. It was a beech tree with heavy roots coming from it, a foot or two, from the ground. The ground fell off from the roots. Had the body been thrown there during life, the agonies of death would have made it slide down the roots on the ground. It rested on the roots as on a pivot, one foot upon the tree, the other leg and the arms stretched out in different directions. It was so placed, as only could have been the body of a dead, and not of a living man who died in the act of placing. The wound on the temple, which on the theory of accident was caused by the beech root, was happily for the truth, on the left temple, when it was the right temple that lay upon the wood. The conspirators had taken in their hurry too, the old unused game bag, and not the one Skinner carried on his saddle; they had forgotten that the saddle on the horse was the one to which no game could be attached; and in their hurry also, they had left shot pouch and powder flask, articles they afterwards procured and threw in a horse pond four feet deep, which were weeks after fished out from the precise point that the confessions of the guilty wretches had designated.

And there the tale of blood, of that day closes. How when all things were ready, a month after, the neighbors met without a word; how they called the plantation roll, and placed each servant in a line so that none could escape the keen eye of scrutiny, or conceal the look of conscious guilt; how those who were believed to know the most were separated from the rest and from each other, so that no conversation could pass, or no word be heard; how the simple question addressed to each, "What has happened wrong on the plantation," brought out the horrible tale of blood and murder; how the answer burst forth even from the principal conspirators, "I knew, Massa Alec, 'twas no use to keep the truth from you;" how the direct testimony came out of those who saw the entrances of the murderers, their exit with the body, and their taking forth of the articles with which they hoped to conceal the deed, and of those who heard the sound of the struggle, and the death cry of agony; how every corroborating circumstance came to light—the blood in the corner, the money hidden in a trunk and secreted in other places, the powder-flask and shot-pouch flung in the pond; how threats made previous to the murder, and endeavors to league in other participants, were detailed; and confessions made the fatal day to fellow servants, and talked about and recited over by the three wretches to a dozen of their companions in servitude; how these confessions were repeated to the gentlemen who made the investigation; how the entire scene was fraught with a calmness, deliberation and solemnity that would have dignified a Court House; how the whole truth came out, and how guilt hung its head submissive to the dread penalty, we can do no more than thus refer to. The three negroes who committed the foul deed, who plotted and rebelled and murdered, were quietly led to prison; and discipline and order once more reigned, where conspiracy and crime had triumphed for a month. As one of the prisoners' counsel himself remarked, there was one bright spot in the black drama, and that was that no summary vengeance was executed. The slaves were yielded to the law, and day before yesterday they came forth from the jail to attend their trial—the ringleader almost the shadow of his former self, so terribly had guilty conscience already punished him—and the same night they were remanded to their cells, hopeless and friendless, never thence to issue except to meet that dread penalty which the laws of God and man alike prescribe.

The prisoners were ably defended by Messrs. Walworth and Shields, whose theory of defence was plausible enough in superstructure; its only want being that it had not a single foot of solid foundation to rest upon. 'Twas a double theory—the one, of being thrown from his horse, or falling therefrom in an attack of palpitation of the heart to which the deceased was somewhat subject; a theory that the Coroner's inquest had taken for granted without investigation; and the other, of its being a conspiracy of the black witnesses to conceal their own guilt by attributing it to the prisoners. Both defences were utterly incompatible with the testimony, direct and circumstantial, and with the confessions made alike to their fellow servants, and to witnesses of the highest credit and respectability. So thought at least the Jury, who were not out of their seats five minutes, and so must have thought every one who heard this remarkable trial. There was not a peg to hang a doubt upon, reasonable or unreasonable; not the first circumstance which could allow a feeling of sympathy to spring up. It was a dark, cold recital of fiendish murder, deliberately planned, barbarously executed and adroitly concealed.

To Mr. Martin, who was associated with the District Attorney, in the prosecution, and to the gentlemen by whose investigations the mystery was developed, great praise is due. The latter received a warm acknowledgment from Mr. Martin in his eloquent speech at the conclusion of the trial. There was no one, however, to testify to the tact, the industry and the ability with which Mr. M. has himself pursued this investigation from June last, until its consummation by the verdict of Tuesday night; the calm decision, the repression of all hasty steps or rash resolves, and the keen, thorough scrutiny, which he has brought to bear on every point. We gladly refer to it as his just due. He has a right to congratulate himself, the sorrowing friends of the murdered man, and the community, upon the laws being vindicated, truth elicited, murder brought to light, the guilty punished, rebellion made an example of, our social institutions rendered more safe, and the negro taught that God has made him in subjection to the white race, and that so he must remain, submissively and cheerfully performing his duty in that situation of life in which it has pleased God to place him.

⊯✝⊱

That is all the evidence I've been able to find. Not as much as you would have liked, I imagine. There's very little about what was happening behind the scenes. Furthermore, except for a single notice in the newspaper, no direct testimony has survived from John McCallin, and the statements from the slaves come to us through Alexander Farrar and Giles Hillyer, hardly disinterested observers. Still, for all their obvious shortcomings, the sources do provide enough information to allow us to see why events unfolded as they did. And to say, I will now attempt to convince you, that the interpretation of the murder arrived at in 1857 was almost certainly wrong.

⊰ 3 ⊱

The Evidence Reconsidered

A historian attempting to solve a problem from the past, whether something as narrow as the murder of an overseer on a plantation in Mississippi in 1857 or as broad as the causes of the Civil War, will ask three basic questions when examining a document. First, how does that document fit in with other evidence specifically relating to the subject under investigation? Does one source—in the case at hand, the newspaper accounts by the Natchez *Courier*—confirm or contradict other sources—most obviously, the letter from Alexander Farrar to Henry Drake? Where there are inconsistencies, is there any clear way of reconciling them? Do the circumstances under which the documents were produced help us make decisions about which statements are reliable?

Second, he or she will want to know whether or not the contents of the document make sense in terms of our understanding of what, for lack of a better term, we might call "human nature." Geologists rely on the principle of uniformitarianism to explain the physical history of the earth. Uniformitarianism states that there are inviolable laws of nature; we can know the past of the earth because we can observe and explain its present. Historians apply their own version of uniformitarianism in attempting to make sense of the human experience. We assume there are certain characteristics of human life that have been constant throughout time and across civilizations. Some of these characteristics are simply the basic drives we share with other animals—for food, for shelter, for sex. But others are unique to our species and presumably go back to long before men and women first began to leave written records—for example, the need for a system of beliefs that explains the daily circumstances of life in a coherent way and allows individuals to come to terms with the knowledge that death is inevitable. What historians often refer to as a "worldview."

Still, human nature explains far less than is popularly imagined. Or put another way, most people seem to underestimate the full extent of diversity that human nature allows. We tend to see our own social institutions and belief system as archetypical, to assume that because of the imperatives of human nature, all societies share the same destiny. Ours is not the first generation to claim naively that it has witnessed the "end of history."

Which brings me to the third and ultimately most important question a historian will ask when examining a document: Does it make sense in terms of what we know about the society that existed at that time and in that place? As I hope to prove, demonstrating that the people of Adams County, Mississippi, almost certainly were mistaken in their interpretation of the murder of Duncan Skinner requires little more than a careful reading of the evidence provided in the previous chapter. But understanding *why* they were mistaken, and speculating on what really happened, that requires going beyond the documents themselves. That requires some consideration of the structure of the antebellum South: its economic system and social relations, its political order and racial ideology. And it is here where the discoveries of historians become indispensable. Because while anybody can take the time to read through a document carefully, and most scholars—historians, at any rate—probably have no greater insight into human nature than anyone else, historians do have the knowledge that comes from devoting a life's work to reading and writing about the past. Speculating on what really happened on that day in May 1857 when Duncan Skinner died, then, will inevitably take us beyond the particulars of the case into the life and times of the Old South.

⛧⛧⛧

The clearest and most detailed description we have of how Duncan Skinner met his death comes from the confession made by Reuben, one of the three slaves subsequently charged with his murder. Although we have two versions of that confession, one in the draft of the letter from Alexander Farrar to Henry Drake dated September 4, the second in the draft written the following day, they vary only in the slightest detail. It would be worthwhile to go over Reuben's testimony one more time. According to what he told the investigators, he, Henderson, and Anderson surprised Skinner in his bed before daylight on May 14 and attacked him with a club. When Skinner broke free, they chased him into an adjoining room, threw him to the floor, and beat him into unconsciousness. They then carried him off in his night clothes into the woods where Reuben snapped his neck, killing him. After that Anderson went back to the cabin to get Skinner's clothes and horse as well as some other items—a gun and game bag among them—that the overseer would ordinarily have taken when he went hunting. He gave the blood-stained nightshirt and club to Jane, who burned them, then made his way back to the other two slaves. Henderson now went off to the stables, while Anderson lifted Skinner on the horse and rode for a distance through the woods before dumping the body onto the trampled roots of a beech tree. Then Reuben fired off one round from the gun and scattered about the various articles Anderson had retrieved from Skinner's cabin. Finally, he and Anderson went back to the cabin, where they unlocked the overseer's trunk and removed his money, returning one last time to the body so they could put the key to the trunk in his pocket.

The other evidence relating to the specific question of how Skinner died comes from articles in the Natchez *Courier* and the indictment handed down by the grand jury. The first mention of the case in the press, a very brief notice published on May 16, contains details that are at odds not only with Reuben's confession but also later accounts in the newspaper: The overseer went to hunt turkeys; he had been shot; he had probably died when his frightened horse threw him. In fact, the only statement made by the *Courier* on May 16 that is consistent with subsequent reports is that Skinner's neck had been broken. We can assume, I think, that the article was put together out of the hearsay and rumor that must have circulated after the discovery of the body and can basically be discounted.

The second article ran in the *Courier* on June 25, no more than a few days after Alexander Farrar and the other whites completed their interrogation of the slaves. In fact, the description of the murder closely follows the testimony offered by Reuben, so closely it would be reasonable to assume that the editor of the *Courier*, Giles Hillyer, received his information from someone involved in the investigation. Still, there is one discrepancy between this second report in the paper and the version of Reuben's confession given by Alexander Farrar. According to Farrar, Reuben testified that he, Henderson, and Anderson broke into Skinner's cabin and attacked him in his bed. The article in the paper stated, "The negroes in the plot went to Mr. Skinner's house just before day, and aroused him on pretence of a child in the family being sick. He opened the door, while in his night clothes, and was knocked down by a blow on his breast from a heavy stick."

The discrepancy is a curious one. Let me offer one possible explanation, and I lay stress on the word "possible." Farrar reported in his letter to Drake that Henderson and Anderson confirmed Reuben's account of the murder. He did not, however, provide the details of their testimony. Perhaps there were minor differences in the statements given by the three slaves. Perhaps Henderson or Anderson remembered that they got Skinner out of bed with some story about a child being ill. ("Perhaps," "maybe," "possibly." By now you should be getting a sense of the conditional nature of much historical interpretation.)

The third article, which ran in the *Courier* on November 19, provided coverage of the trial of the three slaves. It tacitly repudiated the claim made five months earlier that they had attacked Skinner at the door of his cabin.

Presumably Hillyer had come to the conclusion that he was mistaken on this point. But now the paper included a startling new revelation: After Reuben had broken Skinner's neck, Henderson "with a demoniac deviltry that a Nena Sahib might have envied, jumped upon the breast of the dead man, and danced and cut a pigeon wing in triumph over his foe!" It is an arresting image, one that must have shocked *Courier* readers. But where did it come from?

Since the allegation does not appear in the June 25 article or any drafts of the letter from Farrar to Drake, it seems likely that it was raised for the first time at the trial. The *Courier* does not identify who testified for the state, but that information is contained in the court records. Separate summonses were issued to the coroner; to the jury of twelve men he appointed to investigate Duncan Skinner's death; to Alexander Farrar; and to ten slaves, eight on Cedar Grove and two on Magnolia. Assuming the coroner and his jury were called to explain why they had initially ruled the death to be accidental, the allegation must have originated either with Farrar or, more likely, the slaves. Dorcas, Jane, and the other blacks had undoubtedly been threatened with prosecution for their part in the crime if they failed to provide testimony against Henderson, Reuben, and Anderson. Concealing a murder was a felony; aiding someone to commit murder was a capital offense. It takes little imagination to envision that one of them might have felt driven—or been coached—to concoct some story about Henderson dancing on the corpse.

Finally, there is the indictment handed down by the grand jury. A garbled document—tortuous reading, wasn't it?—it claims, on one hand, that Skinner died as a result of the beating he received from all three slaves and, on the other, that he died after Reuben struck him on the temple with a club. This seems to contradict the testimony given by Reuben to the investigating party (and, judging from the *Courier*, repeated by one or more of the witnesses at the trial) that Skinner died when Reuben snapped his neck. According to the indictment, testimony was presented at the grand jury hearing by Jane, Dorcas, and two of the men involved in the investigation, John W. Baird and Alexander Farrar's brother Caleb. There is no obvious reason why any of the four should have offered a version of the murder different from the one provided by Alexander Farrar in his letter to Henry Drake or presented by the prosecution at the trial. Then again, it may just be that the clerk who transcribed the indictment was confused. He wrote up a second indictment the same day, against three slaves of William B. Foules for murdering their overseer, Y. W. McBride. The two documents bear a startling resemblance. In each case the victim was alleged to have "instantly died" both as a result of a beating and because he received "one mortal wound of the depth of one inch and of the breadth of two inches" on his temple. In each case it was a slave named Reuben who was said to have inflicted the fatal blow. Not that I would put much stock in the charge against the second Reuben, either. Testimony presented at the trial of the Foules slaves established that he was home playing with his children at the time McBride was murdered.

I mentioned earlier that when I give the draft of the letter by Alexander Farrar to my students and ask them who killed Duncan Skinner and why, they usually respond simply by repeating the version of the story Farrar reported. This is the answer I expect and, in fact, want, because it provides me with a convenient way of getting them to understand the need to examine documents critically. (Also, it allows me to look clever.) But one year a student replied—and I don't remember the exact words but I have a pretty good recollection of the tone—"Aw, I think that guy—what's his name?—Farrar did it. He killed the other guy. Then he fixed up the whole thing so the slaves got blamed."

Now, you might think I would be pleased by any suggestion of independent thinking. Cynicism is not the same as skepticism, however. Besides, I had prepared a series of questions to lead the students from credulousness into critical thought. I had not anticipated a situation where, in effect, I would have to take them in the opposite direction—where I would have to convince them to suspend a certain amount of disbelief. I don't remember my reply, but if the same situation were to arise now I would take the opportunity to explain that we really have a choice: We can decide that the evidence is so doubtful it does not allow us to draw any credible conclusions about what actually happened. Or we can try and separate out the probable from the possible from the unlikely based on a critical examination of the text of the letter.

Recognizing the fragmentary nature of the historical record is important for anyone interested in how historians recreate the past. It is true that a scholar researching a major political event of the late twentieth century will probably have an overwhelming body of evidence to deal with (although, even then, he or she is likely to have to rely on sources that are slanted and incomplete), but records about incidents that happened long ago and were of purely local interest are frustratingly few and typically contain testimony that would hardly stand up in a court of law.

With that in mind, return to the available evidence for the case at hand. You can decide that the drafts and newspaper accounts are simply too incomplete or too biased to allow us to draw any conclusions. Or you can make the most out of the material available. To my mind, there is more than enough evidence to say how Duncan Skinner came to his death. First, there is Reuben's confession. Add to that the corroboration given to his story, except perhaps in detail, not only by Henderson and Anderson but, if the *Courier* is to be believed, by as many as fifty other slaves on both Cedar Grove and a neighboring plantation, Magnolia. Furthermore, with the exception of the incredible passage about Henderson dancing on Skinner's corpse, the *Courier*'s account of the murder accords exactly with the testimony taken by the investigators. To all that may be added: the statement by Jane, the cook, evidently repeated in court, that she heard the struggle in the overseer's cabin and saw the three slaves carrying off Skinner's body; the evidence of blood stains on the floor; the scars on Henderson's neck that Reuben claimed he received in the fight with Skinner; the distribution of money stolen from the overseer's trunk; and, finally, the powder flask and shot pouch recovered from the pond, where Henderson admitted he threw them.

By now it should be obvious that when I said that the investigation produced the wrong verdict, I did not mean that Henderson, Reuben, and Anderson were innocent. All the evidence suggests that the three slaves killed their overseer and, further, that they carried out the murder more or less in the way Reuben described in his confession. At issue is not who killed Duncan Skinner or how, but why.

⊹

The members of the investigating party had the answer, or at least thought they did. Their explanation was perhaps best summarized in the notice they placed in local newspapers after the August 8 meeting in Kingston: "there is no reasonable ground to doubt that [John] McCallin did suggest to the slaves, upon [Cedar Grove], the possibility, and propriety of their 'putting Skinner out of the way,' to use McCallin's own language, or more plainly, advised them to murder their overseer." In his letter to Henry Drake, Alexander Farrar was even able to pinpoint the precise moment when McCallin instigated the crime: "Henderson the carriage driver states that he went up stairs one night to get McAllin's boots to black, that McAllin, was standing by a window looking out towards the quarter listening to a noise there, occasioned by Skinner whipping some negroes,—that he said, Hen' there is quite a fuss in the quarter to night, and that he (Hen') replied yes, but it is no uncommon thing here. To which McAllin replied, Well if I was you boys, I would get rid of that man. How, asked Henderson? Why: I would put him out of the way. After some further talk Henderson went down stairs with the boots, and in the morning when he returned with them, McAllin rose up in his bed, and said, Hen' how long did that fuss last last night in the quarter? I don't know sir—it is such a common thing here, I didn't pay much attention to it. Well! says McAllin, You boys are a cowardly, chicken hearted set, or you would not stand that man's whipping and beating you so—you would put him out of the way. If you were to do so, then I could marry the widow, and there would be no overseer, and you would all have better times. The Negroes on being asked if they understood what McAllin meant by putting out of the way, replied, why, killing him of course—He further states that this conversation was held the last time McAllin was at the place before the death of Skinner. That he (Henderson) went out among the negroes and they formed the plan to kill Skinner."

Farrar also provided Drake with McCallin's motive: "Dorcas . . . told them, (the negroes), that McAllin said, he was trying to marry their Misstress, and that for some time past he had not been making such good headway, and it was on account of Skinner. That it seemed like Mrs. Sharp had more confidence in Skinner than any body else, that she went by every thing he said, and the only chance he (McAllin) had, was for the negroes to put Skinner out of the way,—That if they would do that, he (McAllin) could then marry their Misstress, and then there should be no overseer, and they (the negroes) should have better times."

The investigators also maintained—and here I return to the notice of the meeting of August 8—that "McCallin, though cognizant of the murder, and knowing those who perpetrated it, concealed the facts from the public, and advised the murderers of the efforts making to discover them." Alexander Farrar again provided the details in his communication with Henry Drake: When McCallin learned that there was going to be an investigation, he came to Henderson at the carriage house "and, said, Hen' do you know what Jesse Skinner is riding about here so much for. I don't know sir, says Hen. Well I can tell you, he is trying to find out who killed his brother, and if you boys dont mind and keep your mouths shut he will find out, for there is a great deal of talk that he was murdered. I have been up to Natches and hear a great deal said there about his being murdered. It is even in the newspaper that he was murdered. And I have come all the way back to put you boys on your guard." According to Farrar, McCallin gave the very same warning to the plough driver.

To the direct testimony implicating McCallin in the crime, Farrar added the following indictment of his character: "McAllin has been known in this neighborhood ever since AD 1838. He then came here to work for Mr. Sharp, and it is believed that from that time until he left here, he kept Dorcas as the negroes term it for a Sweet heart. The evidence of it is so plain, and palpable, that I presume he will not have the hardihood to deny it. He has been in the habit of visiting Mrs. Sharp and remaining with her a week or two at a time. During the epidemic of 1853 he remained with her all the time. He has always been a still quiet man here so much so that no one knows much about him. He would come and go, without its hardly being known that he had been in the neighborhood. His marked attention to Mrs. Sharp, as well as fine dressing has been the subject of remark, and a rumor has prevailed that he was trying to marry her. There is a report here that he has intimated at Waterproof or St. Joseph that he was going to marry her." In the undated second draft Farrar even claimed that when McCallin "first took up with Dorcas she became pregnant, and that he was instrumental in producing an abortion." However, he dropped this allegation from the draft of September 5.

A moment ago I suggested that the confession made by Reuben to the investigating party was basically reliable—that the account he provided of how he, Henderson, and Anderson murdered Duncan Skinner was, except perhaps in some minor details, factually accurate. That does not mean, however, that I think we should take everything Alexander Farrar reported to Henry Drake at face value. After all, he was writing at least in part to counter criticism directed at the investigating party. The editing he did as he worked his way through the three drafts in the Farrar Papers makes it clear that he took great pains to find just the right words and phrases that would effectively refute charges that the interrogation of the slaves had been handled improperly. Here are just a few examples:

In the draft dated September 4, Farrar indicated initially that a number of the slaves on Cedar Grove were "staked down" and whipped. On revision, he dropped all references to use of stakes.

In the same draft Farrar wrote simply that the investigating party had concluded that Lem and Henderson "ought to be whipped." The following day, working on his third draft now, he changed that to "ought to be whipped for lying," as if some excuse for using physical coercion was necessary.

And it was only in the final draft that Farrar made claims about Anderson and Reuben confiding in slaves on Magnolia about having feelings of remorse after the killing. In the undated draft, he wrote simply that the slaves at Magnolia "confessed to having harbored Anderson, that he told them all about the murder of Skinner."

Farrar also made revisions to passages dealing with McCallin and his role in the crime:

In the second, undated draft, Farrar originally wrote that "it seemed" to Dorcas that McCallin was not making headway in his attempt to marry Clarissa Sharpe. Later he altered this passage to read that McCallin "said" to Dorcas that he was not making headway.

In the undated draft Farrar at first wrote that under questioning Henderson "repeated" what the Magnolia slaves said about Dorcas's relations with McCallin. On revision, "repeated" became "repeated precisely."

Similarly, in the undated draft Farrar wrote that the Magnolia slaves testified that McCallin had told Dorcas "when he married her Misstress, he could do more for her." On September 5, "more" had become "a great deal more."

Quite a few other examples might be cited. One of the most striking passages linking McCallin and Dorcas does not even appear in either of the first two drafts: "From what we could gather among the negroes, Dorcas was evidently well pleased at the idea of McAllins marrying her Misstress. She is a smart, sensible woman, and doubtless entertained similar views with McAllin as related to his ability to do more for her, when he married her Misstress, than he could in his present condition. She would point to McAllin and Mrs. Sharp when they would be walking out to gether, and say, you see that man yonder, he will be your <u>master</u> yet."

Not every revision Farrar made had the effect of casting McCallin in a darker light. Two changes actually marginally weaken the case against the carpenter. In the undated draft Farrar wrote: "There is also a rumor that when he first took up with Dorcas she became pregnant, and that he was instrumental in producing an abortion, which rumor I am informed emenated from Mrs. Sharp." As I pointed out earlier, this allegation was dropped from the draft of September 5, perhaps because Farrar suspected that Clarissa Sharpe would be reluctant to substantiate it. Second, Farrar originally indicated in the draft written on September 5 that Dorcas had been McCallin's mistress from the time he first went to work for Absalom Sharpe, in 1838, "until the present." After editing, the phrase "until the present" became "until he left here."

These revisions, and the many more that might be cited, only confirm that Alexander Farrar was not writing to give an impartial recounting of events but to defend the actions of the investigating party and his own reputation. Should we therefore conclude that he fabricated the evidence against McCallin out of whole cloth? In my opinion, no. Not only do you have to make him out to be quite a Machiavellian character, but keep in mind that there were seventeen other men involved in the investigation. Conspiracy theories in American history are usually fascinating but rarely persuasive. Far more likely, Farrar was merely attempting to provide Henry Drake with what he understood to be the truth, but engaged in hyperbole and distortion to counter what he saw as the lies and distortions being spread by McCallin and his supporters. But regardless—whether he willfully sought to mislead or simply tried to place his case in the most favorable light—his words clearly must be approached with caution.

※ ✢ ※

With that in mind we can turn our attention to the substance of the case against John McCallin. Start with the portrait Farrar paints of McCallin's character. It is difficult enough to develop insight into a person you have known for years, let alone take the measure of a man who lived a century and a half ago from drafts of a letter written by someone who regarded him as an enemy. Even so, if we are limited to a single character study of John McCallin, better that it should come from one of his detractors. At least that way we can be reasonably sure that we have heard the worst there is to hear about him. Alexander Farrar implied that John McCallin was only interested in marrying Clarissa Sharpe so he could get his hands on her property. Maybe so. But acquisitiveness was not exactly an uncommon trait in the antebellum South. Observed Dempsey Jackson, "[T]here is no satis-fying man. The more he gets the more he wants. We here make cotton to buy negroes, and so we go on, we find no stopping place this side of the grave, no satisfying our wants, or our ambition until the cold earth is laid upon us." Furthermore, some of the richest men in the Natchez district at the time of the murder had worked their way up from humble beginnings earlier in the century at least partly through providential marriages. It is true that, after about 1830, as the region lost some of its frontier character and the price of land and slaves began to rise, the large planters developed an increasingly elitist mentality. This had consequences for patterns of mar-riage we will want to examine later. For now it is enough to note that, in his dreams of marrying a wealthy woman, John McCallin was hardly unique among the men of his society.

Considerably more damaging for his reputation would have been the charge that he had kept Dorcas as a mistress—considerably more damaging because it marked the carpenter as a traitor to racial convention. Not that sex between white men and black women was unusual in the Old South. The seduction and rape of female slaves by planters happened often enough to lead Mary Chesnut, wife of a South Carolina senator, to write, in perhaps the most quoted passage from her famous diary, "God forgive us, but ours is a <u>monstrous</u> system & wrong & iniquity—perhaps the rest of the world is as bad—this <u>only</u> I see—like the patriarchs of old our men live all in one house with their wives and their concubines, & the mulattoes one sees in every family exactly resemble the white children—& every lady tells you who is the father of all the mulatto children in every bodys household, but those in her own, she seems to think drop from the clouds, or pretends so to think—"

But long-term liaisons across racial lines—relationships characterized by commitment and devotion—were rare. Moreover, typically they involved whites at the extremes of the social spectrum, the very rich and the very poor, who, for different reasons, could afford to flout community standards. Adam Bingaman was one of the wealthiest men in the lower Mississippi Valley. A resident of Natchez and among its leading citizens, he lived openly with a black woman, scandalizing the town. Eventually he moved to New Orleans, where such arrangements had sanction under the name of "plaçage." Meanwhile, at the other end of the spectrum, down in the brothels and alleyways of places like Natchez-under-the-hill, you would find whites—and here I mean men and women both—who had little to lose by taking up with free blacks and fugitive slaves. It was the closest thing that existed in the Old South to genuine equality between the races.

John McCallin was neither very rich nor very poor, and he had aspira-tions that could never be realized if he openly challenged prevailing cus-toms. For that reason I did not at first take seriously the charge that he and Dorcas had carried on an affair for many years. Oh, I could accept that they had slept together once or twice, maybe on several occasions. But even if Absalom Sharpe had been unusually open-minded, it seemed to me unlikely that he would have allowed a man he employed as a carpenter and ginwright to enter into a relationship certain to bring the disapproval of influential neighbors. And surely it was inconceivable that his widow would have let McCallin come and go as he pleased—would have shown him sufficient kindness that he imagined she might some day consent to marry him—if she suspected he was in love with one of her servants. And then there was the testimony of Dempsey Jackson. According to Alexander Farrar, Jackson, a respected planter, opened the proceedings in Kingston by speaking "of his long acquaintance with McAllin—that he had always sustained a good character—and that the meeting ought to proceed with a great deal of calmness and consideration." McCallin "had always sustained a good character." Hardly the description of a social outcast.

So I concluded that the allegation had to be a gross misrepresentation, a story invented by the slaves for purposes I could not fathom or by the investigating party to discredit McCallin. And that continued to be my view right up to the time I was in the final stages of writing this book. Until, in a last-minute scramble to locate additional biographical material, I came across a piece of information that suddenly gave me doubt. Later I will get to the evidence I discovered, but the result has been to persuade me that McCallin and Dorcas may have been much more deeply involved, and for a much longer period of time, than I had originally imagined.

⊰✠⊱

Farrar offered testimony on McCallin's alleged affair with Dorcas to establish that he was a man without scruples. He was well aware, however, that in the end the case against the carpenter hinged on the weight of evidence linking him to the murder. And here he professed to have no doubt. "[W]e cannot conceive of," he wrote to Henry Drake, "how nearly all the leading negroes on a plantation when arraigned and taken off from each other so they could not hear the statements of each other could tell a story agreeing so precisely with each other and a portion of it be true, and the rest false."

Take note of the phrase "agreeing so precisely with each other." Now think back to some memorable event you shared with a friend. A whitewater rafting trip in the Grand Canyon, maybe, or a World Series game. Chances are when the two of you met a day or two later your recollections were already beginning to differ. That breathtaking catch by the center fielder, did it save one run or two? What caused the raft ahead of you to capsize? Now suppose you got together a month later, and with ten or twenty people who were present at the same event. How likely is it that all of you would remember what you had witnessed in exactly the same way, that your accounts would agree "precisely with each other"?

The accord in the testimony of the slaves is cause for suspicion. It points to the weakness in the case against John McCallin, not its strength. Ironically enough, it is Alexander Farrar himself who explains why, although unwittingly. The relevant passage comes in that section of the letter to Henry Drake where he attempted to demonstrate that Duncan Skinner and McCallin could not have been friends: "The negroes on the Sharp place say, that there was no good feeling existing between Skinner and McAllin—that McAllin knew that Skinner had ordered them, never to stop and talk with him, and that if they did, that he would whip them for it, and for that reason he never did stop, and talk with them, unless there was no chance for Skinner to see, or to hear of it. And that all the chance they had to communicate with McAllin, was through Henderson and Dorcas."

Consider that last sentence again: "all the chance they had to communicate with McCallin, was through Henderson and Dorcas." Any knowledge the other blacks had about what John McCallin actually said came from just two slaves: Henderson and Dorcas. But there is more: "We are satisfied, that Dorcas did tell the negroes what they report, and that such conversations between her and McAllin, did take place. . . . Her whole course indicates, McAllins guilt, and that the negroes have told the truth about her. They have made no statement in reference to her, but what she admits to be true, excepting the implication of McAllin." *Excepting the implication of McAllin.* This is a remarkable admission. Dorcas evidently *denied* that John McCallin was behind the killing. "No severe measure has been resorted to, in order to make Dorcas confess," wrote Farrar, indicating that the investigators had not subjected her to physical coercion in an attempt to get her to implicate him. But this disclaimer can hardly be taken at face value. Whipping was a familiar feature of life in the South, used routinely to punish recalcitrant slaves and force the truth (or what slave-owners took to be the truth) out of them. Furthermore, the investigators had relied on physical coercion to make Henderson and his brother Lem confess and had used verbal intimidation to get Dorcas to show them the contents of McCallin's trunk. If Farrar did withhold the whip when he questioned Dorcas it was not out of any sense of compassion or the fear that he would be charged with wrongdoing for beating a female. As the historian Jacqueline Jones notes, "In the severity of punishment meted out to slaves, little distinction was made between the sexes." We may be sure, then, at the very least, that Farrar and the other whites subjected Dorcas to intense psychological pressure.

It could be that her unwillingness to tell them what they wanted to hear was merely an attempt to protect her lover. That clearly is what Farrar wanted the inquiry in Waterproof to believe. But if our concern is the strength of the case against John McCallin, the bottom line is this: Only two slaves had the opportunity to meet privately with him before the murder. Of those two, one disputed that he played a role in the crime. The other was the confessed organizer of the plot, hardly an unimpeachable witness.

⊰✢⊱

John McCallin claimed that he and Duncan Skinner were close friends. That seems extremely doubtful. Skinner had a good working relationship with Clarissa Sharpe, one that allowed him freedom to run Cedar Grove more or less as he chose; he had little to gain and much to lose should she decide to remarry. Common sense suggests that he and McCallin would have regarded each other with suspicion and perhaps animosity. In all probability there was substance to the claim that McCallin made derogatory comments about Skinner to the slaves and promised them that conditions would improve on the plantation once he became their owner. Does that mean he likely conspired at the overseer's death?

Let me ask you this. If you heard that some ambitious junior executive was taking aside the staff at his office and complaining about the boss, would you conclude that he was inciting them to violence? I know, I know. The analogy is far from exact. But grant me this much: The fact that John McCallin saw an opportunity to rise above his modest circumstances, that he thought Skinner stood in his way, that he may have promised the slaves "better times," hardly proves or even suggests that he arranged for the overseer's murder. It presumably goes without saying that the overwhelming majority of white southerners did not regard the pursuit of upward mobility as justification for homicide. If most of my students are prepared to believe that McCallin was an exception, it is undoubtedly because Alexander Farrar seems able to convict him with his own words: "You boys are a cowardly, chicken hearted set, or you would not stand that man's whipping and beating you so—you would put him out of the way." "I have come all the way back to put you boys on your guard." The letter from Farrar to Drake includes directions McCallin allegedly gave Henderson to kill Skinner, warnings McCallin allegedly gave Henderson and the plough driver not to cooperate with the investigation, and instructions Dorcas allegedly passed on to the other slaves from McCallin. The quoted passages are unambiguous. What we want to know is, are they an accurate statement of what McCallin said?

Probably the first thing worth mentioning is that almost certainly Farrar was working from memory when he wrote the letter. There is no indication in the collection of his papers at Louisiana State University that he or anyone else took notes at the time of the investigation, and, in any event, as he worked his way through several drafts, he freely revised statements the slaves supposedly attributed to McCallin. Because he was writing three months after the testimony was taken, we can safely assume that even if he had been inclined to do so, he would have found it impossibly difficult to produce an accurate transcription of what each slave said. As it is, the editing demonstrates he had no such inclination.

But the problem goes deeper, for at the time of the investigation the slaves themselves were attempting to recall statements McCallin had made a month earlier, and, in the case of those individuals whose only contact with him came through Henderson and Dorcas, their testimony was second hand. Consider the warnings that McCallin allegedly gave to Dorcas, Henderson, and the plough driver following the murder (as described in the draft dated September 5): 1) "Dorcas came out to them, and said, that McAllin said, that 'now you have done got Skinner out of the way, and the white folks have been there and can't find it out, all you have got to do is to keep your mouths shut.'" 2) "The plough driver states that McCallin then came over to the horsepen where they were feeding and said to him I don't know whether you boys killed Mr. Skinner or not, but if you did you had better keep your mouths shut." 3) "[McAllin] said, Hen' do you know what Jesse Skinner is riding about here so much for. I don't know sir, says Hen. Well I can tell you, he is trying to find out who killed his brother, and if you boys dont mind and keep your mouths shut he will find out, for there is a great deal of talk that he was murdered."

Note that the same phrase appears in each case: "Keep your mouths shut." It happens, however, that the phrase does *not* appear in the warning quoted from McCallin to Henderson in the previous, undated, draft. For Farrar to have accurately captured what McCallin said, then, all of the following must be true: 1) McCallin used the exact same phrase in speaking with Henderson, Dorcas, and the plough driver. 2) Dorcas borrowed his words when she passed his warning on to the other slaves. 3) When they were interrogated a month later, Henderson, the plough driver, and all the slaves who spoke with Dorcas—although, seemingly, not Dorcas herself—remembered the phrase and repeated it to the investigators. 4) After almost three months more had passed, Alexander Farrar recalled precisely what all the slaves had said, although in the case of the conversation between McCallin and Henderson, only when he came to writing a third draft. It is not impossible that the sequence of events took place as I have just described. It is, however, extraordinarily unlikely. Indeed, the same kind of objections can be made about any of the statements attributed to McCallin in the drafts from Alexander Farrar to Henry Drake, including most notably his alleged exchange with Henderson prior to the murder. Common sense (again) says that Henderson and the plough driver did tell investigators about conversations they had with McCallin and that the other slaves did report on what they'd heard from Dorcas, but that the words they used were different from those reported by Farrar.

Of course, it is possible that the evidence they gave still tended to incriminate McCallin. But then we would want to consider the circumstances under which they were interrogated. A couple of scenarios sound plausible to me.

Scenario 1: After beating a confession out of Henderson, the investigators ask him why Dorcas hid some of the stolen money in McCallin's trunk. Knowing of their personal dislike for the carpenter and hoping at least to avoid further whippings, he confides that Dorcas and McCallin are lovers and makes up a story about McCallin encouraging him to put Skinner out of the way and returning to the plantation after the murder to warn the slaves to keep their "mouths shut." The plough driver, in an effort to deflect attention from his own involvement—remember, on the morning Skinner was killed, he rushed the field hands out to work as usual—decides to confirm Henderson's testimony. As for the other slaves, they present far less damning evidence, saying only that McCallin had promised Dorcas things would improve once he was their master. The investigators, nonetheless, interpret this as corroboration of Henderson's allegations, and Farrar, when he writes to Drake, puts their statements into words that to his mind better convey the true meaning of their testimony.

Scenario 2: As soon as Farrar and the others find out that the money is in McCallin's trunk they jump to the conclusion that he was involved in the murder. They suggest as much to Henderson when they interrogate him, threatening him with an even more brutal beating should he deny it. Seeing little point in trying to protect a white man, Henderson fabricates the story about his exchanges with McCallin. The investigators, now fully convinced, use similar coercive tactics to get the other slaves to make innocuous remarks by Dorcas sound equally sinister and incriminating.

Of the two scenarios, the second more closely reflects John McCallin's reading of events. When Henry Drake wrote to Alexander Farrar requesting an account of the investigation, he noted, "It has been reported here, that Mrs. Sharp's negroes were examined under the lash, & that they were prompted to accuse McAllain." Farrar denied the charge, maintaining that "[t]he confession in relation to him was made in part by Jane on the first day without her receiving a single lash (for we did not punish her at all during the investigation), or without our putting any questions in reference to McAllin." But this was disingenuous. According to Farrar's own account, Jane only made a single reference to John McCallin and that was to mention that a few of the slaves had hidden their gold and silver in his trunk. She said nothing whatsoever implicating him in the murder and at no point in any of the drafts does Farrar claim that McCallin knew about the stolen money.

⊨✠⊭

The final piece of evidence Farrar had to offer was circumstantial and related to McCallin's movements in the days following the discovery of the body. "McAllins leaving [Cedar Grove] and starting home, and then returning the next day, after having been there 8 or 10 days, and the story of Henderson and the plough driver, in connexion with it, is with us irresistable" is the way he put it. Evidently McCallin came to the plantation shortly after Skinner died, quite possibly at the request of Clarissa Sharpe, and remained there for more than a week. He then left for his home in Waterproof only to reappear the following day. The way Farrar saw it, the only possible explanation for his unexpected return was that while in Natchez he learned there was going to be an investigation and rushed back to warn the slaves.

Realistically, however, McCallin could hardly have imagined that anything he had to say to Henderson, Dorcas, or any of his other supposed accomplices would have kept them from confessing or from implicating him once they were put under the lash. In truth, his movements are comprehensible only if you assume he was innocent. Had he actually been behind the murder, almost certainly he would have rushed back to his home in Louisiana the moment he learned there was going to be an investigation, made hasty arrangements to convert as much of his property to cash as possible, and fled the district. I would suggest that the following explanation for his return to the plantation has to be considered far more convincing than the one offered by Farrar:

When McCallin received word that Duncan Skinner had been found dead, he hurried to Cedar Grove. He wanted to comfort Clarissa Sharpe but also, if you believe the investigators' claims that Skinner had sabotaged his attempts to marry her, to see if he could take advantage of the overseer's demise. On arriving at the plantation he learned that a coroner's jury had found the death to be accidental and, having no reason to believe otherwise, hardly gave the verdict a second thought. No doubt it all just seemed like an act of blessed good fortune. After a little more than a week on the plantation he left for his home in Waterproof, carrying a request from Clarissa Sharpe to check in the jails at Natchez and Vidalia for Anderson. (Anderson, of course, was subsequently identified as one of the murderers, but no one at this point was suggesting his disappearance was tied in with Skinner's death.) At one of the jails, however, or perhaps while talking with some friends in town, McCallin heard about the article in the *Courier* and the likelihood there would be an investigation. He rushed back to Cedar Grove to tell Clarissa Sharpe.

Alexander Farrar seemed to believe that any subsequent conversation between McCallin and the slaves was proof of his complicity. But put yourself in McCallin's shoes. During the week he had spent at Cedar Grove following discovery of the body, Jesse Skinner, who apparently was making inquiries on the plantation at the same time, never confided in him that he suspected his brother had been murdered. Neither did Farrar, who, in fact, organized an investigation into the death without saying a word to him. And, this, by Farrar's admission, was before anyone ever imagined that McCallin was implicated in the crime. McCallin believed he had a personal stake in Clarissa Sharpe's affairs. It would hardly be surprising if he decided to make inquiries of his own.

But McCallin was not the only one kept in the dark about plans to interrogate the slaves. Farrar wrote to Henry Drake: "Caution was observed to prevent the design from becoming public. Mrs. Sharp was not apprised of the intention until the morning of the investigation." This is an astonishing disclosure. McCallin would surely have tried to exploit it. Assume he did talk to Henderson and the plough driver. We can imagine what he said to Clarissa Sharpe: "This is your plantation. You have a right to know what happened." So maybe it was true, as Farrar claimed, that the slaves learned about the rumors in Natchez from McCallin. But given how Farrar had treated him and the widow he hoped to marry, it is difficult to make the case he owed anyone an explanation or apology.

Three weeks after writing his letter to Drake—and only days before the meeting in Waterproof was to reconvene to consider any new evidence— Farrar and the planters William Foules and Alfred Swayze came to Cedar Grove to interview Clarissa Sharpe. According to the affidavit they later signed, she told them "that she did not know that McCallin was going to come back—that he never told her what he came back for—and she did not know what he did come back for, unless it was for what the negroes said." But consider the circumstances in which she found herself. If I am correct, McCallin returned from Natchez to inform her that Skinner had been murdered and that Farrar was undertaking plans for an investigation without her knowledge. How candid was she likely to be? Could she really make a statement that at least implicitly would have raised questions about the propriety of Farrar's actions? If she had been a woman of greater self-confidence and independence, perhaps. But, as we shall see, Farrar was the administrator of her husband's estate and the man who served as her financial adviser. She was hardly in a position to contradict his explanation of events. What the affidavit really highlights is that three weeks after Farrar sent his report to Henry Drake, at least some people still had doubts about his interpretation of McCallin's movements. Otherwise, no corroborating testimony from Clarissa Sharpe would have been necessary.

⌗✝⌗

It took extraordinary courage for John McCallin to defy the notice in the newspapers warning him to leave the community. He was not exaggerating when he said that he was putting his life at risk. Even so, it is hard—hard for me, anyway—to feel much compassion for him. On the basis of what we know, he almost certainly was a fortune hunter, he attempted to subvert the authority of the overseer relied on by the widow he hoped to marry, he may well have had a clandestine affair with her servant, and he evidently spread malicious gossip about one of the leading figures in the community, although, granted, Alexander Farrar was spreading malicious gossip about him at the same time. Then, too, some might ask, in a society in which only blacks suffered what the novelist William Styron has called the "abyssal pain" of slavery, how much sympathy should we reserve for any white man?

Still, however we might feel about him, a considered and fair reading of the evidence suggests that John McCallin was a victim of a miscarriage of justice. The testimony the slaves offered against him was clearly unreliable, the circumstantial evidence tenuous at best. When you add to that the fact that he had lived in the area for years without anyone, it seems, suggesting that he was a man of criminal intent, that he had only recently acquired a home and part interest in a store in Louisiana, and that he took his life in his hands when he publicly protested his innocence, the charges against him seem hard to credit. Very likely he was glad to see the end of Duncan Skinner. But, in my view at least, there is no convincing reason to believe he conspired at Skinner's death.

There is an irony here. The system that made John McCallin a victim was ostensibly designed to protect nonslaveholding whites like himself. Because the law of Mississippi barred blacks from testifying against whites, John McCallin could never have been brought to trial. But as should by now be apparent, prohibitions against black testimony in court did not mean that planters like Alexander Farrar regarded the statements of slaves as necessarily untrustworthy. On the contrary, the men who investigated the death of Duncan Skinner were, in the end, prepared to convict McCallin on what amounted to little more than the uncorroborated word of the confessed ringleader of the plot. In a court of law, represented by legal counsel and with his fate in the hands of a jury of his peers, McCallin surely would have been acquitted even if the testimony by the slaves had been admissible. All of which highlights how slender the case was against him. But it also returns us to the question of motive. Because if John McCallin was innocent, then we must look beyond his ambition to explain why Henderson, Reuben, and Anderson murdered their overseer.

4

Slavery

Every southern state had a slave code, or, as it was referred to in the 1857 digest of the *Laws of the State of Mississippi*, "An Act in Relation to Slaves, Free Negroes and Mulattoes." Most of the ninety-three articles in the Mississippi act were concerned with defining the property rights of slaveholders and designating procedures for dealing with slaves and free blacks accused of crimes. But a total of five articles, numbered 4 through 8 in the legislation, outlined the "Duties of Masters towards Slaves":

Art. 4.
No master shall inflict cruel or unusual punishment upon his slave or slaves, or cause or permit the same to be done; and any master, or other person entitled to the services of a slave or slaves, or any person having or taking possession or custody of a slave or slaves, who shall inflict such cruel or unusual punishment on such slave or slaves, or shall authorize or permit such punishment to be inflicted, may be indicted therefor, and on conviction shall be fined according to the magnitude of the offence, in any sum not exceeding five hundred dollars, and imprisoned in the county jail for a term not exceeding twelve months, or both, at the discretion of the court.

Art. 5.
It shall be the duty of owners of slaves to treat them with humanity, to provide for them necessary clothing and provisions, and to abstain from injuries to them extending to endanger life or limb; and if any owner, hirer or employer of slaves, shall have failed to supply them necessary clothing and provisions, or shall have treated them with inhumanity, the person so offending may be indicted therefor, and on conviction shall be fined in any sum not exceeding five hundred dollars, or may be imprisoned in the county jail not exceeding three months, or both, at the discretion of the court.

Art. 6.

Whenever any person shall be charged, under oath, by any citizen of the State, before any justice of the peace, with having violated the provisions of this section, it shall be the duty of such justice immediately to issue his warrant commanding any constable or other officer of his court, to bring before said justice forthwith the slave or slaves upon whom it is alleged such crime has been committed; and it shall be the duty of such justice to appoint three or more respectable slave-holders to examine the person or persons of such slave or slaves, to ascertain if the proof of the infliction of such punishment exists or not on his or her body.

Art. 7.

In all cases where it is established that such punishment has been inflicted, it shall be the duty of such justice to require the accused to give bond and security, in such reasonable sum as said justice may think proper, for his appearance at the succeeding term of the circuit court of the proper county.

Art. 8.

In all trials for offences under this act, it shall be lawful for either party to prove the general character of the accused for cruelty or for humanity to the slaves under his or her control; and the person having the immediate control of such slave, at the time of the infliction of such cruel or unusual punishment, or other unlawful treatment, shall until the contrary appear, be presumed to have inflicted the same.

Slaveholders were occasionally brought to trial under these articles, occasionally even convicted. Community pressure served to reduce instances of outright sadism, if only from time to time and on a haphazard basis. But notwithstanding the presumption of guilt that the law allowed and the apparent mildness of the penalties, the vast majority of people who committed acts of "cruelty" or "inhumanity" could safely assume that they would never be brought to trial, or if brought to trial and of good standing in the community, could reasonably anticipate a favorable verdict from the "respectable" slaveholders selected to sit in judgment on them. Even those individuals who were held in low esteem by their neighbors could expect to escape retribution, at least through the agency of the legal system, due to the provision in the code that prohibited testimony by blacks against whites, the same provision that would have prevented the state from bringing charges against John McCallin.

The weakness of the provisions mandating the responsibilities of masters did not, however, mean that slaves on estates such as Cedar Grove were effectively without protection. On each plantation there was what amounted to an unwritten law that defined the duties of master and slaves. In principle, of course, slaveowners had few duties other than those they imposed on themselves. But in Mississippi, as elsewhere in the South, planters customarily accepted that they had obligations to their slaves, even if those obligations were largely unenforceable by the courts. Or, as the wealthy Natchez planter William Newton Mercer put it with self-serving exaggeration, "One of my greatest responsibilities has been to treat justly and kindly that class of my fellow beings who were made dependent on me by Providence."

The most fundamental obligation of master to slave was to provide the "necessary" food and clothing called for in the slave code, and to that we should add shelter as well. The following list of clothing allotments on Carlisle, a plantation belonging to Stephen Duncan, one of the wealthiest men in the South and a close friend of Alexander Farrar, was fairly typical:

> For each man & boy—for winter garments—2 ¾ yds Jeans for pants & a Blanket coat. 3 Blankets will make 4 coats—
> For each woman & Girl 1 Blanket coat & 5 yds. of Linsey for gowns—
> For each child—1 slip of Linsey & 3 of Cotton. An average of 1 ½ yds. to each will make a slip—
> For each Man & Boy—5 ½ yds. of Lowells or Osnaburgs for 2 pair pants—& 8 yds of 4/4 cotton for three shirts each—
> For each woman & girl—2 ½ yds. Lowells or Osnaburgs for Petticoats—& 13 yds 4/4 shirting for 3 shifts and 1 gown—
> The women who do not work out get no Blanket coat & get but 1 pair shoes—
> All who work out get Blanket coats & 2 pairs shoes. One pair Boots is equal to 2 pairs shoes.

Each adult slave was given a ration of one peck of cornmeal and three to four pounds of salt pork or bacon per week. They would supplement these provisions with meat and fish caught during their spare hours, with chickens and eggs—Jane, the cook on Cedar Grove, and her husband, Burrell, hid their share of the money stolen from Duncan Skinner in their hen house—and with vegetables grown in gardens allotted to them specifically for that purpose. As for housing, it varied widely from plantation to plantation, with some small number of slaves living in brick cabins with plank floors and glass windows. Most, however, had to make do with rude shacks.

Abolitionists at the time, and many historians since, have characterized the food, shelter, and clothing provided by southern planters as inadequate. Field hands often went around in ragged clothes, children in tattered shifts; cabins were generally poorly ventilated, too cold in the winter, too warm in the summer; many slaves had next to no furniture or eating utensils; the slave diet was appallingly unbalanced by present-day nutritional standards. But planters insisted that the average slave was better off in a material sense than many northern and European laborers, and recent scholarship has suggested that this view was not entirely unfounded. In any case, for our purposes what is important is that planters regarded the providing of food, shelter, and clothing as something more than simply a means of protecting the value of their investment. It was, as I pointed out, an obligation.

And they acknowledged other obligations as well—the obligation to provide medical care for their slaves, for example. Planters and overseers attended to sick laborers themselves but did not hesitate to call in doctors when necessary. Clarissa Sharpe set aside a room in the L-shaped building next to the main residence at Cedar Grove as an infirmary. A statement of account in the Farrar Papers indicates that Dr. G. G. Groves made a total of forty trips in 1856 to treat slaves on Bonne Ridge plantation in Catahoula Parish, Louisiana, which Alexander Farrar had acquired from Clarissa Sharpe the previous year. The bill for his services amounted to more than $350.

When slaves were seriously injured in an accident or when they lived beyond the age when they could serve as productive laborers, their owners were expected to provide for them. Admittedly, the subsistence afforded was often meager, and not a few of the elderly and infirm had to turn to family members or friends for assistance. But, as slaveowners were often heard to ask, how many free laborers in the North received even meager compensation from their former employers once they had outlived their usefulness?

Planters also accepted the responsibility to provide their slaves with regular breaks from labor. Sunday was a day of rest and, on many plantations, Saturday afternoon as well. Time was set aside for celebrations at certain moments during the work year—for instance, following the harvest. And slaves were allowed a number of traditional holidays, including Independence Day (ironically enough) and Easter Monday. Even unfeeling slaveowners gave their hands three days off at Christmas, while generous masters allowed five days to a week and hosted a grand barbecue with drinking and dancing and gifts. Recalled one Mississippi slave from the distant perspective of the 1930s, "Christmas was de time o' all times on dat old plantation. Dey don' have no such as dat now. Every child brought a stockin' up to de Big House to be filled. Dey all wanted one o' de mistis' stockin's, cause now she weighed nigh on to three hundred pounds. Candy and presents was put in piles for everyone. When de names was called dey walked up and got it." Slaves expected small tokens at other times as well, for example when they put in extra labor or worked especially hard. More often than not, most planters obliged, making gifts of some tobacco, or colorful ribbons, or a little cash to purchase items in town.

Why *did* the planters oblige? Why did they provide Christmas presents and medical care and shelter for the elderly? After all, as the historian Ulrich Phillips observed some years ago, "Theoretically the master might be expected perhaps to expend the minimum possible to keep his slaves in strength, to discard the weaklings and the aged, to drive his gang early and late, to scourge the laggards hourly, to secure the whole with fetters by day and bolts by night, and to keep them in perpetual terror of his wrath." A variety of explanations have been proposed as to why planters chose a more benign—or perhaps I should say "less barbaric"—course, but, according to the scholar widely acknowledged today as the leading authority on slavery in the Old South, Eugene Genovese, there were two main contributing factors. First was the closing of the African slave trade by Congress in 1808. With legal imports shut off and with the supply of illegal imports uncertain, slaveholders had to foster conditions that would encourage slave men and women to reproduce. The emergence of a rough numerical equality between the sexes during the eighteenth century proved essential, but clearly if the slave population were to grow, laborers would have to survive beyond young adulthood and experience at least some minimal stability in their lives, as well as hold some expectation for minimal stability in the lives of their children. It therefore tells us something that the life expectancy of southern slaves in the nineteenth century was substantially higher than that of slaves in the Caribbean and at least equal to that of laborers in western Europe. Despite a high infant-mortality rate, the slave population grew rapidly by natural increase, almost as rapidly as the white population.

The second factor Genovese cites is the residency pattern of southern planters. With the exception of Haiti, which secured independence early in the nineteenth century, the principal islands of the Caribbean were colonies. Many of the men who owned large plantations in the West Indies kept homes in England or France or Spain. They rarely if ever saw their slaves, instead entrusting the operation of their estates to managers whose sole responsibility was to produce profits as large and as rapidly as possible. Under the circumstances, there was no possibility of a bond forming between slaveowner and slave and little likelihood of masters developing a sense of responsibility for their laborers. In the southern states, however, planters lived on their plantations or, if they chose to take up residence in a town such as Natchez, visited them regularly. They knew their slaves by name and inevitably came to see them as human beings—inferior human beings, to be sure, but human beings all the same. And to justify holding human beings in bondage—justify not only to others, but themselves as well—they had to convince themselves that slavery provided benefits to laborers as well as to masters, which meant they had to acknowledge a measure of obligation to their slaves.

The idea of reciprocity is central to what Genovese has called the "paternalism" of the antebellum plantation: Planters came to see the labor of the slaves as a legitimate return for the care and protection they provided. At the same time, the slaves saw the gardens, holidays, and gifts, the food, shelter, clothing, and medical care, as a claim they had on their owners for services involuntarily rendered. In a very rough sense, then, or so the argument goes, the master-slave relationship took on the appearance of the relationship between a father and child. The master provided the necessities of life, while at the same time insisting on the right to monitor the social lives of his laborers and to instruct them in proper moral behavior; the slaves returned what at least passed for obedience. Ideally the relationship took the form described in 1860 by E. N. Elliott, president of Planters' College, a small academy located in Port Gibson, Mississippi, about thirty miles north of Natchez:

> Slavery is the duty and obligation of the slave to labor for the mutual benefit of both master and slave, under a warrant of protection, and a comfortable subsistence, under all circumstances. . . . Nor is the labor of the slave solely for the benefit of the master, but for the benefit of all concerned; for himself to repay the advances made for his support in childhood, for present subsistence, and for guardianship and protection, and to accumulate a fund for sickness, disability, and old age. The master, as the head of the system, has a right to the obedience and labor of the slave, but the slave has also his mutual rights in the master; the right of protection, the right of counsel and guidance, the right of subsistence, the right of care and attention in sickness and old age. He has also a right in his master as the sole arbiter in all his wrongs and difficulties, and as a merciful judge and dispenser of law to award the penalty of his misdeeds.

The concept of paternalism has come to dominate discussion of the antebellum plantation ever since Genovese first introduced it almost thirty years ago. It is important to be clear what he means by the term, but also what he does not mean. What he does not mean is that slaveholders were kindly or benevolent. Southern slavery was, he says, "cruel, unjust, exploitative, oppressive." Planters routinely used the whip to compel obedience, freely treated female slaves as sexual objects for their own pleasure, and bought, sold, gambled, and swapped men and women, boys, girls, and infants. But because they could neither profitably nor in good conscience model themselves on Ulrich Phillips' hypothetical master, they put into place rules and regulations on their estates—what I earlier referred to as the "unwritten law" of the plantation—that supposedly were reciprocal in nature and accorded master and slave responsibilities appropriate to their respective stations in life. Of course, that true reciprocity existed was a fiction. The ideal described by E. N. Elliott was never approximated—never remotely approximated—in reality. But that does not mean that planters were unconstrained by a sense of obligation, merely that their sense of obligation was only one, and not the most important, factor determining their relations with their slaves.

I have drawn on the concept of paternalism in my own research and use it as an organizing theme in my course on the history of the Old South. Like Genovese, I take pains to clarify my meaning. I emphasize to my students that in describing the planters as paternalistic I do not for a moment wish to suggest they were, as a class, compassionate or benevolent. They were first and foremost businessmen, who engaged in the production of cotton (or tobacco, or hemp, or rice, or sugar) because it brought them profits, and who used slave labor above all because it was cheaper than the free-labor alternative. But it would be a mistake, I argue, to assume that their daily interaction with their slaves was dictated solely by financial consider-ations. When, for example, planters provided care for the infirm, it was not—at least not in most cases—because they perceived some immediate eco-nomic benefit to be gained. Rather, they took it for granted that slaves who had been incapacitated were nonetheless entitled to continued support. When they gave holidays to their slaves, they did not as a rule refuse time off to laborers who had been troublesome. The obligation to provide a break from work existed independent of any personal feelings toward individual slaves.

And how do my students react to all this? Let's just say this is one of those times I referred to earlier in which teacher and students draw differ-ent conclusions from the same material. No matter how much you try to deny it, they say to me, a system that was "cruel, unjust, exploitative, op-pressive" must, by definition, have been something other than "paternalis-tic." That the term itself, paternalism, depends on drawing comparisons—even heavily qualified comparisons—between the way planters treated their slaves and a father treats his children is particularly offensive. What father would sell his own sons and daughters?, they invariably ask me.

It is important to listen to your students, and to keep an open mind. In the case of paternalism, after almost twenty years of teaching about slavery I have finally come around to their way of thinking. I figure, if a word sug-gests one meaning to professional historians and something else to the rest of society, then arguably those historians who want to influence thinking beyond the classroom should look for another way of characterizing what-ever it is they are attempting to describe. Paternalism, I have come to be-lieve, does imply a level of benevolence that is inconsistent with the nature of the relationship between most masters and most slaves.

But many of my students want to go farther. They challenge the idea that the majority of planters could ever have felt a genuine sense of duty toward their slaves. Aware from lectures and assigned readings that slaves were frequently subjected to humiliation and physical abuse, that during the nineteenth century a planter who purchased a slave could expect, on average, a return of 10 percent a year, substantially more than he or she could earn from investment in railroad stock or most manufacturing enterprises, that hundreds of thousands of slaves experienced the trauma of sale at some time during their lives, they tend to assume that statements by slaveholders testifying to their feelings for their laborers are mere rhetoric, not to be taken seriously. In that regard they echo the view presented by historian James Oakes in his influential interpretation of the Old South, *The Ruling Race*. Oakes maintains that the planters' materialism precluded them from developing any meaningful sense of social obligation. To the extent that slaveowners provided their hands with care and protection beyond the basic food, shelter, and clothing required to keep up their strength, it was simply to make them more cooperative and efficient workers.

The historical record in and of itself does not really allow us to speak with anything approaching certainty about the motives of most slaveholders. It would obviously be naive simply to take their words at face value. And while we can try to draw inferences from their behavior, any industrious historian can turn up countless instances of planters who treated their slaves with apparent concern and even affection, as well as countless instances of planters who treated their slaves with callous indifference if not brute inhumanity. It really all comes down to your understanding of human nature. Many of my students seem to assume that a hunger for profit will inevitably overwhelm any inclination to act unselfishly. Or, to borrow a central concept of sociobiologists, that altruism itself can be explained in terms of self-interest.

I am somewhat less cynical (and a product of different times). Without a doubt the primary concern for any planter was to advance his own material interests and secure the financial well-being of his family; in the South this meant acquiring ever greater numbers of slaves and larger tracts of land. But my understanding of human nature tells me that the ideas individuals hold about the appropriate means for advancing their material interests will depend to a significant extent on the context in which they find themselves. History shows, for example, that societies similar in their devotion to profit, but different with respect to their organization of labor, can produce quite different views of social obligation. I've already drawn a comparison between the Old South and the Caribbean. Now let's turn our attention to the urban North during the early stages of industrialization.

At the time of the American Revolution, production of manufactured goods was carried out by artisans working in their own homes assisted perhaps by journeymen and apprentices. The craftsman served as something of a father figure to his laborers; they lived with him or boarded nearby and he viewed them as dependents, like other members of his family. He took it to be his responsibility to see that they were adequately fed and clothed and also to ensure that they lived useful, moral lives. In short, his relationship with his laborers, much more than the relationship between a southern planter and his slaves, might legitimately be described as "paternalistic."

During the first half of the nineteenth century, however, significant improvements in transportation—the building of turnpikes and canals, the invention of steamboats and railroads—led to a transformation in the organization of labor in northern cities. As it became easier to move goods across country, substantial new markets opened up. Few artisans had the resources to take advantage of the expanded demand, and so merchants began to gain control of the process of manufacturing, eventually rationalizing production by bringing workers into a "central shop," forerunner of the modern factory. The workers, many of whom were immigrants, were paid a wage—usually a fairly insubstantial wage—and out of that, plus money earned by their wives and children, were expected to provide for their own support. Not surprisingly, the view of human obligation that the manufacturer adopted differed starkly from the view of human obligation held by the master craftsman. To the manufacturer, all workingmen were independent and therefore should be expected to take responsibility for their own lives and the lives of their families. After all, were they not free to sell their labor in the marketplace and did not the marketplace accord its benefits in a fair and just manner? (It's not only slave societies that produce fictions.)

Southern planters were every bit as materialistic as northern manufacturers, but inevitably they developed a way of looking at relations with their laborers that was appropriate to the situation in which they found themselves. In order to protect his investment, the slaveholder—any slaveholder—must provide his laborers with food, shelter, and clothing. Should he come to believe that they have a legitimate claim on him for these things—or, more strongly, that such basic necessities are theirs by right—then his relationship to them will tend to take on a paternalistic aspect. Very few southern planters ever formally admitted that slaves had rights, and offhand I can think of no instance where a slaveowner knowingly put his own economic survival at serious risk to ensure the well-being of his laborers. All the same, it would be a mistake to conclude that the Mississippi planter conceived of his responsibilities to his slaves in the same nakedly exploitative way as a Londoner who owned an estate in Jamaica, just as it would be a mistake to imagine that an eighteenth-century artisan in rural Massachusetts held the same attitude toward his journeymen as a nineteenth century Boston manufacturer did toward his wage laborers. The point I wish to make is that a commitment to production for profit did not—and does not—preclude the development of a wide range of beliefs, some seemingly contradictory, about human obligation.

The determination of planters to advance their own material interests existed in tension with their sense of responsibility to their laborers. The nature of this tension is perhaps best revealed in the ambivalence they exhibited toward the buying and selling of slaves. They did both, of course, but they held most slave dealers in low regard and many of them also attempted to preserve family relationships. Clarissa Sharpe, as we have seen, instructed in her will that the slaves on Cedar Grove were not to be sold for twenty-one years subsequent to her death and, in any sales that took place after that time, family groups were to be kept together. Without question, she had more on her mind than mere financial considerations when thinking about the disposition of her estate. Still, it appears that she did assume one day her slaves would end up on the market. The contradictory influences evident in Clarissa Sharpe's thinking were evident in the thinking of planters generally. Which is why comments like the following, taken from a letter written to Alexander Farrar in 1859 by his son, away at Harvard, should always be read with a double meaning: "I am afraid that the fever has got in the quarters and you may lose valuable lives."

⛬✟⛬

It was in this situation, with its inherent tension between the planters' material interests and their sense of duty, that the overseer found himself. His principal responsibility, as he well understood, was to produce profits. The respected Natchez planter John Carmichael Jenkins noted in his journal, December 21, 1854: "Engaged a Mr. Wickwere to oversee River Place for next year. I am to pay him at a rate of 900 Dolls & if he makes 600 Bales of cotton & full crop of Corn agree to pay him 1000." Manuals for overseers instructed them how best to get the work out of their laborers necessary to ensure themselves such bonuses:

> It is indispensable that you exercise judgment and consideration in the management of the Negroes under your charge. Be *firm*, and at the same time *gentle* in your control. Never display yourself before them in a passion; and even if inflicting the severest punishment, do so in a mild, cool manner, and it will produce a tenfold effect. When you find it necessary to use the whip—and desirable as it would be to dispense with it entirely, it *is* necessary at times—apply it slowly and deliberately. . . . The indiscriminate, constant and excessive use of the whip, is altogether unnecessary and inexcusable. . . . Never threaten a negro, but if you have occasion to punish, do it at once, or say nothing until ready to do so. A violent and passionate threat, will often scare the best disposed negro to the woods. Always keep your word with them, in punishments as well as in rewards. If you have named the penalty for any certain offence, inflict it without listening to a word of excuse. Never forgive that in one, that you would punish in another, but treat all alike, showing no favoritism. By pursuing such a course, you convince them that you act from principle and not from impulse, and that you will certainly enforce your rules.

But as much as planters demanded that their overseers ensure large profits, they also directed them, if with somewhat less evident conviction, to provide slaves with decent care. William Minor of Natchez, whose extensive holdings in the Mississippi Valley included both cotton and sugar plantations, instructed his overseers to "treat all the negroes with Kindness and humanity, both in sickness and in health." And the manual for overseers cited above included the following advice in regard to slave religious observances: "You will find that an hour devoted every Sabbath morning to their moral and religious instruction, would prove a great aid to you in bringing about a better state of things amongst the negroes. It has been thoroughly tried, and with the most satisfactory results, in many parts of the south. As a mere matter of interest, it has proved to be advisable—to say nothing of it as a point of duty."

Note the use of the terms "interest" and "duty" again. If other overseers had been accorded the kind of latitude Clarissa Sharpe apparently allowed Duncan Skinner, then no doubt they would have resolved the tension between the two on their own terms, as Skinner presumably did. But most planters seem to have distrusted their overseers almost as much as they distrusted their slaves. Indeed, they counted on slaves and overseers to inform on each other. Consider, for instance, the following series of entries from a journal kept in 1859 by Benjamin L. C. Wailes, who served with Alexander Farrar on the board of directors of Jefferson College, a private academy for young men in Adams County. Fonsylvania was his plantation near Warrenton, south of Vicksburg.

> Thursday, June 2—On returning from the College yesterday about 5 O'clock in the evening, found letters from Mr Owens, and Rogillio, my overseer, from which I learned that some disorders had taken place on the plantation, and two of the negroes had absconded, and giving rather unfavorable reports of the crop. Owens hints at some deficiency existing in Rogillio and asks me to come up and make some changes.
>
> Saturday, June 4—Met with Mr Pettit at Warrenton and he told me there had been great abuses at the plantation; that it was the current opinion of the neighborhood that my overseer had not been acting correctly; that the crop was in the grass and very unpromising and that he had advised Dr Beall to write to me on the subject. Tried to get the particulars from Owens, and got from him a confirmation of the crop negligence and unfitness of the overseer. Sent cab back and mounted the old brown, and riding through the crop examining my cotton in the Owens field, saw some of the women plowing their corn patches in a distant part of the field, one of whom I found to be Jane the wife of John, one of the absentees and learned from her that Clem, the brother of John and the other runaway, had just passed by her. Rode in the direction pointed out by her and called to him, and he came out of bushes nearby and followed me home to Fonsylvania, and a few minutes after John also came in to me. Heard their version of the difficulty, which being mainly corroborated from sources not altogether friendly

to them, was mote to be relied upon. Sent for Rogillio the overseer to the house and got his account of the matter, which showed, that, as to Clem, at least, he had acted under a misconception, and that the difficulty had been created very unnecessarily. Shall make further investigations.

Sunday, June 5—A number of the negroes called in to-day to give me their account of the causes of the disturbances on the place during the past week or two, and though several were hostile and unfriendly to each other, there was a general correspondence in their statements, as well as accounts of white persons in the neighborhood. From all of which I gather that the overseer has been indolent, seldom in the field with the hands; that he is deficient in judgment and temper, and brutal in his conduct to the negroes. In short, I satisfy myself of his unfitness for the situation in which he was placed. That he had driven the boys John and Clem off the place with loaded fire arms and in fear of their lives. He had been neglectful and inattentive to the sick, and, although recommended to me as a religious man, proved passionate and profane, and in short brutish in his disposition toward the negroes.

Monday, June 6—Discharged Rogillio this morning.

Tuesday, June 7—Gave out the negroes's summer clothing, and gave them a war talk. Did not punish any of them in consideration of their improper treatment, although two or three of them merited a little flag-ellation. They have gone to work with good spirit and I trust my lecturing will not be lost upon them.

No doubt many overseers, Rogillio perhaps among them, were incompetent at what they did. Most, however, were also victims, if that is the right word, of the unrealistic expectations of their employers. Planters knew full well the difficulties involved in producing a crop. But, shielded from the day-to-day problems of coercing labor from recalcitrant slaves, they found it easier to tell themselves that there was no necessary contradiction between "interest" and "duty," that any difficulties were a result of mismanagement by the overseer.

It was easier to tell the slaves that as well. Many slaves were, understandably, susceptible to the comforting fiction that it was the overseer who was the principal agent of their hardships. That most overseers came from the lower class and were looked upon with scarcely concealed contempt by planters only fed this illusion. Some remarks made to an interviewer many years after the Civil War by James Lucas, who had been a slave on a plantation near Natchez, illustrate the point: "[M]arsters wid out wives wuz de debble. Hit really wuzn't de marsters so much ez hit was dey po' white obberseers. Law miss, obberseers wuz wuss den bulldogs. Sometimes dey put people in stocks en whipped dem but what de marster didn't know didn't hurt him."

We know little about the background of Duncan Skinner. Census records indicate that he was born in Darlington County, South Carolina, that his father, Lemuel Skinner, was a farmer, that his mother was named Nicy, and that he had ten brothers and sisters. His tombstone tell us his age, 37, at the time of his death. A notice of estate sale run by Jesse Skinner in the Natchez *Courier* several months after the murder suggests he owned a slave woman named Susan and her three children. If so, he was more successful than most overseers. We know one other thing about him as well. We know that he was cruel. In Darlington County the Skinners had a reputation for their hair-trigger tempers. With that in mind, recall the testimony given by Henderson under interrogation, as reported by Alexander Farrar: "Henderson the carriage driver states that he went up stairs one night to get McAllin's boots to black, that McAllin, was standing by a window looking out towards the quarter listening to a noise there, occasioned by Skinner whipping some negroes,—that he said, Hen' there is quite a fuss in the quarter to night, and that he (Hen') replied yes, but it is no uncommon thing here. To which McAllin replied, Well if I was you boys, I would get rid of that man. How, asked Henderson? Why: I would put him out of the way. After some further talk Henderson went down stairs with the boots, and in the morning when he returned with them, McAllin rose up in his bed, and said, Hen' how long did that fuss last last night in the quarter? I don't know sir—it is such a common thing here, I didn't pay much attention to it."

Alexander Farrar had no reason to fabricate Henderson's testimony about Skinner's vicious streak. On the contrary, because it shows that the slaves had good reasons of their own for wanting the overseer out of the way, it tends to weaken the case against John McCallin. We also know from Farrar's account that the slaves told the investigators, "It seemed like Mrs. Sharp had more confidence in Skinner than any body else. That she went by every thing he said." So the possibility was remote that they might have convinced her to dismiss Skinner by resorting to the tactics used by the laborers on Fonsylvania to bring about the firing of Rogillio. Under the circumstances, there would appear to be little doubt why Henderson, Reuben, and Anderson murdered their overseer: he was brutal. It hardly seems likely they had to get the idea from some nonslaveholding white carpenter.

⊣✦⊢

When the investigators came to Cedar Grove they decided to interrogate Jane, the cook, first, reasoning, as Alexander Farrar explained to Henry Drake, that the murder "could not happen without her knowing it." Most plantation laborers in the South were field hands, but a minority, such as Jane, served as cooks or servants or artisans or in other specialized roles. When Frederick Olmsted visited the lower Mississippi Valley during the 1850s, he stopped at a plantation outside Natchez that had 135 slaves, including "3 mechanics (blacksmith, carpenter, and wheelwright), 2 seamstresses, 1 cook, 1 stable servant, 1 cattle tender, 1 hog-tender, 1 teamster,

1 house servant (overseer's cook), and one midwife and nurse." To become a cook, such as Jane, or house servant, or artisan, you had to demonstrate some talent for the task required, but you also had to show a devotion to the interests of your owner. No planter was going to entrust his horses to a carriage driver who habitually mistreated them and no planter's wife was going to turn over her kitchen to a slave who was careless with the dishes or routinely burned the roast. This does not mean that servants were invariably assumed to be trustworthy. Before retiring for the night Jane had to turn over the keys to the kitchen to Duncan Skinner.

In return for their service, slaves who worked in and around the house or at a craft could look forward to privileged treatment. Servants, in particular, were better fed and received more respectable-looking clothing than field hands, and, much more important, they could reasonably expect their families would be spared if the owner decided to put members of the slave force up for sale. Still, not all laborers wished to be servants. Maids and carriage drivers were on call all the time, including Sundays and holidays. Furthermore, servants had to spend many hours in enforced intimacy with whites—a privilege in the minds of the whites perhaps, but presumably a source of discomfort to most slaves. Incidents such as the following, recorded in July 1856 by Eliza Magruder, a teenager who lived on her uncle's plantation near Natchez, were common: "I was very much provoked with Lavinia this morning, for telling me a falsehood as well as being impertinent, Aunt Olivia boxed her ears for it." Plantation mistresses who suspected their husbands of sexual infidelity with a servant could be particularly vindictive.

It was for that reason, because of the physical and psychological costs experienced by house servants, that artisans, such as Reuben, who was a carpenter, held the most widely desired positions in the hierarchy of slave occupations. In addition to receiving better food and clothing than field hands, skilled laborers also enjoyed an unusual degree of autonomy. They could, within limits, control the conditions and pace of their own labor. Furthermore, as can be seen in many surviving antebellum plantation buildings and cultural artifacts, some were able to find meaningful expression for their artistic sensibilities. For the males there might also be the opportunity to travel about the countryside, as it was common for planters to hire craftsmen out for short periods of time, or, if they owned more than one place, to move them around from plantation to plantation as need dictated. At the time of Absalom Sharpe's death in 1851, Reuben was working on Bonne Ridge, the Sharpe estate in Louisiana. The only reason we know he was a carpenter is because the probate records of Catahoula Parish, in noting that he was to be assessed as part of the slave force on Cedar Grove, mention his occupation in passing.

Because of the privileges available to them and the high regard in which they were held by their owners, some servants and artisans came to look upon field hands with unconcealed disdain. Joseph Holt Ingraham, a New Englander who took a teaching position at Jefferson College in the 1830s, claimed to have overheard the following conversation in Natchez between two "well-dressed, smart-looking" carriage drivers waiting for their masters at a slave auction:

> "You know dat nigger, they gwine to sell, George?"
> "No, he field nigger; I nebber has no 'quaintance wid dat class."
> "Well, nor no oder gentlemens would. But he's a likely chap. How much you tink he go for?"
> "I a'n't much 'quainted wid de price of such kind o' peoples. My master paid seven hundred dollar for me, when I come out from ole Wirginney—dat nigger fetch five hun'red dollar I reckon."
> "You sell for only seben hun'red dollars!" exclaimed the gentleman upon the coach-seat, drawing himself up with pride, and casting a contemptuous glance down upon his companion: "my massa give eight hundred and fifty dollars for me. Gom! I tink dat you was more 'spectable nigger nor dat."

Ingraham found the social climate in Mississippi so completely to his liking that he decided to settle there, so make of his testimony what you will. But it is clear enough that on some of the very largest plantations, where servants and artisans lived in their own quarters and where they were allowed to pass their status on to their children, they saw field hands as their natural inferiors. That the privileged slaves were almost invariably light-skinned, often because they were related to the master, only fed into this sense of caste.

Nevertheless, the evidence suggests that the vast majority of servants and skilled workers felt a bond with ordinary laborers. While visiting Natchez, Frederick Olmsted watched as a "white gloved and neatly dressed" mulatto groom on horseback "bowed politely, lifting his hat and smiling to a very aged and ragged negro with a wheelbarrow and shovel, on the foot path." Indeed, even Ingraham recognized that respect for the elderly crossed what we might call class lines. He commented, "negroes have a peculiarly strong affection for the old people of their own colour. Veneration for the aged is one of their strongest characteristics."

In any case, on only a small fraction of plantations was the slave force large enough to allow for the existence of an elite whose sole purpose was the production of crafts and looking after the needs of the owner and his or her family. On places the size of Cedar Grove, with fewer than a hundred slaves, most servants and artisans began their working lives as field laborers and almost all were expected to help out with the crops during the harvest and at other times of the year. Servants and specialized workers commonly had husbands or wives who were field hands, and, except for those maids who were required to be available to their mistresses at all hours, they lived in the slave quarters. This does not mean that house servants and artisans on plantations like Cedar Grove did not from time to time put on airs and that field hands did not from time to time view them with distrust and perhaps resentment. But overall the two recognized their common interests and shared a common culture. It is revealing that, after they murdered Duncan Skinner, Henderson, Reuben, and Anderson divided up his money among all the slaves on the plantation.

Feelings of community could last well beyond the time when individuals were separated by sale. The slave John Beck sent the following letter to Alexander Farrar, his former owner, in July of 1856:

> Dear friend after a tender of my respects to you and your mother & all the rest of the family & c
>
> I pen you these few lines to inform you that I am in good health hoping this will finde you enjoying the same blessing.
>
> I am going to write your negroes a few lines & I will request you if you pleas to write me an answer for them and direct it to Osyka Mississippi Pike.
>
> I send my respects to Julian Love respects &
>
> Give My respects & Love to Molinda my former Wife, Molinda I wish to know how many children you have & who you have got for a husband & if there is any thing in my power that I can do for you let me know & I will do it. Molinda I maried a very fine looking yellow Girl I thought that I could enjoy my self as well as I did with you but it was a mistake, we lived together about two years and we desolved & quit, we have been quit about six months.
>
> I send my love & respects to Edward Burns & all the balance of the black society two numerous to mention.
>
> Mary Ann sends her respects to Stephen Pain she has got Four children Anderson, Joe, Jary & Harriet her son she had by him is out on pearl river living with Wm. Varnado and is doing well, he is a man nearly grone.
>
> I met with a bad misfortune last February year I got my thigh broke & it is about one inch and a half shorter than the other I am living with my younge master Lewis H. Varnado & I am well pleased with my home.
>
> I want to know how the crops are in that country.
>
> They are not very good here cotton is tolerable corn is not so good nothing more at present you must excuse my bad writing & spelling. Direct your letter to Osyka Miss. Pike Co. Send to John E. Beck.

John Beck must have been a privileged slave—a servant most likely—because he felt free openly to use a last name and because, although it was against the law, he had learned how to write, perhaps even was given instruction by Alexander Farrar. The letter suggests he had an unusually close relationship with Farrar. By referring to his former owner as a "friend," Beck adopted a familiarity that the great majority of planters would have regarded as offensive under all but the most exceptional circumstances. Still, we want to be careful here. Beck clearly had no choice but to communicate through Farrar if he hoped to get a message to the laborers on Commencement. What his letter shows above all is the enduring nature of feelings binding members of the slave community.

Ties among slaves extended across boundaries of plantations as well as across time. It was fairly common for husbands and wives to live on separate estates, seeing each other only on weekends. Many slaves preferred these sorts of marital arrangements—"broad marriages" they were called—above all because they normally spared partners the distress of seeing each other beaten or subjected to other forms of abuse. In addition, most masters allowed their slaves to get together with laborers from neighboring estates over the Christmas holidays and for special festivities during the year. For example, following the harvesting of corn in the late fall, planters generally invited slaves from nearby plantations to participate in a shucking competition followed by a feast and dance. In view of the contact that routinely took place between slaves on different estates, it is surprising that Alexander Farrar would offer Dorcas's knowledge of Y. W. McBride, the overseer who was murdered on the Foules place, as proof that she enjoyed a close relationship with John McCallin: "McBride was an entire stranger in our community, no one knew him here before he came to oversee for Mr. Foules, and after that, he was not known off of the place by but few. McAllin did know him. And we think that he must have had some conversation with Dorcas concerning him." Far more likely, however, Dorcas learned about McBride through the grapevine that linked slaves across Adams county. The Skinner murder provides additional evidence of the feeling of community that bound blacks on different estates. When Anderson ran away, he received shelter on Magnolia, a neighboring plantation. Needless to say, the slaves who hid him did so at great personal risk.

As I indicated, servants and artisans attained their status at least in part by being cooperative and working in seeming good faith to serve the interests of their masters. It might sound contradictory, then, to say that privileged slaves, males in particular, were disproportionately represented among runaways. The contradiction is more apparent than real, however. Close contact with whites allowed many slaves to see through the paternalistic pretensions of their owners. Furthermore, in the course of carrying out duties that routinely placed them in the presence of planters, servants overheard conversations about abolitionists and acts of resistance by slaves and congressional debates over the status of slavery in the western territories that only heightened their longing for freedom. For that reason, and because they had far more opportunities than field hands to learn to read and write and, in the case of artisans and carriage drivers, to travel about the countryside, they were in a much better position to entertain the possibility of flight. The apparent cooperation of privileged slaves, then, was just that—*apparent* cooperation. Servants and artisans made themselves useful, but to secure privileges for themselves, not—not in the great majority of cases, anyway—out of blind devotion to the interests of their masters.

I said "to secure privileges for themselves." What I should have said was, to secure privileges for themselves and others in the slave community. Servants stole food from the kitchen to distribute in the quarters, warned other slaves when their cabins were to be searched, and forged passes so field hands could slip away to visit family members on other plantations. Carpenters made furniture for family and friends, and seamstresses produced clothing. The same qualities of intelligence and resourcefulness that led planters to select particular slaves for positions of responsibility made those slaves potentially effective leaders in the quarters. Their devotion to the interests of the slave community as a whole was one major reason why on most plantations they were held in high regard by field hands.

Then, too, artisans and servants would have indirectly benefitted from the tendency of some slaves to seek reaffirmation of their personal worth in identification with the rich and powerful men and women who owned them. Interviews with former slaves carried out under the auspices of the Works Progress Administration in the 1930s reveal numerous instances of individuals who appear to have lived in the reflected glory of their masters. The following testimony comes from Charley Davenport, who was a field hand on a plantation not far from Cedar Grove:

> Aventine where I wuz bawn en bred wuz acrost Second Creek. Hit wuz a big plantation wid 'bout a hundred head ob people libin dare. Hit wuz only one ob us marster's places cause he wuz one ob de richest en highest quality gentlemen in de whole country. Ize tellin you de trufe, us didn't b'long to no white trash. Our marster wuz de Honorable Mister Gabriel Shields hisself. Ebbery body knows 'bout him. He married a Surget. Dem Surgets wuz pretty debblish fur all dey wuz de richest fambly in de land. Dey wuz de out fightenist, out cussinest, fastest ridin, hardest drinkin, out spendinest folks I ebber seed. But Lawd, Lawd, dey wuz gentlemen eben in dey cups.

Davenport also assured the white woman who interviewed him that Abraham Lincoln showed up on Aventine before the Civil War "jest a rantin and preachin' bout us bein his black brudders. Ole Marse didn't know nothin 'bout hit 'cause hit was sorta secret like." So you have to wonder whether maybe he was just pulling her leg all along. Still, it would be remarkable if, given the vulnerable position in which they found themselves, slaves were entirely able to resist the view that the close association servants and skilled workers had with "quality gentlemen" conferred a kind of quality of its own.

For a variety of reasons, then, servants often had considerable standing among the field hands, which is why it makes perfect sense that the planters who conducted the investigation into the death of Duncan Skinner would start with Jane. They could reasonably expect that, as the cook, she would have full knowledge of goings-on in the quarters. They also would no doubt have assumed that her privileged status within Clarissa Sharpe's household meant that she would be more inclined than other slaves to be cooperative. It must have come as something of a shock, then, to discover that she had participated in the effort to conceal the murder, attempting to scrub the blood stains off the floor of Skinner's cabin and burning his nightshirt and the club used to beat him. They would have been equally surprised, no doubt, to hear that Reuben, long allowed the freedom as a carpenter to travel between Cedar Grove and Bonne Ridge, had been involved in the crime. But surely the most astonishing revelation would have been that Henderson, the carriage driver, was the central figure behind the plot. We know from probate records that his privileged position on the plantation traced back to before Absalom Sharpe's death, so obviously he had long been regarded as conscientious and trustworthy. There is no suggestion that he had more reason than other slaves to hate Skinner. On the contrary, the way he apparently phrased his references to the overseer, saying "he didn't pay much attention" to the beatings because they were so "common," makes it sound as if he himself was not one of the usual victims. Indeed, as carriage driver, Henderson probably only had to deal with Skinner on an occasional basis.

There was, of course, another privileged slave who figured prominently in the investigation. Dorcas must be regarded as something of an enigma. Like Jane, she participated in the attempt to cover up the crime. From the draft of the letter written by Alexander Farrar on September 5 we learn, "when her Misstress sent over word to Skinner that morning by Dorcas, she sent word back that Mr. Skinner had taken a cup of coffee before day light,— and, given out his breakfast—and said that he would be back to it—that he was going out to kill some squirrels." Furthermore, she was trusted by the field hands to hide their share of the stolen money. Yet, for all her apparent commitment to the other slaves, she seems to have set herself above them, pointing to McCallin when he was out walking with Clarissa Sharpe and saying (if we can trust Farrar), "you see that man yonder, he will be your master yet." "Your" master, not "our" master, as if she stood apart from the rest of them because of her position as a house servant or her supposed intimacy with their would-be owner.

Up to now I have been operating under the assumption that it was either Henderson or the members of the investigating party who came up with the story that McCallin was behind the crime. But is it possible that Dorcas played a contributing role? Following the murder, Henderson must have been concerned that the solidarity of the slave community would break down. Could it be that he approached Dorcas and persuaded her to assure the field hands that McCallin was pleased to see Skinner eliminated and wanted them to keep their "mouths shut"?

Of course, we could speculate endlessly and in ever more creative, far-fetched ways about the conversations that took place between the slaves. Exactly who said what to whom lies beyond anything that can reasonably be inferred from the documents. Still, certain things seem clear: Loathing for Skinner was widespread in the quarters and likely many, if not all, of the slaves on the plantation took part in what presumably were very heated discussions about how to get rid of him. Furthermore, given the risks that they were apparently prepared to take and the privileges they stood to lose if the plot was discovered, Reuben, Jane, and Dorcas must all have spoken with feeling. Nonetheless, it appears from the evidence that it was Henderson who was primarily responsible for the decision to kill the overseer and that it was Henderson who came up with the plan that he, Reuben, and Anderson attempted to put into effect. What followed was really nothing less than an execution: an execution carried out in the name of all the slaves on Cedar Grove but planned—"coolly planned" as the Natchez *Courier* put it—by the carriage driver who was seemingly their acknowledged leader.

One more thing: Apparently slaves on the surrounding plantations learned of the killing almost as soon as it took place. The slaves on Mandamus were evidently emboldened by the event to do away with their own overseer; the Magnolia slaves hid Anderson. Yet, although a full month passed between the discovery of the body and the investigation, there is not the slightest suggestion in the historical record that any slave on Mandamus, or Magnolia, or any other plantation betrayed the confidence of the murderers. The execution of Duncan Skinner was carried out by three men on Cedar Grove but they were acting with at least the acquiescence, and more likely the approval, of all the slaves in the vicinity.

⊷✢⊶

The plot to execute Duncan Skinner was hardly unprecedented in the Natchez district. Eliza Magruder wrote in her diary on July 30, 1856: "Found them in a stew at the Ridges, the negroes have been behaving very badly, attempted to poison the Overseer, and have been punished very severely for it." Still, although it was fairly common for a slave to react violently to a beating or to the abuse of a family member, the planned murder of an overseer was not exactly an everyday occurrence. Even less frequent were premeditated attacks on owners, and you can count on the fingers of one hand the number of insurrections in the South involving more than fifty slaves. The best-known uprising, in part because it inspired a novel by William Styron, took place in Southampton County, Virginia, in 1831. Led by the messianic preacher Nat Turner, it lasted over two days and resulted in the death of more than fifty whites. An abortive rebellion near Richmond in 1800 and another in Charleston in 1822 organized by a free black named Denmark Vesey have also attracted considerable attention from scholars. Unfortunately, we know little about the single largest uprising, outside New Orleans in 1811. It involved as many as 500 slaves.

Still, organized revolt was far more common in the Caribbean. When historians write about resistance in the Old South they mainly concern themselves with those small-scale acts of opposition that characterized daily life: feigning illness (especially effective for pregnant women), deliberately misunderstanding instructions, "accidentally" breaking equipment, and theft. Then there were the many slaves, like John and Clem on Fonsylvania, who ran away—"stole themselves," as the slaves liked to put it. The phenomenon was so common that Samuel A. Cartwright, a prominent Louisiana physician, concluded that blacks were uniquely susceptible to a rare disease in which victims experienced a compulsive urge to run away from home. "Drapetomania," he called it. (So you can see, purportedly serious intellectuals were offering biological explanations for social disorders long before Charles Murray came along.) Drapetomania must have risen to epidemic proportions around Natchez, because on his travels through the district Frederick Olmsted encountered an old black man who told him: "Heaps o' runaways, dis country, sah. Yes, sah, heaps on 'em round here." The same day that Henderson, Reuben, and Anderson went on trial, Dempsey Jackson ran this notice in the *Courier*:

$75 REWARD

For the following described fellows: NEWTON, a black fellow 26 or 28 years of age; has been for the last three years my family carriage driver; cuts off his words short in talking; about 5 feet 8 inches high.

ENNIS, about 18 years old, small and of copper color; small featured; a shrill voice, and a devil of a little rascal; will belong to everybody but his master, when taken; baste him well and the truth may be got from him.

LOUIS, has been raised in this county; a smart rascal; about 18 years old; he is plausable; has been sent to town on errands since he was ten years old, and has, as a natural consequence with our low grog shops and free negroes, become a finished rascal; his father was half negro, his mother full negro, so he is light copper color, and as smart a rascal as is in this county.

I will give $25 a piece for them, secured in jail so I can get them.

The substantial evidence of resistance in the South raises an interesting question: When slaves broke tools or disrupted the work process or, like Newton, Ennis, and Louis, ran away, were they expressing opposition to slavery itself or to the particular conditions they faced *within* slavery? That is, was their goal to undermine the system or simply make it less oppressive? The temptation is to say that it was both: Slaves were sending a message to their owners that they would never be reconciled to bondage but, at the same time, they wanted specific abuses eliminated. However, the protection that slaves secured was based on the willingness of their owners to fulfill their self-imposed obligations under plantation law. That willingness in turn depended on whether masters felt that slaves were living up to their own, reciprocal obligations. If laborers basically went about their business in at least a seemingly compliant manner, then they could expect not only that their owners would feel a responsibility to provide them with decent care—decent in the mind of the planter, anyway—but also that they would listen when slaves came to them with complaints and take steps to remedy any justifiable grievances—again, justifiable in the mind of the planter. Should it happen, however, that slaves who committed acts of resistance to protest some perceived wrong continued to be just as troublesome after their concerns were addressed, their owner would obviously lose his incentive to accommodate them or, in the extreme case, cease to feel an obligation to ensure that they received humane treatment.

Take, for example, the events I described earlier on the Fonsylvania plantation of Benjamin Wailes. The overseer Rogillio had been "brutish" in his treatment of the laborers, two of whom had fled to nearby woods. When Wailes arrived at the plantation to investigate, the runaways came out of hiding and gave him their version of what had happened. He then interviewed other slaves on Fonsylvania as well, all of whom apparently confirmed the account given by the fugitives. There were other reasons why Wailes decided to let Rogillio go—"the crop was in the grass and very unpromising"—but, still, a significant factor in his decision was quite clearly the desire to placate his laborers. Now, suppose he then brought in a new overseer who treated the slaves with much greater forbearance. And suppose the slaves continued to be uncooperative, continued to run away. What reason would he have for listening to their complaints in the future?

I am not suggesting that individual slaves did the equivalent of a cost-benefit analysis every time they told a lie to their owner or shattered a hoe against the stump of a tree when they caught the overseer looking the other way. But each slave, even when committing an unpremeditated act, operated according to certain assumptions—maybe reflected upon in quiet moments in the quarters, maybe discussed with other slaves, maybe not—about what treatment, if any, warranted cooperative behavior and what consequences could reasonably be expected when someone acted in opposition to the expressed interests of his or her master. The nature of those assumptions presumably predisposed some individuals to operating largely within the system and some to working ceaselessly against it.

With that in mind we can return to the question I raised a moment ago: Were most acts of resistance intended to express opposition to slavery itself or to the conditions blacks faced within slavery? In an ideal world we would be able to determine the answer by reading through testimony left by the slaves. But while such testimony exists, largely in the form of interviews conducted with former slaves under the auspices of the W.P.A. and autobiographies produced by or ghostwritten for fugitives who escaped to the North or Canada, that testimony is of limited reliability, at least for addressing the specific question that concerns us here. The fugitives tended to be exceptional individuals who came from regions bordering the free states. Their experiences were at a far remove from those of, to use the obvious example here, slaves who lived on plantations in the Natchez district. In any event, the accounts they provided were seriously slanted by their desire to serve the cause of antislavery in the increasingly heated political atmosphere of the 1840s and 1850s. As for the W.P.A. "slave narratives," they have significant shortcomings: The men and women interviewed were trying to remember events that had taken place more than 70 years earlier; most of them had only experienced slavery as children; a large proportion of the individuals who posed the questions and recorded their answers were white women; conditions during the depression of the 1930s were exceedingly harsh and impoverished elderly blacks were hardly likely to say anything that they feared might threaten their chance for government assistance.

Without reliable testimony from the slaves themselves, the best we can do is try to infer motives from behavior. This, too, presents complications. The historical record includes slaves who appear never to have compromised, even to the point of self-destruction, as well as slaves who seem to have completely identified with the interests of their masters. But, if you will forgive the heavily qualified nature of the following generalization, the view of the majority of historians seems to be that most of the time most slaves were concerned with securing the best conditions they could under the existing circumstances. The decision made by the two slaves on Fonsylvania to go into hiding would, in this regard, be fairly typical. They fled to the woods because of mistreatment by their overseer but returned when given the chance to present their version of events to their owner. Even fugitives who escaped to the North or Canada, when describing what prompted them to flight, usually referred to some specific grievance—being sold or threatened with sale, most commonly—although, not surprisingly, they also testified to a burning desire to be free.

When I first began to look at the evidence related to the murder of Duncan Skinner, I assumed that the slaves involved were motivated by nothing more than a desire to eliminate a cruel overseer. After all, Skinner was evidently brutal like Rogillio and the slaves on Cedar Grove appear to have had some expectation that they would enjoy "better times" once he was eliminated. But as I began to examine the evidence more closely I came to see that an alternative interpretation—one far more radical in its implications—was at least possible. Recall that the murder of Skinner apparently led to the murder of Y. W. McBride, overseer on the nearby Mandamus plantation, and that the statement released after the public meeting in Kingston referred to "the general restless state" of slaves in the area. Add to that the allegation recently made by the historian Winthrop Jordan that a major slave revolt was only narrowly averted at Second Creek, a few miles from Cedar Grove, during the first months of the Civil War, and you have a basis for arguing that a spirit of insurrection was widespread throughout the neighborhood and that the murder of Duncan Skinner, rather than being an isolated response to the actions of a particular overseer, was part of a concerted attack on slavery itself, akin, you might say, to a raid in a guerrilla war.

Still, notwithstanding these second thoughts, in the end I have concluded that my initial reading of events was probably correct. For one thing, I personally do not find the evidence Jordan offers for an attempted uprising in 1861 all that persuasive. What he refers to as a "conspiracy" looks to me more like idle boasting by a handful of slaves and overreaction by their owners. No need to take my word for it, though. Read his award-winning book *Tumult and Silence at Second Creek* and reach your own conclusions. As for the rest of it: Apparently the slaves on Mandamus had good reasons for wanting McBride out of the way. According to Alexander Farrar (although the allegation is admittedly unproven), John McCallin described McBride to Dorcas as "a through going man, (meaning thorough we supposed) and take him up one side, and down the other, he was a full match for Skinner, and had got what he deserved." Furthermore, one of the slaves convicted of murdering McBride had a short time before suffered the humiliation of being reduced to a field hand from the privileged position of driver (foreman of a gang). And the men who wrote the notice in the newspapers that referred to the "restless state" of the slaves in the neighborhood clearly wanted to turn popular feeling against John McCallin, so it made sense for them to attempt to link him to a broad pattern of disturbances. In the final analysis, however, the main objection to treating the murder as an act of insurrection is that to do so it is necessary to go well beyond anything the slaves appear to have said under interrogation. You can only carry inference so far. All the same, the mere fact that the evidence does allow for two very different interpretations illustrates just how much guesswork is involved in trying to sort out the true meaning of individual acts of resistance.

⇥✛⇤

No historian thinks that those slaves who devoted themselves to securing improvement within the system believed that slavery was legitimate. The overwhelming majority were simply realists, aware that the possibility of waging successful rebellion was vanishingly remote in a society in which whites were united and had sufficient numbers and more than enough force to put down any attempted uprising. Still, for slaves, realism carried a heavy price. It meant frequently accepting abuse in silence, living with the likelihood that at some time you would be separated by sale from loved ones, and consciously adopting behavior that conformed to degrading stereotypes.

Fifty years ago, influenced by a growing awareness of how psychologically damaging such behavior could be, scholars argued that slaves had no distinct culture of their own, or rather, that what culture they had was borrowed from their owners. The most famous work advancing this thesis was *Slavery: A Problem in American Institutional and Intellectual Life*, by Stanley Elkins. Published in 1959, it drew an analogy between the conditions slaves faced in the South and Jews experienced in Nazi concentration camps. Elkins claimed that, like the Jews, slaves were victims of a "total" institution that denied them the opportunity to form meaningful relationships and compelled them to see their interests as identical with those of their masters.

During the civil rights era, however, such interpretations increasingly fell out of favor. With blacks organizing, often at great personal risk, to secure protection of their voting rights and an end to segregation, historians grew dissatisfied with studies that represented slaves as little more than victims of white oppression. Researchers started to investigate black family structure, religion, and folk culture and discovered ample evidence that slaves took determined steps to establish control over their own lives. An important pioneering work was *The Slave Community*, by John Blassingame. Blassingame identified what amounted to a separate world in the quarters, a world in which slaves operated with a significant degree of independence and according to a set of values quite distinct from those of their masters, values rooted in the African past.

Historical interpretation often proceeds in a dialectical manner. Put in a grossly simplistic way, a first generation of scholars produces what becomes the standard view on a subject, the following generation offers a critique and constructs its own orthodoxy, and the third generation proposes some sort of synthesis. The generation of scholars that reinterpreted slavery during and after the civil rights era provided an important corrective to earlier accounts by showing slaves as active in shaping their own history. The breadth of the studies they produced means that we now know a good deal more about the experiences of slaves than of nonslaveholding whites. But perhaps inevitably, they tended to downplay those aspects of life in the quarters that might cast their subjects in a less favorable light. So, for example, they had little to say about husbands who abused their wives and parents who beat their children, they barely acknowledged the darker currents of superstition and fear running through slave religion, and they treated with neglect those slaves who harbored the suspicion that black skin was a badge of inferiority. As a result, one unintended and ironic consequence of their research has been to overshadow the very real capacity of slavery to do damage, to produce victims. Because if slaves were unqualifiedly successful in forming warm and supportive family relations and developing a rich, autonomous cultural life, then how oppressive could the system have been, really? Part of the obligation facing the coming generation of historians is to restore that depth of feeling for the profound costs of slavery without, however, abandoning the insights of recent research.

Having said that, those insights are essential for understanding how slaves on plantations such as Cedar Grove found meaning in their lives and resources to resist in a world that placed their fate in the hands of men like Alexander Farrar and Duncan Skinner. Take what we have come to know about the slave family. In a famous report written some thirty years ago, Daniel Patrick Moynihan argued that the "deterioration of the Negro family"—by which he meant, in particular, instability associated with single-parent, female-headed households—could be traced back to slavery. But beginning with a pathbreaking study by Herbert Gutman in 1976, historians have demonstrated quite clearly that most slaves were able to establish family relationships that were instrumental in helping individuals cope with the trials of everyday life. Two-parent nuclear families represented the ideal, although, depending on the stage of development of a particular plantation (for example, whether the slave force was stable or expanding), other forms may have predominated, including some based on fictive kinship.

Legally slaves could not marry. But it was in the interests of planters to encourage unions because marriage fostered a measure of order in the quarters and increased the likelihood that laborers would choose to have children. Some small number of planters literally forced individual women and men to marry, but on most estates masters left the choice of partners up to the slaves themselves, reserving only a right of veto (which they may have exercised no more often than they did in cases involving their own children).

In January 1855, as a result of a ruling by the probate court of Adams County, eight families on Cedar Grove were put up for sale at public auction. Clarissa Sharpe reacquired the slaves in question shortly thereafter, but since one of the families involved was headed by Anderson and a second included Jane, we know a little bit about their family background. Anderson was 40 at the time of the sale, and married to a wife, Betty, ten years younger. They had six children living with them: Mahala, 17 (meaning either that Betty was only 13 when she gave birth for the first time or Mahala had a different mother); Clarissa, 9; Osborne, 7; Benjamin, 5; Gordon, 3; and Lydia, 1. Jane was 30, her husband, Burrell, 38. They had three boys: Cyrus, 10; Archy, 8; and John, 6.

If Anderson was a typical husband and father, he would have spent some of his spare time hunting and fishing to supplement the family diet, and working around the cabin. His wife, Betty, would have done the cooking, cleaning, and mending and also would have tended the family garden; in addition, she would have had primary responsibility for looking after the children during those hours when she and Anderson were not at work. Jane, of course, would have had similar duties. Although this division of labor may appear to suggest that the slave family was patriarchal, historians generally acknowledge that husbands and wives operated on a level of somewhat greater equality than husbands and wives in free households. Notes historian Deborah Gray White, the typical wife "had considerable autonomy within the slave marriage." The point being not, of course, that slaves anticipated late-twentieth-century liberal sensibilities. Rather, the circumstances under which men and women formed relationships tended to work against firm role differentiation. Men were not providers in the usual sense; it was the planter who had responsibility for seeing that families had basic food, shelter, and clothing. Furthermore, notwithstanding the importance of their domestic duties, women spent the greater part of their day doing the same kind of work as men. Although more women than men were household servants and more men than women were artisans, most slaves on a plantation, whether male or female, worked in the fields, planting, weeding, and harvesting the crop. Perhaps the greatest leveling factor, however, was the tenuous position of the slave father. I noted earlier that many planters attempted to keep families together when they bought or sold slaves. But to be entirely accurate, they concerned themselves principally with keeping women with their children. A man would have a reasonable expectation that some time during his life he would be separated by sale from other members of his family. That was one very important reason why about four out of every five fugitives were male.

Without question, the most important role parents had was to provide their children with a strategy for survival in a society that could be at once capricious and heartless. They had to do this in a context in which parents and young children spent most of the day apart (infants and toddlers being left in the care of elderly slave women) and all slaves were subject to the authority of their owners. I like to ask my students how, if they were a slave father or mother, they would get the point across to a three- or four-year-old about the absolute necessity of appearing subservient around whites and keeping the confidences of the quarters. The few with children of their own just shake their heads. As one former slave commented some years after the war, "Mothers were necessarily compelled to be severe on their children to keep them from talking too much."

I actually think the best account of the disturbing tendency toward violence that must have existed in more than a few households can be found in Richard Wright's autobiographical *Black Boy*, which describes his childhood in Mississippi fifty years after the Civil War. The segregated society in which Wright grew up was very different from the world of slavery that his grandparents had known. Still, in both systems black parents faced the challenge of teaching their children to be submissive and discrete. A young boy who did not "know his place" was a danger not only to himself but to his family and other members of the black community. Wright, who was a rebellious child anyway but also had the dangerous habit of asking pointed questions, received frequent, vicious beatings from older relatives. In part the adults were just taking out their frustrations on him, but in part they were trying to make him understand, in apparently the only way they could imagine, the need for blacks in the South to bend to arbitrary authority. "I was lashed so hard and long that I lost consciousness," he wrote of one whipping he received from his mother. "I was beaten out of my senses and later I found myself in bed, screaming, determined to run away, tussling with my mother and father who were trying to keep me still." He was four years old at the time.

Fortunately for slave children, there were other, more benign ways for adults to provide them with strategies for survival. Folktales, for example. In the quarters after work was done and on weekends, slaves liked to get together and spin stories. Most popular were the "trickster" tales involving a sly slave named John or, much more often, artful animals such as Brer Rabbit. Tricksters sought to secure by guile what they could not hope to win by force. (After the Civil War, Joel Chandler Harris made characters such as Brer Rabbit household names in America through his Uncle Remus stories, which Walt Disney, in turn, in characteristically pasteurized form, transformed into the commercial success of *Song of the South*.)

The trickster stories served many purposes for slaves. They provided entertainment, they acted as morality tales, and they offered lessons in the remorseless arbitrariness of power. They also, in portraying instances of the weak outwitting the strong, allowed slaves momentary feelings of vicarious satisfaction. Just by way of example, imagine it is a Saturday evening on Cedar Grove in early 1857. Anderson is sitting around the fire with his children. One of the children—nine-year-old Osborne, say—asks him to tell a story. Anderson breaks into a smile, then starts into his own version of a popular tale making the rounds in Mississippi back then:

> De rabbit is de slickest o' all de animals de Lawd ever made. He ain't de biggest, an' he ain't de loudest but he sho' am de slickest. If he gits in trouble he gits out by gittin' somebody else in. Once he fell down a deep well an' did he holler and cry? No siree. He set up a mighty mighty whistling and a singin', an' when de wolf passes by he heard him an' he stuck his head over an' de rabbit say, "Git 'long 'way f'om here. Dere ain't room fur two. Hit's mighty hot up dere and nice an' cool down here. Don' you git in dat bucket an' come down here." Dat made de wolf all de mo' onrestless and he jumped into the bucket an' as he went down de rabbit come up, an' as dey passed de rabbit he laughed an' he say, "Dis am life; some go up and some go down."

Singing and dancing were as much a part of slave life as storytelling. Masters reserved the right to monitor the social activities of their slaves and not infrequently came by the quarters during celebrations, if only for their own entertainment. Slaves were guarded in what they said when whites were around, although, as the distinguished folklorist Roger Abrahams has demonstrated, even in the presence of their owners they found ways of making "moral commentary" on their situation by joking in an ironic way that planters appear not to have found, or chose not to treat as, threatening. Away from the eyes of whites, however, blacks could be much more caustic. The famous abolitionist Frederick Douglass, himself an escaped slave, recounted the following song in his autobiography:

> We raise de wheat,
> Dey gib us de corn;
> We bake de bread,
> Dey gib us de cruss
> We sif de meal,
> De gib us de huss,
> We peal de meat,
> Dey gib us de skin
> And dat's de way
> Dey take us in.

One of the most popular songs sung by slaves had to do with the patrols made up of whites—nonslaveholders mainly, like John McCallin—sent out at periodic intervals to check up on their activities:

> Run, nigger, run, patteroller'll ketch yer,
> Hit yer thirty-nine and sware 'e didn' tech yer.
>
> Poor white out in de night
> Huntin' fer niggers wid all deir might.
> Dey don' always ketch deir game
> D'way we fool um is er shame.
>
> My ole mistis promus me
> When she died she'd set me free,
> Now d'ole lady's ded an' gone,
> Lef dis nigger er shellin' corn.
>
> My old master promus me
> When he died he'd set me free,
> Now he's ded an' gone er way
> Neber'll come back tell Judgement day.
>
> Run, nigger, run, patteroler'll ketch yer,
> Hit yer thirty-nine and sware 'e didn't tech yer.

So-called secular songs such as these (as opposed to the spirituals, which I will get to in a moment), as well as the trickster tales, demonstrate that slaves had a powerful sense of the injustice of their condition but also show that they were acutely aware of the realities of power in the South. However, it is largely in their religion that we find evidence of that conviction, so widely shared, that one day they would be delivered from bondage. We have learned a great deal over the past thirty years about the sacred world of the slaves. It seems that some African beliefs and practices survived with little alteration in parts of the South through the antebellum period and beyond. During the 1850s, blacks occasionally gathered in the swamps outside of Natchez to take part in rituals involving magic and witchcraft. Still, long before that time, Christianity had become the dominant faith in the quarters, although the Christianity practiced by the slaves differed in important respects from the religion of their masters.

The main wave of conversion in the South took place during the late eighteenth and early nineteenth centuries, not coincidentally a time when evangelicalism was sweeping through the white population. However, missionary work continued in the slave quarters right up to the Civil War. In part planters were developing a growing concern for the spiritual needs of their laborers. A neighbor came looking for Alexander Farrar to ask if three of her slaves could attend Sunday services at Commencement. She confessed to Farrar's wife, Ann, that it "hurt her conscience" to see them go without religious instruction. Planters fulfilled their spiritual duties to their slaves by bringing in preachers (black and white) to conduct services, by preaching to the slaves themselves, and, in some small number of instances, by building chapels on their estates. And many of the churches in the neighborhood—for example, the First Presbyterian, in Natchez, where Joseph Stratton served as minister—had balconies where slaves could sit during services.

Of course, planters had very specific ideas about which particular Christian themes were suitable for their laborers. Slaves were instructed to be obedient to their masters, to leave punishment of the wicked to God, and to wait for their reward in heaven. Or as one Mississippi slave cynically recalled years after the Civil War: "atter de white fokes preachin' den de preacher preached to us darkies. He would jes tell us not to steal our master's meat from de smoke house, or cotton or tatoes or 'lasses an' like that. An' do not kill each other."

We are back in that gray area where it is difficult to sort out what the planters were doing out of a sense of obligation from what they were doing to advance their financial interests. Recall the advice I quoted some time back from a manual for overseers: "You will find that an hour devoted every Sabbath morning to their moral and religious instruction, would prove a great aid to you in bringing about a better state of things amongst the negroes. It has been thoroughly tried, and with the most satisfactory results, in many parts of the south. As a mere matter of interest, it has proved to be advisable—to say nothing of it as a point of duty." No doubt some planters had no other purpose in bringing Christianity to the quarters than making their laborers submissive. Others—many fewer, I imagine—were only concerned with serving God. Statements made at the time, however, such as the advice to overseers quoted here, suggest that most saw no contradiction between the two, or, rather, assumed that teaching their slaves to be obedient and hard-working and to be accepting of their condition *was* serving God.

There was no guarantee, however, that slaves would practice Christianity exactly as their masters intended. All Protestant sects sought converts in the quarters, as did the Catholics, but the Methodists and Baptists were by far the most successful, in part because they were open to having blacks become preachers but also because they were willing to allow for the emotionalism—the manifestations of spiritual release—that many slaves expected in their religious observances. For example, Methodism contained strict injunctions against dancing, but as the famous British geologist Sir Charles Lyell observed on a tour through the South in the 1840s, "At the Methodist prayer-meetings, they are permitted to move round rapidly in a ring, in which manoeuvre, I am told, they sometimes contrive to take enough exercise to serve as a substitute for the dance." This practice, the "ring-shout," was popular throughout the slave states. Here is a description by a northern Unitarian minister who witnessed it in the Sea Islands of South Carolina during the Civil War:

> After the praise meeting is over, there usually follows the very singular and impressive performance of the "Shout", or religious dance of the negroes. Three or four, standing still, clapping their hands and beating time with their feet, commence singing in unison one of the peculiar shout melodies, while the others walk around in a ring, in single file, joining also in the song. Soon those in the ring leave off their singing, the others keeping it up the while with increased vigor, and strike into the shout step, observing most accurate time with the music. This step is something halfway between a shuffle and a dance, as difficult for an uninitiated person to describe as to imitate. At the end of each stanza of the song the dancers stop short with a slight stamp on the last note, and then, putting the other foot forward, proceed through the next verse. They will often dance to the same song for twenty or thirty minutes, once or twice, perhaps, varying the monotony of their movement by walking for a little while and joining in the singing. The physical exertion, which is really very great, as the dance calls into play nearly ever muscle of the body, seems never to weary them in the least, and they frequently keep up a shout for hours, resting for only brief intervals between the different songs.

It was not only a distinctiveness of style that marked Christianity in the quarters. In part because of their own religious traditions, in part because of the particular circumstances in which they found themselves, slaves interpreted the word of God in ways quite different from those of their masters. Slaveowners preached that they should expect freedom only in the afterlife. But African religions did not make a clear distinction between the now and the hereafter. Significantly, in the Christianity of the slaves, Moses and Jesus were figures of equal prominence. As Eugene Genovese argues, "The slaves . . . merged them into the image of a single deliverance, at once this-worldly and otherworldly." Of course, in the presence of whites, slaves could not afford to draw out the "this-worldly" dimension explicitly. But off by themselves they could more freely and openly exult in the potentially revolutionary implications of Christian belief.

The fullest expression of the slave faith in deliverance can be found in the "sacred songs," or spirituals. Spirituals were not reserved for the Sabbath and church but used, as the eminent cultural historian Lawrence Levine notes, as "rowing songs, field songs, work songs, and social songs." Often marked by a very evident sorrowfulness ("Sometimes I feel like a motherless child"), they nonetheless convey a strong belief in the possibility of transcendence ("Sometimes I feel like a feather in the air, / And I spread my wings and I fly"). The promise of earthly liberation was so plain in some spirituals that they could not be sung when whites were around. Here is one example provided by William Wells Brown, who escaped from slavery in Missouri:

> O, gracious Lord! When shall it be,
> That we poor souls shall all be free;
> Lord, break them slavery powers—
> Will you go along with me?
> Lord, break them slavery powers,
> Go sound the jubilee!

But often the message was more ambiguous about when and where deliverance would come: now or later, in this world or the next. Mississippi slaves—maybe the slaves on Cedar Grove who conspired to murder Duncan Skinner—sang the following verse in one of their spirituals:

> But some ob dese days my time will come,
> I'll year dat bugle, I'll year dat drum,
> I'll see dem armies, marchin' along,
> I'll lif my head an' jine der song.

To the extent that Christianity gave slaves assurances of their importance to God and promised them ultimate deliverance, it served as a powerful weapon in their struggle to resist debasement. At the same time, it allowed them to devote their energies to securing the best conditions they could within slavery without abandoning their commitment to the goal of liberation. Still, precisely because their religion allowed them to concentrate on working toward improvement in their immediate circumstances, and because it encouraged them to believe that deliverance would come only at the hands of God, a certain conservatism took hold in the quarters, a patience. And in that sense, while it is true that planters failed in their efforts to get slaves to see bondage as divinely ordained, Christianity did in its own way serve to inhibit insurrection.

But as we know from the "liberation theology" of our own times, Christian faith can also lead to calls for revolution. Southern planters understood that, or why else would Alexander Farrar have written to William B. Foules only days before the execution of Henderson, Reuben, and Anderson: "If the negroes are brought out in public to be hung and they get up and talk out that they are prepared to die—that they have got religion, and are ready to go home to heaven & c & c—it will have a bad effect upon the other negroes, hence I think to prevent unfavorable impressions that the best plan would be to hang them all privately and have them brought out in the country and buried by the negroes upon the spot where the murders were committed."?

Here, then, was the real threat for slaveowners: slaves who committed acts of "social treason" and said that they were "ready to go home to heaven." Or far worse, charismatic leaders like Nat Turner—might Henderson have become one?—who heard the voice of God and then proclaimed the Day of Judgment at hand. The planters who investigated the death of Duncan Skinner knew that. They knew that slaves were not reconciled to their fate and that there was always a possibility that any number of them might, without warning, rise in rebellion. They knew, too, that Skinner had been a cruel overseer and that the slaves on Cedar Grove had good reasons for wanting him dead. Yet knowing that—knowing *all* that—they still persisted in blaming the murder on John McCallin. A charitable explanation would say that they were simply negligent, that they failed to examine the evidence with sufficient care. McCallin, however, saw their actions in a far more sinister light. He charged they were out to frame him.

⇥ 5 ⇤

The Question of a Frame-Up

John McCallin apparently gave three reasons why the men who investigated the death of Duncan Skinner would want to frame him: to protect the sanctity of their class; to rid themselves of a political opponent; and to cover up criminal activity by Alexander Farrar. We can take each of these allegations in turn.

According to the letter Farrar wrote to Henry Drake, McCallin claimed that "the community here being a rich, proud and haughty one, they wanted to drive him off, because he was a poor mechanic and they did not want to see him elevated along side of them." Deeds on file in the Tensas Parish courthouse, located in St. Joseph, Louisiana, indicate that in September of 1854 McCallin acquired a half interest in a small store in Waterproof for $125 and then two years later purchased a home there for $250. Assessment rolls for the parish in 1857 show that he also owned two horses worth $125. Measured against the heightened aspirations of white men in the society, his attainments appear unimpressive. In the words of Joseph Holt Ingraham, who, like McCallin, came to the Natchez district in the 1830s:

> A plantation well stocked with hands, is the *ne plus ultra* of every man's ambition who resides at the South. Young men who come to this country, "to make money," soon catch the mania, and nothing less than a broad plantation, waving with the snow white cotton bolls, can fill their mental vision, as they anticipate by a few years in their dreams of the future, the results of their plans and labours.

John McCallin undoubtedly caught "the mania" after arriving in the lower Mississippi Valley, but by the time he had achieved a stake in the society, plantation ownership lay beyond the "labours" if not the "plans" of

113

all but the most exceptional of men in his modest circumstances. Presumably that is why he set his sights on marrying Clarissa Sharpe. But he was scarcely "poor" in 1857. The home, horses, and part interest in a store suggest that he was a moderately successful carpenter and ginwright who had converted his talents into a respectable stake in the society.

Still, he would not have been wrong when he complained that the men who investigated the murder of Duncan Skinner held him in contempt. There is evidence of a growing elitism among planters in the district during the decades leading up to the Civil War. Large slaveholders such as Alexander Farrar were wealthier than everyone else, but they also deliberately set out to create a lifestyle that would distinguish them from others by more than just land and slaves. They built imposing mansions and elegant gardens, many of which serve as tourist stops today. They raced purebred horses at the Pharsalia racetrack near Natchez or down in Metairie, outside New Orleans. They bought elegant carriages so that their wives and daughters could drive into town to shop at the numerous stores that catered to the elite, stopping, if there was time, for an hour or two of "private entertainment" at the "ice cream saloons" of John Botto. And they hosted each other with lavish indulgence. John Quitman, a wealthy Natchez slaveowner who attempted to organize an invasion of Cuba during the 1850s aimed at overthrowing the government ("filibustering," such military adventures were called), has left us a description of a day's visit at the home of a friend:

> Mint-juleps in the morning are sent to our rooms, and then follows a delightful breakfast in the open veranda. We hunt, ride, fish, pay morning visits, play chess, read or lounge until dinner, which is served at two P.M. in great variety, and most delicately cooked in what is here called the Creole style—very rich, and many made or mixed dishes. In two hours afterward every body—white and black—has disappeared. The whole household is asleep—the *siesta* of the Italians. The ladies retire to their apartments, and the gentlemen on sofas, settees, benches, hammocks, and often, gipsy fashion, on the grass under the spreading oaks. Here, too, in fine weather, the tea-table is always set before sunset, and then, until bed-time, we stroll, sing, play whist, or croquet. It is an indolent, yet charming life, and one quits thinking and takes to dreaming.

Such scenes of decadent idleness—did you think of *Gone with the Wind*?—were inevitably rare in a society in which men had to devote most of their days to business. Still, a studied attitude toward leisure played an important role in the lifestyle planters attempted to effect. But perhaps the principal way the large slaveholders sought to set themselves apart was by ensuring that their children acquired "breeding." At a time when public education in the southern states was virtually nonexistent—the Natchez

Institute, a school that provided for over 500 students each year, represented a conspicuous exception—planters hired tutors to instruct their younger sons and daughters at home and sent older children to private academies. Alexander Farrar advertised for a tutor at Commencement. Candidates for the position included a Yale graduate who felt it prudent to write in his letter of application, "On the subject of slavery I am entirely neutral."

One of the more popular private academies for boys in the lower Mississippi Valley was Jefferson College, located in the town of Washington, six miles to the east of Natchez. Alexander Farrar served on its board of directors. The school curriculum included Greek, Latin, rhetoric, and philosophy, in keeping with the view that a classical education was appropriate for young men destined to occupy an elevated place in society. For young women of the Natchez district there were, among other schools, the Elizabeth Female Academy and the Fayette Female Academy. At such institutions the daughters of planters learned to speak foreign languages, play musical instruments, and paint. Both boys and girls took private lessons in dance and "manners."

Following graduation from a local academy, many young men went on to study at the University of Virginia or one of what today are the Ivy League colleges. Yale and Princeton even provided quarters for servants. Later, for those whose families were exceptionally wealthy, there might be a "Grand Tour" of the cultural centers of Europe, where they would adopt what they took to be the proper bearing and habits of "gentlemen." Here is a passage from the diary of the 21-year-old son of a close friend of Alexander Farrar, describing a day in Paris:

> [T]here is a good deal of sameness in the life one leads—one 24 hours seem cut out precisely after the preceding 24—still notwithstanding it is a monotony which never varies—a repetition which is always pleasing. I generally get up about 12—breakfast read the paper & lounge until 2. Get into the carriage & shop or see sights till 4 then drive in the Bois— dine at 6—generally at Trois Frères—then go to some theatre & afterwards to Mabille or Chateau des Fleurs—Jardin D'Hiver or Chateau Rouge & then to bed.

Just in case the point of all these educational and cultural advantages might be lost on the children themselves, their parents were at pains to spell it out for them. "I hope," wrote James Foster of Hermitage plantation near Natchez to his young son away at school in Tennessee, "that you are resolved that you will faithfully and indefatiguably labour to see what you can accomplish in the way of improvement in your mind, and in your temper and manners; for it is in the cultivation of the mind, the subduing and controling of the temper, and the grace and elegance of manner, that we find that which places men in a portion above the vulgar herd."

And in another letter: "The approbation of God and the good opinion of the better part of society is that for which we live." Children of planters felt the heavy weight of their parents' ambitions. Alexander Farrar's 21-year-old son wrote from Harvard in 1859, "I am trying my dear Father to give you the pleasure of one day realizing your expectations, but although I write this with tears of hope blinding me, still I cannot trust myself to say I shall succeed."

Travelers to the region differed over whether planters actually achieved the gentility to which they so clearly aspired. A British nobleman who spoke at the First Presbyterian Church in Natchez in 1839 described his audience as "among the most elegant both in dress, appearance, and ease and polish of manners, that I had yet seen in the United States." Just a few years before the Civil War another British visitor observed, "there is as refined society to be found in Natchez as in any other part of the United States." The most flattering portrait of the planters comes from Joseph Holt Ingraham, who praised the large slaveholders for having "an '*air distingué*'", and in the highest degree aristocratic." He admitted that he did not like to apply the term "aristocratic" to Americans, but added, "no other word will express so clearly that refinement and elegance to which I allude, and which everywhere indicate the opulence and high breeding of their possessors."

Still, not every traveler formed such a lofty impression of the local planters. Frederick Olmsted, whose views were clearly shaped by his opposition to slavery, commented:

> The farce of the vulgar rich has its foundation in Mississippi, as in New York and in Manchester, in the rapidity with which certain values have advanced, especially that of cotton, and, simultaneously, that of cotton lands and negroes. Of course, there are men of refinement and cultivation among the rich planters of Mississippi, and many highly estimable and intelligent persons outside of the wealthy class, but the number of such is smaller in proportion to that of the immoral, vulgar, and ignorant newly-rich, than in any other part of the United States.

But whether or not they had gentility or merely pretended at it, the planters of the Natchez district clearly saw themselves as a class apart, or more accurate, a caste above. An employee at a local manufacturing firm noted that they "were slow to regard any as their equals except those of their own class." Or consider the advice from the wife of a prominent Natchez planter to her son: "Avoid as much as possible low company. Associate with the refined for your manners soon tell what company you keep—Recollect dear son that you have a name to preserve." People who feel they have "a name to preserve" are very particular about marriage partners. In the Natchez district of the Old South, intermarriage among members of the elite became so common that—to borrow a turn of phrase from the historian

D. Clayton James—"the proverbial Philadelphia lawyer would have been baffled by the complex family relations."

So there can be little question that John McCallin was right when he suggested that the planters of the community resented his attempt to marry into their exclusive social circle. And the fact that Clarissa Sharpe allowed him to stay at Cedar Grove on a regular basis and to keep a trunk with clothes there may well have made them wonder. But they almost certainly took his prospects much less seriously than he did. Clarissa Sharpe, for all that she might have found McCallin an attractive and—who knows?—maybe sensitive and sympathetic companion, was far too much a product of her society and, as we shall see, far too dependent on the good will of Alexander Farrar to accept a marriage proposal from a man who was, in the view of her friends and neighbors, beneath her.

⛭

Like the great majority of Irish Catholic immigrants, John McCallin was a Democrat. Alexander Farrar, on the other hand, was a leading figure in the American Party. Henry Drake, in his letter to Farrar, indicated that it had been alleged (by whom he did not say) "that the meeting, at which Mr. Jackson presided, was a meeting of the American party, for the purpose of making nominations, & that after that business was attended they took up McA.'s case, as a kindred subject. McAllain's friends are trying to make the impression, that the whole thing is a mere political persecution." On the narrow question of the reason for the meeting at Kingston, the charge reported by Drake was most certainly unfounded. The Natchez *Courier* was the official paper of the American Party; at no point during July and August did it carry a notice about a nomination meeting in Adams County or publish a list of candidates selected to run for office. Still, even if McCallin's supporters were in error on that particular point, they may nonetheless have been correct in seeing the attempt to implicate him in the murder as politically motivated. Before evaluating their claim, however, it would be useful to say a word about the restructuring of American politics in the 1840s and 1850s.

The early 1840s arguably represented the high water mark of American nationalism between the Revolution and the Civil War. Thanks to the construction of canals and the introduction of steamboats, and, later, railroads, communities across the country were more closely linked together than ever before. Nor were the ties purely economic. People in all regions shared a commitment to democracy, to evangelical Protestantism, to at least some forms of social reform—temperance, in particular—and, not least critically, to white supremacy.

I find many people assume that the steps taken to abolish slavery in the North following the Revolution must have reflected a certain sympathy toward blacks. But as Alexis de Tocqueville famously observed in the 1830s, "The prejudice of race appears to be stronger in the states that have abolished slavery than in those where it still exists; and nowhere is it so intolerant as in those states where servitude has never been known." Blacks in the North were for the most part denied the vote, prevented from serving on juries or testifying against whites, restricted to menial labor—"nigger work," it was called—and segregated in schools, hospitals, even cemeteries. Indiana and Oregon went so far as to pass laws barring black immigration. Indeed, it was in significant measure because of the historical record of northern discrimination that Chief Justice Roger Taney of the Supreme Court felt justified in ruling, in the famous Dred Scott decision (handed down, as it happened, only weeks before Henderson, Reuben, and Anderson murdered Duncan Skinner), that blacks were not citizens of the United States. At the time the Constitution was adopted, he claimed, they "had for more than a century been regarded as beings of an inferior order," adding in words that have come to haunt his reputation ever since, "so far inferior that they had no rights which the white man was bound to respect."

It is true that, during the 1830s, national harmony was seemingly threatened by the appearance of a small yet vocal band of abolitionists dedicated to securing the immediate and unconditional end to slavery in the South. Initially they abstained from politics, fearing its corrupting influence, but by the end of the decade many abolitionists were campaigning for candidates supporting antislavery initiatives. Still, it can hardly be said that they captured the hearts and minds of northern voters. In 1840 and 1844 when a former Alabama slaveholder-turned-abolitionist, James Birney, ran for president under the banner of the Liberty Party, he received less than 3 percent of the popular vote in the North. The apathetic and in many places hostile response to his candidacy was a sign that most northern whites were just not that concerned about the continued existence of slavery in the South. Granted, if it could be done peacefully and in a costless way, many more than 3 percent would have been pleased to see the institution eliminated. But whether slavery lived or died hardly fired the imagination.

What did fire the imagination, both North and South, was the promise of national expansion. It is our "manifest destiny," wrote the New York editor John L. O'Sullivan, who coined the term, "to overspread and possess the whole of the continent which Providence has given us for the development of the great experiment of liberty and federated self-government entrusted to us." And it was in an effort to help America realize its "manifest destiny" that James Polk, shortly after he became president in 1845, sought to purchase Mexico's two northern provinces, California and New Mexico. The Mexican authorities understandably had little interest in surrendering land of such immense potential wealth. But their rejection of his offer merely tempted Polk into using the tenuous excuse of a boundary dispute to instigate a war. Three years later American troops had won by force what the administration had failed to achieve through negotiation. The Treaty of Guadalupe Hidalgo, signed in 1848, added more than 500,000 square miles to the United States, including much of the present-day Southwest. It was "a crowning fulfillment of American nationalism," wrote the late David Potter, one of America's most brilliant historians. Yet, as he noted, it was "an ironic triumph for 'Manifest Destiny,' an ominous fulfillment for the impulses of American nationalism. It reflected a sinister dual quality in this nationalism, for at the same time when national forces, in the fullness of a very genuine vigor, were achieving an external triumph, the very triumph itself was subjecting their nationalism to internal stresses which, within thirteen years, would bring the nation to a supreme crisis."

The problem—the source of the stresses—lay in the absence of any law or constitutional provision defining the status of slavery in the newly acquired territories. What this meant was, some sort of political settlement would have to be negotiated. And—and here is the critical point—there was a profound difference in the minds of most northerners between allowing slavery to continue in jurisdictions where it already existed and permitting it to enter new territories. Because while few northerners had any thought of moving south, a great many entertained the possibility that they—or if not they themselves, their children—might one day want to relocate in the West. They were not prepared to see planters move into the territories and buy up extensive tracts of farmland or introduce slaves, who might depress the market for free labor. Furthermore, and not incidentally, most had no wish to settle in a community where they would have to live among blacks, free or slave. Some minority of individuals shared the view of the future president Abraham Lincoln that slavery was immoral, and restricting it to the states where it currently existed would in time lead to its extinction. But among those northerners who were vehemently opposed to its expansion were many who were quite prepared to see it continue and prosper in the southern states. As they well recognized, as long as blacks were tied down in the South by bondage, they would have no legal opportunity to move elsewhere.

It was not the first time national expansion had revealed a tendency to provoke sectional strife. In 1819 northern and southern congressmen and senators had found themselves at odds when Missouri Territory, part of the Louisiana Purchase, sought admission as a slave state. Months of acrimonious debate left witnesses wondering about the future of the nation. In the end, however, the desire for national unity prevailed and the conflict was resolved through negotiated settlement. By the terms of the Missouri Compromise, Missouri became a slave state while the northern section of Massachusetts was turned into the free state of Maine. In addition, Congress divided the remaining land of the Louisiana Purchase along the line 36° 30'. In territory north of the line slavery was prohibited; south of the line it was to be allowed.

For a generation after the Missouri Compromise, politicians were effectively able to contain the brushfires of sectionalism that flared up now and again. The two major parties of the late 1830s and early 1840s, the Whigs and Democrats, maintained broad national constituencies by carefully side-stepping issues likely to promote divisiveness between North and South. After the Treaty of Guadalupe Hidalgo, however, that was no longer possible. When northern congressmen proposed slavery be kept out of the new territory, southern politicians reacted quickly, organizing across state and party lines, calling local meetings, and raising the threat of secession. (And to get a sense of the role of contingency in history, consider this: If the Civil War had broken out in 1851 rather than a decade later, the commander-in-chief of the Union forces would have been, not Abraham Lincoln, but Millard Fillmore.)

The controversy was eventually resolved by the Compromise of 1850, although "compromise" is hardly the best term to describe what was actually a deal built on deft manipulation of sectional voting patterns. Still, a case can be made that, had no further questions about the territories been brought before the House or Senate and had the Supreme Court continued its historic pattern of avoiding definitive rulings on slavery, tensions would have muted for a time, certainly well beyond April of 1861, when the first shots of the Civil War were fired. In 1852 the nondescript Franklin Pierce won a decisive victory in the presidential election, and it seemed that the country was in for an extended period of sectional harmony under the ascendancy of the Democratic Party.

The reconciliation artificially contrived in 1850 proved short-lived, however. Ironically, once again it was an attempt to fulfil a nationalist vision that led to sectional antagonism. Many Americans were convinced that the best way to restore a sense of unity would be to build a railroad across the country. Among them was Stephen Douglas, a young senator from Illinois who had played an instrumental role in securing passage of the Compromise of 1850. Now chairman of the Committee on Territories and acknowledged champion of the Midwest, Douglas was determined that the proposed transcontinental line follow a northern route with a terminus in Chicago. He faced opposition, however, from senators who favored a more southerly route, through St. Louis or perhaps New Orleans. For a time efforts to get approval of the legislation necessary for the development of a line—any line—foundered on narrow sectional voting. In the end, however, a number of prominent Democratic senators from the slave states agreed to give their votes to Douglas provided he used his influence to push through legislation setting aside the Missouri Compromise and replacing the prohibition against slavery in the northern portion of the Louisiana Purchase with "popular sovereignty."

I find that the doctrine of popular sovereignty is often misunderstood by students. First proposed by Democratic senator Lewis Cass of Michigan in 1847, it called for the people of a territory to decide for themselves whether slavery would be allowed within their borders. The mistake students frequently make is to assume that the doctrine somehow applied to the *states*. In fact, the right of the states to legislate on slavery was implicitly written into the Constitution, as even most radical abolitionists conceded. If Mississippi suddenly decided that it wanted to abolish the institution, it had the authority to do so. If Massachusetts for some reason should decide to restore slavery, it had the authority to do so as well. What popular sovereignty promised was simply to extend a well-established right of the states to the territories. A vast section of America still had territorial status in the 1850s: a considerable part of the Louisiana Purchase as well as Utah and New Mexico, created out of the land acquired in the Mexican War.

When Stephen Douglas acceded to the demands of southern Democrats, many in the North who formerly had thought popular sovereignty would serve to prevent the expansion of slavery now saw the doctrine as an instrument of sectional aggression, a cover for introducing slave labor into free territory. Douglas was not, as his critics claimed, indifferent to slavery. He assumed any territory organized under popular sovereignty would remain free. But he also believed that popular sovereignty was a more democratic way of deciding the issue than leaving it up to Congress and that the interests of national unity would be better served by building a transcontinental railroad than preserving the Missouri Compromise.

The legislation rescinding the Missouri Compromise, the Kansas-Nebraska Act, created two new territories, leaving the future of slavery in each to be decided by popular sovereignty. It took Douglas three and a half months to get it through the Senate and it was another two months before it passed the House. President Pierce signed the bill into law May 30, 1854, the date at which secession and Civil War probably became inevitable. The Second Party System—the system of Democrats and Whigs—now collapsed under the weight of sectional animosity. Northerners were outraged that the Democrats had championed a proposal opening up western territory to the possibility, if not necessarily the fact, of slavery. Douglas joked grimly that he could have traveled from Boston to Chicago by the light of his burning effigies. In elections in 1854 and 1855 the number of Democratic congressmen from the North plummeted from 91 to 25. Their party had become, in effect, the party of the South. The question that remained was, what would become the party of the North?

Logically, you might imagine, it would be the Whigs. But for a variety of reasons the party had declined dramatically by the time of the Kansas-

Nebraska Act. Although a wide range of new parties now rose to attempt to fill the political vacuum, in the end there emerged two principal contenders. The better known of the two today—the one that still survives—was the Republican Party. Republicans saw the expansion of slavery to be the single most critical question confronting the nation. The other was the American Party.

The origins of the American Party lay in demographic changes reshaping the face of American society. Beginning early in the century but especially during the decade following 1845, immigrants flooded into the United States. At the time the Second Party System began to break apart, fully 14 percent of the nation's 25 million people were foreign born. By 1860 more than one-quarter of white adult men were immigrants; in the North the figure stood at one-third. The impact of this demographic upheaval was most strongly felt in northern cities, where the number of immigrants often approached or exceeded the total of native-born residents.

Among the newcomers the single largest group was the Irish. Between 1820 and 1860, 2 million Irish men, women, and children crossed the Atlantic to the United States, most of them driven from their homes by the infamous potato famine of the 1840s. A majority were Catholics, John McCallin included. To many in America, then an overwhelmingly evangelical Protestant country, Catholics represented a dangerous and alien element. Tensions grew rapidly, most particularly in those urban centers in the North where the Irish concentrated. During the two decades or so before the Civil War arsonists burned down as many as twenty Catholic churches, and mob violence against Irish Catholics was common. In Philadelphia, where McCallin lived for several years during the 1830s, rioting lasted for two months in 1844.

There was a nativist backlash of another sort as well. One reason the Whigs went into decline was the party leadership misread the political implications of the upsurge in immigration. In an attempt to expand their base they made overtures to immigrants and Catholics. The principal result, however, was to alienate the Protestant workers who represented the core of their constituency. Native American clubs, calling for curbs on immigration and restrictions on rights of the foreign born, had been around for a number of years. When one of those clubs, the Order of the Star-Spangled Banner, reinvented itself as the American Party or "Know Nothings" in the early 1850s, disaffected Whigs streamed into its ranks. (The nickname "Know Nothings" came about not for the reason you might imagine. Party members were initially pledged to secrecy and responded to questions about their activities by saying, "I know nothing.") In the end, however, outside of certain localities, the cause of antislavery proved more compelling to northerners than the cause of nativism, and, in any case, Republican politicians were more than willing to exploit anti-Catholic sentiment. The American Party faded into relative insignificance. In the presidential election of 1856, the Republican candidate, the explorer John Frémont, although he narrowly lost to the Democrat James Buchanan, won a majority of the electoral votes in the free states, paving the way for Abraham Lincoln to capture the presidency in 1860 without taking a single electoral vote—in fact, taking precious few votes at all—in the South.

All of which brings us back to the allegation that John McCallin was a victim of "political persecution." The vast majority of northern Whigs, Abraham Lincoln among them, sooner or later found their way into the Republican Party. However, for southern Whigs, such as Alexander Farrar, the Republicans hardly represented a serious option. There were the Democrats, of course, and not a few Whigs elected to join the party of their traditional rivals. However, many Whig planters in the Natchez district—and the area around Kingston was a stronghold of Whig support—found the Democrats too insistently sectional, too open in their ambition for secession. And then there were the personal animosities that had developed over the years. And so, like Farrar, they turned to the American Party almost by default.

I am not suggesting that planters in the lower Mississippi Valley were indifferent to the consequences of immigration. Natchez had a significant foreign-born element, a majority of whom, like John McCallin, were Democrats. The elite of the American Party looked upon most immigrants with unconcealed disdain. Benjamin Wailes, a friend of Alexander Farrar, wrote the following entry in his diary in June of 1857 after stopping by a barbecue in honor of the leading Democrat of Adams County, General John Quitman:

> A rough, dull affair; a long tiresome indifferent speech in defense of fillibustering, the conquest of Cuba, annexation of Mexico, etc, etc., and announcing himself a candidate for re-election for congress. A large proportion of the company consisted of foreigners from Natchez, and the fag end of democracy. Not twenty men of prominence or high respectability present.

But there were no profound ideological divisions between Know Nothing and Democrat in the Natchez district—most important, no disagreement over slavery—and leadership of both parties was in the hands of planters, businessmen, and professionals. As the journal entry by Wailes suggests, class more than party defined personal allegiances among members of the elite. After Quitman died in 1858, Farrar headed the executive committee of three (which also included William T. Martin, prosecuting attorney at the trial of Henderson, Reuben, and Anderson) charged with raising $50,000 for erection of a monument to the dynamic military leader and politician.

The barbecue Wailes mentioned took place only days after the investigation into the death of Duncan Skinner. One wonders whether John McCallin and his workingmen friends from Natchez were there. Certainly

McCallin was correct in thinking that his association with the Democratic Party was a further reason for Alexander Farrar and the other Know Nothings who took part in the investigation to be suspicious of him. Yet the available evidence on the political affiliations of men involved in the case—and it is limited—casts serious doubt on his claim that the charges against him were politically motivated. Farrar wrote Henry Drake that at the meeting in Kingston, "There were more democrats present than usually vote at the Kingston precinct," including Alexander Boyd, a brother-in-law of Clarissa Sharpe. According to Farrar, when the investigators first gathered signatures from prominent local citizens in support of their findings, Boyd declined to commit himself, saying "that he was an old man and did not want to pledge himself to any course that might lead to violence, but as to McAllins guilt he did not doubt it." Farrar added: "He made the same statement publickly at the last meeting, and then signed a paper with some near 40 others, approving of the action of the meeting." However, the document referred to, with its forty or so signatures, has seemingly not survived.

It does not appear that any of the men who took part in the investigation were Democrats; if they had been, surely Farrar would have mentioned it in his letter to Drake. However, two of the planters who signed the public statement supporting the findings against McCallin, and Alfred Swayze, who accompanied Farrar to take testimony from Clarissa Sharpe about McCallin's unexpected reappearance at the plantation after the murder, are listed as members of the Democratic Party executive for Adams County in notices in the *Mississippi Free Trader*. But perhaps the most compelling reason for rejecting the theory that the charges against McCallin constituted "political persecution" was the failure of the *Free Trader* to come to his defense. The newspaper, with its circulation of over 4,000, was the Democratic organ in Adams County. Yet, while the editor, James McDonald, ran all public notices relating to the investigation, including McCallin's response to the charges against him, he chose not to offer a personal opinion on the case or even discuss the substance of the evidence. Presumably he either believed the accusations against McCallin or concluded that a nonslaveholding carpenter was too inconsequential to merit the attention of the planters and merchants who were the *Free Trader*'s most important subscribers.

※✠※

During the early years of the nineteenth century in the United States, when a woman got married she, for all intents and purposes, lost any claims to an independent identity. Matrimony, if she was fortunate, would bring her material well-being and a measure of security. But it also placed her in a position of subservience to her husband, who, on the occasion of their wedding, automatically acquired title to any property she owned. And for the newly married woman a whole series of legal disabilities followed. Historian Suzanne Lebsock has provided a brief list in a seminal study of Petersburg, Virginia:

> Because the wife owned nothing, she could perform no transactions. Although she was entitled to act in her husband's stead under some circumstance—the wife could enter a store and charge groceries to her husband's account, for example—she had no standing as an economic agent. She could make no contracts; she could not sue or be sued in her own name; she could not execute a valid will; she could neither purchase nor emancipate a slave. And since she had no legal capacity to transact business for herself, she certainly had no capacity to transact for others. The married woman was not eligible to serve as a trustee, executor, administrator, or legal guardian.

Mississippi was actually in the vanguard of states seeking to expand the rights of married women. In a ruling in 1837, the State Supreme Court found that a Chickasaw woman had legal title to property she had held prior to her marriage. The property in question was a slave. Then two years later, in 1839, the state legislature enacted the first statute in the United States allowing wives to own property in their own name. Still, the "Woman's Law," as it was commonly known, was far less forward looking than it might at first appear. Passed in the depths of a depression, its main purpose seems to have been to allow married men a convenient means of escaping debt by transferring their property to their wives. This became a popular strategy among members of the antebellum elite for holding on to their land after the Civil War.

More important for what concerns us here, during the 1850s in Mississippi and Louisiana, the wife of a husband who died intestate was not his legal heir. She was entitled to her "dower" rights (not to be confused with the dowry she may have brought to her marriage), which in Mississippi meant, if, like Clarissa Sharpe, she had no surviving children, she received one-half his personal property as well as the use of one-half his land for the remainder of her lifetime. However, she did not hold formal title to the real estate and after her death it automatically transferred to her husband's heirs. According to the law of Louisiana, the widow of a landowner whose principal place of residence was outside the state inherited nothing at all unless, as a result, she found herself without means of support.

When he died in early 1851, Absalom Sharpe left no will. Whether this was intentional or simply an oversight is unknown, but the consequence was to ensure that all the land he owned—Cedar Grove; a tract of more than 700 undeveloped acres up in Washington County, Mississippi; and Bonne Ridge, a plantation of around 2,200 acres in Catahoula Parish, Louisiana—would pass on to his brothers and sisters rather than his wife. At least some widows were prepared to challenge the workings of the law. In December of 1852, Susan Conner of Berkeley plantation begged her "kindly neighbor," Alexander Farrar, "to prevail on Mrs. Sharpe to refuse any compromise, and join me in a <u>Protest</u> against the claims of our husbands claimants under the clause in the code Napoleon, which deprives non-resident wives of any right whatever except they are proven to be in necessitous circumstances." Conner had instituted a suit in the courts of Louisiana to recover Arcola plantation, property of her late husband, and had appealed to the governor of Mississippi to use his influence on her behalf. Her active efforts "to recover her just rights," she confessed, had not been without cost for her reputation in a society in which women were expected to defer to the judgments of men. "There is a great hue & cry raised against me as a womans rights woman," she acknowledged, "but, I am not one except where the U.S. and reason, give me a right to be a rights woman. I care not a copper to be a governor a Legislator, or any other 'or, but if I can protect my own rights, and those of others, I hold it my duty to resist the united world, with my <u>single Will</u>."

But Clarissa Sharpe did not, so far as we know, join Susan Conner in her suit or her overtures to the governor of Mississippi. Rather, she seems to have placed her fate in the hands of Alexander Farrar. For reasons that are not spelled out in the historical record but presumably in response to some sort of formal request, the Probate Court of Adams County named Farrar and Clarissa Sharpe co-administrators of all that portion of Absalom Sharpe's estate lying within the borders of Mississippi. In Louisiana nonresidents unrelated to the deceased were barred from serving in the capacity of administrator and Clarissa Sharpe assumed legal responsibility for the management of Bonne Ridge. But documents in the Farrar Papers, including letters to overseers and lawyers as well as financial and court records, make it clear that it was Farrar who actually supervised the operation of the plantation. And it was almost certainly in his role as administrator—de jure in Mississippi and de facto in Louisiana—that he took the actions that led John McCallin to accuse him of swindling Clarissa Sharpe and perhaps even plotting the murder of Duncan Skinner and McCallin himself to ensure their silence.

Absalom Sharpe had eight brothers and sisters. Several had predeceased him, however, and that meant that all their children—and some of their grandchildren, since a number of the children had themselves died—had claims on his estate. In total the legal heirs numbered more than fifty and were spread across, at a minimum, four states in the North as well as Texas. They had little interest in dividing up acreage and slaves in Mississippi and Louisiana. What they wanted was cash. For her part, Clarissa Sharpe was more than willing to oblige them if, by doing so, she could hold on to Cedar Grove. And so Alexander Farrar set himself the task of negotiating terms for her to buy them out.

Reaching a settlement proved to be a complicated matter, however, much more difficult than he had originally imagined. The surviving documents relating to the estate, which can be found in the Farrar Papers, and in the records of the Adams County Probate Court and the District Court of Catahoula Parish, would fill a weighty volume. A hint of the difficulties he faced is suggested by a passage in a letter sent to him by one of the lawyers he hired to handle the negotiations:

> You have already discovered that it has become quite difficult to treat with the heirs, on account of the interference of third persons in the way that you speak of. And I find that the heirs themselves have been writing to each other, and posting one and another up, upon what has been done, and what is doing, and have become quite jealous, as to what may be the real value, or worth of their interests in the Estate.

This letter was written in the fall of 1854, more than three and a half years after Absalom Sharpe's death, so you get some idea of how protracted and involved the negotiations were. In fact, the legal wrangling would continue for another four years. As the passage suggests, some claimants believed that the appraisals of the property secured by Farrar were artificially low. And in early 1855, as a result of petitions they presented before the Adams County Probate Court and the District Court of Catahoula Parish, all the land and slaves belonging to the estate were put up for sale at public auction.

It is clear from the evidence available to us today that the heirs had a legitimate grievance. In the inventory made at the time of Absalom Sharpe's death, Henderson, Reuben, and Anderson were appraised at $800, $750, and $650 respectively. But in the court-ordered assessment following their trial, Henderson was found to be worth $1,500, Reuben $2,000, and Anderson $1,400. Still, if the heirs thought the sale would set things right, they must have been sorely disappointed. When Cedar Grove and the land in Washington County went on the block in Natchez, there was only one bid submitted: by George Baynard, a local planter. Not coincidentally, Baynard was Alexander Farrar's brother-in-law. The price he paid, one dollar per acre for the land in Washington County, eight dollars per acre for the slightly more than 900 acres on Cedar Grove, and about $20,000 for the 54 slaves, was considerably below market value. Cedar Grove was evaluated at $20,000 in the 1860 census rolls, and by Farrar's own reckoning, the Washington County property was worth $10,000. As for the slaves, even a conservative estimate would place their value at $45,000. The only logical conclusion is that Farrar used his considerable influence and feelings of good will for Clarissa Sharpe to discourage competing offers. The same scenario was played out in Catahoula Parish when Bonne Ridge went up for sale, only this time with Farrar as the uncontested bidder. The price he paid of under $43,000 was $7,000 less than what he estimated the plantation to be worth, *independent of its 32 slaves.*

Following the auctions, in what was certainly part of a prearranged deal, Clarissa Sharpe recovered title to the entire estate. She then signed an agreement with Alexander Farrar that called for the property to be divided between the two of them. She was to keep Cedar Grove and all but 20 of its slaves. He would take the land in Washington County, Bonne Ridge and its labor force, plus the additional 20 slaves from Cedar Grove. Farrar estimated the value of his share of the property at $88,000: $10,000 for the land in Washington County, $50,000 for Bonne Ridge, and $28,000 for the 52 slaves. To compensate Clarissa Sharpe he agreed to waive an existing debt of more than $26,000, give her an additional $25,000, and accept responsibility for paying off the outstanding financial obligations to the heirs, estimated to be around $36,000.

The question is, did Farrar use his position as administrator of Absalom Sharpe's estate for personal gain? The Washington County land was undeveloped but it lay in what would become the richest cotton-growing region in the United States following the Civil War. Still, in 1855 its value was purely speculative. The documentary evidence does not exist to allow us to say with certainty whether or not a figure of $50,000 for Bonne Ridge was fair market value, but the total is sufficiently high to suggest that it may have been. The soil along the Tensas River, where Bonne Ridge was located, was deep and rich, and 2,200 acres was a lot of land. Still, the fact that there were only about 30 slaves on the plantation at the time Farrar acquired it suggests that a considerable stretch of the property was unimproved.

It is really only the evaluation of the 52 slaves that raises serious questions. Farrar apparently came up with the figure of $28,000 largely on the basis of an inventory of the slaves on Bonne Ridge made at the time of the auction. In that inventory, no doubt put together under Farrar's supervision, none of the laborers, even individuals in their early 20s, were appraised at over $1100. Yet, during the 1850s what were known as "prime field hands" routinely went for $1500 in the Natchez district. And as we have seen, skilled artisans, such as Reuben, could be expected to bring even higher sums. Taking into account the apparent undervaluation of the slaves, Farrar acquired property worth at least $100,000 and probably more on the order of $110,000 to $120,000—in other words, a good 25 percent or so above what he paid for it.

Ironically, the strongest suggestion that he used the estate to advance his own fortunes comes from Farrar himself. Banks were institutions of secondary importance in the plantation South; when a planter wished to borrow a large sum of money—to buy more slaves or land, say—he or she would normally turn to a wealthy neighbor. In 1858, less than three years after taking possession of Bonne Ridge, Farrar approached one of the richest men in the district, Jacob Surget, with a request for a loan of more than $20,000. Added to advances he had already received from Surget, this would make his total debt $30,000. As security he offered a mortgage on the plantation, including the more than 50 slaves he had acquired in his agreement with Clarissa Sharpe. In the note he wrote to Surget requesting the loan, he stated, "I consider that the security offered is worth considerable over four times the amount mentioned." Of course, under the circumstances, he had good reason for exaggerating the value of the property.

Alexander Farrar did very well, then, from his management of Absalom Sharpe's estate. But so did Clarissa Sharpe. According to the "allotment of dower" ordered by the probate court of Adams County in 1851, she was to receive only 44 of the 92 slaves on Cedar Grove and possession for life (though, remember, not ownership) of just 508 acres on the plantation. The remainder of the land and slaves in Mississippi was to go to the heirs, as was Bonne Ridge and all its laborers, since she could hardly claim to be in "necessitous circumstances." Thanks to the efforts of Alexander Farrar, however, she acquired legal title to Cedar Grove and got to keep more than 70 slaves. By the time the census enumerator came around in 1860, she had expanded her labor force to 91, almost exactly the number of slaves on the plantation at the time of her husband's death, and her property—land and slaves together—was estimated to be worth nearly $100,000.

Not that claims that Alexander Farrar had acted fraudulently were necessarily unfounded. He had assuredly used his influence to secure low valuations on the property at the time of its appraisal and, later, to discourage other planters from submitting competing bids when the land and slaves were put up for sale at public auction. It was not Clarissa Sharpe who was the victim of his actions, however, but her late husband's relatives. Whether or not Farrar actually broke the law is unclear, but the end result was that the heirs realized at least $50,000 less from the sale of their share of the estate than they would have if the property had been either appraised or sold at fair market value. My own guess is that $70,000 would be closer to the actual figure.

In an assessment made of him before the Civil War, the local representative of the R. G. Dun & Co. Agency described Alexander Farrar as a man of "proverbial integrity." It is worth noting, however, that on at least one occasion prior to the events related here he engaged in financial activities that, in the minds of some individuals who knew him well, cast a shadow over his reputation. It was following the death of his father, Daniel Farrar, in 1845. Alexander, the oldest son, became executor, taking responsibility for administering an estate that included half a dozen plantations and heavy financial obligations. As each of his brothers and sisters married, he allowed them to take up residence on one of the properties. But, claiming that management of the outstanding debt required his continued oversight, he refused to agree to a formal distribution of the estate. This evidently caused griping by one or two family members that he was misusing his authority for personal gain.

More damaging to his reputation was his behavior following the Civil War. Emancipation of the slaves left him with debts he had no prospect of liquidating. In a desperate attempt to stave off bankruptcy, he transferred his landholdings, not to his wife as so many planters did, but to a close friend. The Dun agent who provided an estimate of his character in 1875 must have wondered at the antebellum entry in the company ledger about his "proverbial integrity." Farrar, he wrote, was "Hopelessly insolvent & dishonest."

Still, his fraudulent activities after the war came at a time when he was in dire financial straits. The available evidence suggests that in 1855, when he negotiated the terms of his agreement with Clarissa Sharpe, he showed genuine regard for her interests. So John McCallin's accusation that he swindled her appears to be without foundation. What is important, however, is not whether Farrar acted properly but whether he was *thought* to have acted properly. "Above all else," the historian Bertram Wyatt-Brown tells us, "white Southerners adhered to a moral code that may be summarized as the rule of honor." For a member of the planting elite such as Farrar, this meant that not only his ability to exercise influence in the society but also his "inner conviction of self-worth" depended on the assessment of him made by the community as a whole. In other words, honor was reputation. So even if the probate court was satisfied that he had lived up to his obligations as administrator and even if his agreement with Clarissa Sharpe was voluntarily arrived at and legally binding, Farrar faced a loss of standing, and perhaps a good deal more, if the judgment of the community was that he had abused his authority for personal gain. No one was likely to think less of him for taking advantage of Absalom Sharpe's relatives, almost all of whom lived in the North. But southern men were duty bound to protect their women—this was a cardinal tenet of the code of honor—and allegations that he had swindled a widow whose business affairs had been entrusted to him and then perhaps, to conceal his wrongdoing, arranged for the murder of her overseer would have done irreparable damage to his reputation. It is with understandable bitterness that he wrote to Henry Drake: "I have lived to but very little purpose, in this life, if in the community in which I am known, it is even rendered necessary for me to deny such vile and infamous charges."

Farrar hardly had to worry about unsubstantiated rumors originating with John McCallin. A nonslaveholding carpenter was too inconsequential a figure to exert significant influence over public opinion. But what if McCallin were merely repeating concerns expressed to him by Clarissa Sharpe? McCallin was a regular guest at Cedar Grove, after all. The two of them must have spent a lot of time alone, strolling around the plantation grounds together, sitting in the parlor. Surely they would have talked about her dealings with Farrar, if only because McCallin imagined he had a stake in her husband's estate. And who knows, maybe she even hinted to him that Farrar had pressured her to sign over Bonne Ridge and the land in Washington County. Or maybe McCallin himself raised doubts in her mind that Farrar had paid enough for the property.

Still, whatever reservations and resentments Clarissa Sharpe may have expressed to John McCallin in the privacy of her own home, it is almost inconceivable that she would have voiced them in public. Think back to the testimony she gave regarding McCallin's unexpected reappearance at Cedar Grove more than a week after the murder. In the statement she made to Farrar and two other planters she charged that she did not know why he returned "unless it was for what the negroes said" (that is, to warn Henderson, Reuben, and Anderson). But as we have seen, almost certainly McCallin came back to let her know about rumors that Skinner had been murdered. Her unwillingness to offer testimony that would have tended to exonerate him on that occasion indicates just how reluctant she must have been to cross Alexander Farrar. And we have to assume that if Farrar had asked her in the presence of other planters whether she believed he had cheated her, she would have vehemently denied it.

Having said that, it is worth pointing out that the outrage Farrar felt over the "vile and infamous" charges does at least provide a credible motive for him to frame McCallin for murder. But if the idea ever crossed his mind, he surely rejected it, and not just because of the difficulty he would undoubtedly have faced in convincing at least some of the other seventeen men in the investigating party to go along. The simple fact is, there was no need to trump up charges against McCallin if the object was to drive him from the district. The accusation that he had spread malicious rumors about one of the most respected figures in the community would itself have been enough. White southerners, Bertram Wyatt-Brown has noted, "reacted to defamation harshly and immediately." And usually, he might have added, without recourse to the legal system. A duel was not an option in this case; gentlemen did not duel with social inferiors. But intimidation through the press was an entirely acceptable alternative. The investigating party made known their findings against McCallin by taking out a notice in the local newspapers. Had they believed his real crime was slander rather than murder that notice would undoubtedly have read something like this:

> MR. JOHN MCCALLIN, having made vile and infamous charges against a man of proverbial integrity in this community, we hereby warn him not again to make his appearance among us; and we, the undersigned do hereby pledge ourselves to enforce the warning herein given.

⋈✠⋈

John McCallin believed he was a victim of a conspiracy. But, to my mind, a more persuasive interpretation says that because the men of the investigating party held him in contempt, they allowed their judgment to become clouded, and, because they allowed their judgment to become clouded, they did not examine the testimony against him with a critical eye. And if this were an isolated case—if it were rare for an innocent white to be implicated in an act of resistance by slaves—we could probably leave it at that. But, in fact, such incidents were quite common in the Old South. In the thirty years or so leading up to the Civil War, whites were routinely held to be responsible when slaves committed premeditated murder or plotted rebellion or were thought to be plotting rebellion.

Most often the accused were individuals of dubious character or little standing in the society—outsiders, you might say. In the supposed conspiracy at Second Creek, investigators concluded that two or perhaps three white men were involved, one an Irish immigrant unknown to local residents. John McCallin did not exactly count as an outsider; if he had, there would hardly have been sufficient interest in his claims of innocence to justify the holding of public meetings, first in Kingston and later in Waterproof. But he clearly was not someone of unquestioned respectability either, nor, being a nonslaveholding carpenter and Irish Catholic, of significant influence. Still, I don't want to leave the impression that only white men of doubtful reputation or of working-class or immigrant background were at risk. On occasion even planters found themselves cast as scapegoats. Furthermore, when, for whatever reason, there were no local individuals who seemed suited to the role, nameless "abolitionists" could always be conjured up. If historians took seriously every alarm about clandestine antislavery activity raised in the antebellum South, you would have to believe that there existed cells of revolutionaries in every swamp and cave below the Potomac.

For many whites accused of inciting slaves to violence, the designated punishment, as it was in the case of John McCallin, was expulsion from the community. Still, some paid with their lives. In the summer of 1835 rumors of a planned slave insurrection north of Jackson led to a state of panic in central Mississippi, with vigilante groups taking control of three counties. By the time the hysteria had subsided, at least two planters had been implicated in the alleged conspiracy and maybe a dozen whites had been hanged. In Texas in 1860, following a series of mysterious fires, a dozen more whites died along with about an equal number of slaves. It is impossible to say how many innocent whites lost their lives in similar incidents during the last three decades before the Civil War. Likely the total would run into the hundreds. Those who were beaten or driven from their homes must have numbered many more.

It is for that reason that any consideration of why John McCallin was blamed for the murder of Duncan Skinner must go beyond the personalities involved in the case. Because, while it is undoubtedly true that the men who interrogated the slaves allowed their feelings of antagonism for McCallin to cloud their judgment, it is also the case that they brought to their interpretation of the evidence a predisposition to believe that someone white was behind the crime. So we must ask how it was that southern slaveholders routinely attributed acts of resistance by slaves to white agitation. Which is another way of saying, it is time to survey the history of what George Fredrickson has called "the black image in the white mind." We begin in the early colonial period.

⇥ 6 ⇤

Black Images, White Minds

Slavery in the United States—or to be perfectly accurate, black slavery—traces its beginnings back to 1619, when a Dutch man-of-war sold twenty "Negars" in Jamestown. This was twelve years after the founding of the colony. But Africans lived in the imaginations of English men and women long before settlement of the New World, indeed long before the existence of a New World to settle was known. Medieval authors, among them Geoffrey Chaucer, made references to blacks in their writings, drawing on the literature of ancient Greece and Rome as well as allusions in the Bible. And by the Middle Ages, Africa was the subject of many travel accounts, most an exotic mixture of fact and fantasy.

The first contact between England and Africa took place in the early sixteenth century when traders made their way down to the Guinea coast in search of commercial opportunities. In 1555 one such trader named John Lok brought several African men to London, intending to teach them the English language and English customs so they could serve him as interpreters. As far as we know, these were the first blacks to arrive at the shores of the kingdom. Africans in the abstract had been a source of wonder to the English. In the flesh they seemed alien, unsettling. Toward the end of the century, with their numbers growing, Elizabeth I wrote to the lord mayors of several principal cities encouraging that the Africans "be sente forth of the land." Five years later, in 1601, she issued a proclamation licensing a German merchant to transport blacks from England to Spain and Portugal. They are "infidels," she complained, "having no understanding of Christ or His gospel."

Africans were conspicuously different from the English in other ways as well, of course. They seemed primitive, uncivilized. Reports circulated that they practiced cannibalism, carved tattoos into their faces, engaged in human sacrifice. Richard Eden, a popular writer who published accounts of early English expeditions to Africa, concluded that they were "a people of beastly lyvynge, without a god, law, religion, or commonwealth." The "beastly lyvynge" comment was not necessarily meant as metaphor. Traders discovered chimpanzees in the same place where they first confronted Africans. Elizabethans had heard about baboons and monkeys, but not apes without tails that stood upright and had some superficial resemblance to human beings. It was said that male chimpanzees were driven by lust to assault African women, which in turn fed into fevered fantasies in the English mind about the sexual desires of Africans. This was long before Darwin, long before anyone imagined evolution or the genetic links between apes and humans. No one was saying exactly that Africans were beasts themselves. And yet . . .

And then there was the question of color. It is striking that when the English first encountered Africans they almost invariably described them as "black," apparently recognizing no distinctions between individuals of different shades. Now, black was a term with fearful connotations in sixteenth-century English society. Here are some definitions from the *Oxford English Dictionary* of the day:

> Deeply stained with dirt; soiled, dirty, foul. . . . Having dark or deadly purposes, malignant; pertaining to or involving death, deadly; baneful, disastrous, sinister. . . . Foul, iniquitous, atrocious, horrible, wicked. . . . Indicating disgrace, censure, liability to punishment, etc.

The color black, in short, suggested evil. White, on the other hand, was associated with purity, goodness. Complemented by red, it represented female beauty. (You may have seen pictures of Elizabeth I with chalky face and rouged cheeks.) Meanwhile, some commentators claimed that black skin had its own dark significance. They took as their source a passage from Chapter 9 of the Book of Genesis, where Noah in fury calls down God's wrath against his own son, Ham. Various versions of the biblical story made the rounds, but one of the most popular can be found in a book published by the adventurer George Best in 1578:

> It manifestly and plainely appeareth by Holy Scripture, that after the generall inundation and overflowing of the earth, there remained no moe men alive but Noe and his three sonnes, Sem, Cham, and Japhet, who onely were left to possesse and inhabite the whole face of the earth: therefore all the sundry discents that until this present day have inhabited the whole earth, must needes come of the off-spring either of Sem, Cham, or Japhet, as the onely sonnes of Noe, who all three being white, and their wives also, by course of nature should have begotten and brought foorth white children. But the envie of our great and continuall

enemie the wicked Spirite is such, that as hee coulde not suffer our olde father Adam to live in the felicitie and Angelike state wherein hee was first created, but tempting him, sought and procured his ruine and fall: so againe, finding at this flood none but a father and three sonnes living, hee so caused one of them to transgresse and disobey his fathers commaundement, that after him all his posteritie shoulde bee accursed. The fact of disobedience was this: When Noe at the commandement of God had made the Arke and entred therein, and the floud-gates of heaven were opened, so that the whole face of the earth, every tree and mountaine was covered with abundance of water, hee straitely commaunded his sonnes and their wives, that they should with reverence and feare beholde the justice and mighty power of God, and that during the time of the floud while they remained in the Arke, they should use continencie, and abstaine from carnall copulation with their wives: and many other precepts hee gave unto them, and admonitions touching the justice of God, in revenging sinne, and his mercie in delivering them, who nothing deserved it. Which good instructions and exhortations notwithstanding his wicked sonne Cham disobeyed, and being perswaded that the first childe borne after the flood (by right and Lawe of nature) should inherite and possesse all the dominions of the earth, hee contrary to his fathers commandement while they were yet in the Arke, used company with his wife, and craftily went about thereby to dis-inherite the off-spring of his other two brethren: for the which wicked and detestable fact, as an example for contempt of Almightie God, and disobedience of parents, God would a sonne should bee borne whose name was Chus, who not onely it selfe, but all his posteritie after him should bee so blacke and lothsome, that it might remaine a spectacle of disobedience to all the worlde. And of this blacke and cursed Chus came all these blacke Moores which are in Africa, for after the water was vanished from off the face of the earth, and that the lande was dry, Sem chose that part of the land to inhabite in, which nowe is called Asia, and Japhet had that which now is called Europa, wherein wee dwell, and Africa remained for Cham and his blacke sonne Chus, and was called Chamesis after the fathers name, being perhaps a cursed, dry, sandy, and unfruitfull ground, fit for such a generation to inhabite in.

Still, for all the evidence that the English—indeed, Europeans generally—were predisposed to see black skin as a curse, the historical record contains a measure of ambiguity. For one thing, initial interpretations of why Africans were black tended to focus on climate, not divine retribution. Richard Eden: They are "so scorched and vexed with the heate of the sunne, that in many places they curse it when it riseth." No doubt the biblical explanation gained increased currency after it became widely known that Africans who settled in England did not produce light-skinned children and peoples in tropical regions of the New World were not themselves black. Even so, it is hard to say how many people took the story seriously. Consider the following comment from a clergyman in 1627: "As for the foolish tale of *Cham's* knowing his wife in the Arke, whereupon by divine curse his son *Chus* with all his posterity, (which they say are *Africans*) were all blacke: it is so vaine, that I will not endeavour to retell it." Furthermore, during the fifteenth and sixteenth centuries European artists began to portray blacks in a newly favorable light, commonly representing one of the Magi as black and giving certain saints identifiable African characteristics. And then there is Shakespeare's Othello, who, for all his failings, has principles and noble bearing.

My concern here, however, is not with the depth of color prejudice in Elizabethan society but rather the way in which beliefs about slavery intersected with perceptions of Africans. Englishmen prided themselves on their liberties. They did not, however, suppose that freedom was the inherent right of all individuals. Quite the contrary, they assumed slavery to be divinely ordained, part of the natural order. More than that, as the distinguished historian of antislavery thought, David Brion Davis, has demonstrated, they shared with other Europeans the view, stretching back at least to Aristotle, that the institution was intricately linked to the progress of Western civilization. True, the English were slow to take up the slave trade themselves, even though by the end of the sixteenth century the Portuguese had been selling Africans to the Spanish colonies of the New World for almost 100 years. But that was because they initially looked upon the peoples of Africa more as potential consumers and producers than commodities; they had no objection to the slave trade in principle.

The men and women who immigrated to Virginia in the early seventeenth century were products of Elizabethan culture and there is no reason to assume that they suffered a crisis of conscience when Dutch ships arrived at the colony carrying human cargo. Certain individuals were meant to be slaves. But what was it about the particular individuals unloaded at the docks of Jamestown that indicated they were marked for bondage? Was it their paganism, their "beastly lyvynge," their want of "civilization"? Or was it, perhaps, their color?

Testimony that would allow us to answer this question with certainty has not survived from early Virginia, and, in any case, since slavery was regarded as part of the natural order, it is doubtful that many colonists felt inspired to write down their views on the reasons for its existence. I am talking about unspoken assumptions here. We do know that during the Middle Ages the English identified slavery with godlessness—or what they thought of as godlessness—and not with skin color or other physical attributes. We also know that by the nineteenth century, southern planters would come to hold devout Christians in bondage and regard slavery as the normal condition for all people of African heritage. But the time I am talking about now, the early years of colonial Virginia, represents something of a period of transition between the two views.

To get my students to try and sort through the influences at work, I usually invite them to engage in a little counterfactual history. Suppose, I say, the Atlantic slave trade had not yet come into existence at the time when Jamestown was first settled. How would the colonists have reacted to a proposal to enslave Africans? And to what extent would their reaction have differed if the Africans had been Christian? Civilized? White? Or to take the case that would presumably be most relevant for isolating the significance of physical characteristics: What if, when the English first confronted them, Africans already enjoyed English liberties, spoke the English language, wore English clothes, and practiced English customs? What if they were observant, God-fearing Anglicans? In other words, what if they were just like the English in every respect except for their color, hair, and facial features. But most students seem to find this a problematic exercise. Arguably, some leaps of imagination are too difficult to make.

Winthrop Jordan, who, in his magisterial study *White over Black*, has done more than any other historian to illuminate the origins of American race consciousness, addresses the issue in this way:

> [I]t seems likely that the colonists' initial sense of difference from the Negro was founded not on a single characteristic but on a congeries of qualities which, taken as a whole, seemed to set the Negro apart. Virtually every quality in the Negro invited pejorative feelings. What may have been his two most striking characteristics, his heathenism and his appearance, were probably requisite to his complete debasement. His heathenism alone could never have lead to permanent enslavement since conversion easily wiped out that failing. If his appearance, his racial characteristics, meant nothing to the English settlers, it is difficult to see how slavery based on race ever emerged, how the concept of complexion as the mark of slavery ever entered the colonists' minds. Even if the colonists were most unfavorably struck by the Negro's color, though, blackness itself did not urge the complete debasement of slavery. Other qualities—the utter strangeness of his language, gestures, eating habits, and so on—certainly must have contributed to the colonists' sense that he was very different, perhaps disturbingly so.

Jordan also allows that the available evidence "suggests that for Englishmen settling in America, the specific religious difference was initially of greater importance than color." I would put it somewhat differently, I think, or rather make a somewhat different point. I would argue that heathenism was the necessary link through which the black skin and other physical characteristics of the Africans first became associated in the English mind with bondage.

During the early eighteenth century, the Society for the Propagation of the Gospel, an Anglican organization, had difficulty convincing slaveholders in the southern colonies to allow missionaries in the slave quarters. Part of the reason was the fear expressed by planters that, once their laborers had been baptized, the moral justification for slavery would be destroyed. The society discouraged such thinking, but the planters remained reluctant, even after various colonial assemblies enacted statutes making it legal for one Christian to own another. Old views on the rationale for slavery had apparently not yet entirely disappeared.

⊱✠⊰

Turn ahead to the Revolutionary era. Baptist and Methodist preachers crisscross the Virginia countryside, by and large receiving an enthusiastic reception from slaves and free blacks. Some masters are concerned about the leveling implications of the evangelical message, but few now fear that conversion might one day lead to emancipation. On the contrary, many planters have come to believe that Christianity will teach their slaves humility and obedience.

But there are new currents of thought abroad in the land. For the first time slavery is under serious attack. There had been criticism of the institution earlier, by Quakers mostly, who argued that it was contrary to Scripture and the egalitarian leanings of Christian doctrine. But the emergence of a widespread antislavery movement rested largely on arguments about natural rights first advanced a century earlier by John Locke. Locke himself had found ways to reconcile his philosophical commitment to human liberty with the reality of American slavery. But as colonists began to draw on his ideas to raise resistance to British policies, they perhaps inevitably found themselves questioning the morality of holding blacks in bondage. On the face of it, after all, slavery would seem to be incompatible with the "self-evident" truths mentioned in the Declaration of Independence: "That all men are created equal; that they are endowed by their Creator with certain inalienable rights; that among these are life, liberty, and the pursuit of happiness."

In fact, not all slaveholders acknowledged the existence of a contradiction between slavery and the principles embodied in the Declaration. Many did, however, including the author of that famous document, Thomas Jefferson. And Jefferson, a wealthy Virginia planter, along with other influential southern statesmen, now called for steps to be taken leading to emancipation of the slaves. Wrote George Washington in 1786: "I never mean—unless some particular circumstance should compel me to it—to possess another slave by purchase; it being among my first wishes to see some plan adopted, by which slavery in this country may be abolished by slow, sure and imperceptible degrees."

Still, the qualifying phrase Washington included—"unless some particular circumstance should compel me to it"—draws attention to the pro-

visional nature of the commitment to emancipation made by many planters. And provisional not just in the sense that they were unprepared to sacrifice their financial interests. Judging by the comments they made, most
slaveholders were more concerned about the disorienting effects of slavery
on the moral compass of masters than the incalculable damage it inflicted
on slaves. Jefferson, for one, who showed some measure of compassion for
blacks, referring to them variously as "unfortunate beings" or "unfortunate
people," reserved much of his sympathy for the children of slaveowners:

> The whole commerce between master and slave is a perpetual exer-
> cise of the most boisterous passions, the most unremitting despotism
> on the one part, and degrading submissions on the other. Our children
> see this, and learn to imitate it. . . . The parent storms, the child looks
> on, catches the lineaments of wrath, puts on the same airs in the circle
> of smaller slaves, gives a loose to his worst of passions, and thus nursed,
> educated, and daily exercised in tyranny, cannot but be stamped by it
> with odious peculiarities. The man must be a prodigy who can retain
> his manners and morals undepraved by such circumstances.

The fact is, the opposition to slavery did not even signify a decline in
the level of color prejudice in the society. Some passages from Jefferson's
Notes on the State of Virginia, written in 1781–82, illustrate the point:

> The first difference which strikes us is that of colour. Whether the
> black of the negro resides in the reticular membrane between the skin
> and scarf-skin, or in the scarf-skin itself; whether it proceeds from the
> colour of the blood, the colour of the bile, or from that of some other
> secretion, the difference is fixed in nature, and is as real as if its seat
> and cause were better known to us. And is this difference of no impor-
> tance? Is it not the foundation of a greater or less share of beauty in the
> two races? Are not the fine mixtures of red and white, the expressions
> of every passion by greater or less suffusions of colour in the one, pref-
> erable to that eternal monotony, which reigns in the countenances, that
> immoveable veil of black which covers all the emotions of the other race?
> Add to these, flowing hair, a more elegant symmetry of form, their own
> judgment in favour of the whites, declared by their preference of them,
> as uniformly as is the preference of the Oranootan for the black women
> over those of his own species. The circumstance of superior beauty, is
> thought worthy attention in the propagation of our horses, dogs, and
> other domestic animals; why not in that of man?

In behavior, too, Jefferson found blacks wanting:

> They seem to require less sleep. A black, after hard labour through
> the day, will be induced by the slightest amusements to sit up till mid-
> night, or later, though knowing he must be out with the first dawn of

the morning. They are at least as brave, and more adventuresome. But this may perhaps proceed from a want of forethought, which prevents their seeing a danger till it be present. When present, they do not go through it with more coolness or steadiness than the whites. They are more ardent after their female: but love seems with them to be more an eager desire, than a tender delicate mixture of sentiment and sensation. Their griefs are transient. Those numberless afflictions, which render it doubtful whether heaven has given life to us in mercy or in wrath, are less felt, and sooner forgotten with them. In general, their existence appears to participate more of sensation than reflection. To this must be ascribed their disposition to sleep when abstracted from their diversions, and unemployed in labour. An animal whose body is at rest, and who does not reflect, must be disposed to sleep of course. Comparing them by their faculties of memory, reason, and imagination, it appears to me, that in memory they are equal to the whites; in reason much inferior, as I think one could scarcely be found capable of tracing and comprehending the investigations of Euclid; and that in imagination they are dull, tasteless, and anomalous.

Some of the claims made by Jefferson were new but others clearly traced back to the days when English traders first arrived on the coast of Africa. I imagine you picked out his offhand remark about "the preference of the Oranootan for the black women."

Winthrop Jordan has oberved that, on matters of race, Jefferson was "a sounding board for his culture." Still, in one respect he was quite untypical. Most opponents of slavery in the South attributed what they saw as the intellectual and moral failings of slaves to the primitive conditions supposedly existing in Africa. Given time and contact with whites, they argued, blacks would rise appreciably on the scale of humanity. Jefferson, on the other hand, regarded their behavior and mental capacity as innate. In that sense he anticipated the views of both antebellum planters and more recent apologists for racial discrimination.

I spoke earlier of the "color prejudice" of Elizabethans but refrained from calling them "racist." The sixteenth-century English did not have a concept of "race," or at least did not have a concept of race as a biological classification reflecting a fundamental division of humanity. Historians generally refer to them as "ethnocentric," meaning that cultural considerations more than physical appearance dictated their sense of who they were and where they stood in relation to other peoples. Indeed, the crude, derogatory images they held of the Irish worked against any tendency to see all light-skinned individuals as representatives of a single "white race." With Jefferson, however, we have quite clearly arrived at an ideology that today we would call "racist": *Human beings divide naturally into biological categories—races—whose members share identifiable physical characteristics, most notably skin color. Race is a primary determinant of mental capacity, behavioral traits, and moral sensibility. Accordingly, races can be ranked hierarchically.* I earlier commented that Jefferson had some compassion for blacks. It should be clear that I meant in comparison with others in his society. Then again, you don't have to be mean-spirited to hold racist beliefs.

In any case, whatever the moral limitations of the antislavery movement, it did produce some noteworthy results. Although no state south of Pennsylvania elected to abolish slavery, many individual slaveholders chose to free some or all of their laborers. George Washington, for example, following a common practice, provided for the manumission of his slaves after his death. As a result of such actions, and because a considerable number of slaves had escaped during the Revolution, the size of the free black population in the South grew rapidly. In 1810 it stood at more than 100,000. This represented almost 9 percent of the total black population in the region, up from only 5 percent twenty years earlier.

By that time, however, by 1810, the support for antislavery had begun to decline. During the following decades few masters expressed a desire to free their slaves and, in any case, most southern states passed laws making manumission difficult if not impossible. Part of the change in attitude can be traced to a technological breakthrough. In 1792, a New Englander, Eli Whitney, invented the cotton gin, which separated seeds from cotton bolls much more rapidly than slaves were able to do by hand. As a consequence, planters could now commit many more acres to cotton production and yields rose rapidly, from about 6000 bales in 1792 (each bale weighing around 400 pounds) to 180,000 bales in 1810. Meanwhile, the new opportunities presented by the cotton culture hastened expansion westward. The first cotton gin arrived in Natchez, then a relatively young settlement, in 1795. Output rose from only 36,000 pounds in 1794 to 1,200,000 pounds two years later. During the nineteenth century planters like Absalom Sharpe and Alexander Farrar would build their fortunes on cotton. In 1860 production in the Natchez district reached well over 400,000 bales, or about 10 percent of the total for the entire South.

Slavery was profitable during the colonial era, so it would be misleading to suggest that economic forces were driving the institution toward extinction before Whitney came up with his invention. There can be little doubt, however, that the rapid expansion of cotton production in the early nineteenth century made the elimination of slavery that much harder to imagine. But if economic considerations had been all that were at stake, it is doubtful that state legislatures would have resorted to the extreme measures they did to prevent manumission. By the Revolutionary era, however, slavery had become more than simply a labor system; it was now a form of race control as well. And that created a profound dilemma for planters like Jefferson, who had a principled commitment to abolition but believed deeply in the inferiority of blacks. How could the slaves be freed without endangering social peace? How could blacks be incorporated into the polity? To Jefferson the obstacles seemed overwhelming:

> Deep rooted prejudices entertained by the whites; ten thousand recollections, by the blacks, of the injuries they have sustained; new provocations; the real distinctions which nature has made; and many other circumstances, will divide us into parties, and produce convulsions which will probably never end but in the extermination of the one or the other race.

Jefferson wrote these remarks during the Revolution. They took on added meaning a decade later when slaves on Saint-Domingue rose in rebellion and slaughtered their masters, taking control of the French colony early in the nineteenth century and establishing the independent Republic of Haiti. Slaveholders in the South noticed a substantial increase in acts of resistance by their slaves after word began to spread about the bloodshed in Saint-Domingue. The most striking instance was an abortive rebellion in Virginia in the summer of 1800 organized by a blacksmith named Gabriel— "General Gabriel," they called him. Had his plan succeeded, hundreds of armed slaves would have marched on Richmond.

Then again, blacks in the South hardly needed the example of Saint-Domingue to tell them slavery was immoral. Many of them had lived through America's own war for independence, had educated themselves in the meaning of "liberty" and "equality." And here was the irony: The same Revolutionary rhetoric of natural rights that gave rise to the conviction among many planters that slavery should be abolished led to acts of resistance by slaves that seemed to demonstrate the indispensability of the institution. Today we would probably say that southern slaveholders faced a "Catch-22": Retain slavery and obliterate the moral fabric of the nation; eliminate it and risk self-destruction. "[W]e have the wolf by the ears," wrote Jefferson, in perhaps his most memorable metaphor, "and we can neither hold him, nor safely let him go. Justice is in one scale, and self-preservation in the other."

For planters, slavery had become a "necessary evil." That was the term they used, a "necessary evil." Jefferson and other notable southerners of his generation continued to favor abolition, but conditionally, only if blacks could be removed from the United States. Another famous opponent of slavery, though of the next generation, would share Jefferson's belief in colonization. While working out the details of his Emancipation Proclamation, Abraham Lincoln attempted to negotiate arrangements for the massive transplanting of American blacks to Liberia or Haiti. Just another example of why hostility toward slavery should not be confused with a commitment to racial equality.

Turn ahead once more, this time to 1857, the year Duncan Skinner was murdered. With a vocal antislavery movement extending its influence in the North and increasing calls for abolition from abroad, slaveholders have become passionate and outspoken in defense of their "peculiar institution" (their euphemism, not mine). They no longer think of slavery as a "necessary evil." Now it is a "positive good." The arguments they offer to justify its existence, through tracts, pamphlets, and newspapers, in sermons and political addresses, are many and varied, at times crude, at times subtle and sophisticated.

They argue from constitutional principle. In 1837 the famous South Carolina statesman, John Calhoun, presented a series of resolutions in the Senate affirming the rights of the individual states to control their "domestic institutions." Here is one of those resolutions:

> Resolved, That in delegating a portion of their powers to be exercised by the Federal Government, the States retained, severally, the exclusive and sole right over their own domestic institutions and police, and are alone responsible for them, and that any intermeddling of any one or more States, or a combination of their citizens, with the domestic institutions and police of the others, on any ground, or under any pretext whatever, political, moral, or religious, with the view to their alteration, or subversion, is an assumption of superiority not warranted by the Constitution, insulting to the States interfered with, tending to endanger their domestic peace and tranquility, subversive of the objects for which the Constitution was formed, and, by necessary consequence, tending to weaken and destroy the Union itself.

They argue from economics. David Christy was a northern journalist, but his book *Cotton Is King*, published in 1855, was popular across the South. "COTTON IS KING," proclaimed Christy, "and his enemies are vanquished."

> Slavery is not an isolated system, but is so mingled with the business of the world, that it derives facilities from the most innocent transactions. Capital and labor, in Europe and America, are largely employed in the manufacture of cotton. These goods, to a great extent, may be seen freighting every vessel, from Christian nations, that traverses the seas of the globe; and filling the warehouses and shelves of the merchants, over two-thirds of the world. By the industry, skill, and enterprise, employed in the manufacture of cotton, mankind are better clothed; their comfort better promoted; general industry more highly stimulated; commerce more widely extended; and civilization more rapidly advanced, than in any preceding age.

They argue from Scripture. Thornton Stringfellow was a wealthy slave-holder and Baptist minister who had a plantation near Fredericksburg, Virginia. This is how he concluded one of his essays enumerating biblical justifications for slavery:

> We will remark, in closing under this head, that we have shown from the text of the sacred volume, that when God entered into covenant with Abraham, it was with him as a slaveholder; that when he took his posterity by the hand in Egypt, five hundred years afterwards to confirm the promise made to Abraham, it was done with them as slave-holders; that when he gave them a constitution of government, he gave them the right to perpetuate hereditary slavery; and that he did not for the fifteen hundred years of their national existence, express disappro-bation toward the institution.
>
> We have also shown from authentic history that the institution of slavery existed in every family, and in every province of the Roman Empire, at the time the gospel was published to them.
>
> We have also shown from the New Testament, that all the churches are recognized as composed of masters and servants; and that they are instructed by Christ how to discharge their relative duties; and finally that in reference to the question which was then started, whether Christianity did not abolish the institution, or the right of one Christian to hold another Christian in bondage, we have shown, that "the words of our Lord Jesus Christ" are, that so far from this being the case, it adds to the obligation of the servant to render service with good-will to his master, and that gospel fellowship is not to be entertained with persons who will not consent to it!

They argue from natural science (or what passed for natural science). Josiah Nott was a prominent physician in Mobile who wrote extensively on the anatomical differences between the races. The following passage comes from a public address he gave in 1844:

> When the Caucasian and Negro are compared, one of the most strik-ing and important points of difference is seen in the conformation of the head.
>
> The head of the Negro is smaller by a full tenth—the forehead is narrower and more receding, in consequence of which the anterior or intellectual portion of the brain is defective.—The upper jaw is broader and more projecting—the under jaw inclines out, and is deficient in chin; the lips are larger and correspond with the bony structure; the teeth point obliquely forward and resemble in shape those of Carnivorous animals; the bones of the head are thicker, more dense and heavy. . . .
>
> In animals where the senses and sensual faculties predominate, the nerves coming off from the brain are large, and we find the nerves of the Negro larger than those of the Caucasian. . . .

The arm of the African is much longer than in the Caucasian—a Negro of 5 feet 6 has an arm as long as a white man of 6 feet. The arm from the elbow to the hand is much longer in proportion, than in the white man. . . .

In the two races the lower limbs are in their relative proportion reversed—in their *entire* measurement, the legs of the African are shorter, but the thigh longer and flatter. . . .

Now it will be seen from this hasty sketch, how many points of resemblance Anatomists have established between the Negro and Ape. . . . In short, place beside each other average specimens of the Caucasian, Negro and Ourang Outang, and you will perceive a regular and striking gradation—substitute for the Negro a Bushman or Hottentot from the Cape of Good Hope, and the contrast is still stronger.

With Nott, the supposed similarity in the characteristics of Africans and chimpanzees remarked upon by sixteenth-century English traders had taken on new meaning. There are, he concluded, "rational grounds for believing" that blacks and whites belong to different species: "The difference to an Anatomist, between the Bushman or Negro and the Caucasian, is greater than the difference in the skeletons of the Wolf, Dog and Hyena, which are allowed to be distinct species; or the Tiger and Panther."

The doctrine of "polygenesis," or separate creations for the two races, gained a certain currency among antebellum southerners and even found some favor in the North. However, any interpretation of black inferiority that placed science in opposition to the teachings of the Bible inevitably ran into substantial opposition in a society so devoutly committed to evangelical Protestantism.

We do not know what opinions Alexander Farrar held on polygenesis, although we can take it for granted, I think, that he was well informed on the subject. We can assume as well that he and the other slaveholders who investigated the murder of Duncan Skinner would have agreed with John Calhoun on the right of states to control their own "domestic institutions," with David Christy on the central importance of cotton to the world economy, and with Thornton Stringfellow on the scriptural basis for slavery. In recent years, however, the proslavery spokesman who has drawn most attention from historians interested in the thought of southern planters is George Fitzhugh, a journalist for the Richmond *Enquirer*, perhaps the most influential paper in the Old South. In two provocative books published in the 1850s, *Sociology for the South; or the Failure of Free Society* and *Cannibals All! or Slaves Without Masters*, Fitzhugh attempted to demonstrate that slavery was inherently superior to free labor both materially and morally. Operating on the assumption that "every social structure must have its substratum," he repudiated the traditional American commitment to equality and denied that the interests of society as a whole were advanced by unrestrained competition among individuals seeking personal gain:

The bestowing upon men equality of rights, is but giving license to the strong to oppress the weak. It begets the grossest inequalities of condition. Menials and day laborers are and must be as numerous as in a land of slavery. And these menials and laborers are only taken care of while young, strong and healthy. If the laborer gets sick, his wages cease just as his demands are greatest. If two of the poor get married, who being young and healthy, are getting good wages, in a few years they may have four children. Their wants have increased, but the mother has enough to do to nurse the four children, and the wages of the husband must support six. There is no equality, except in theory, in such a society, and there is no liberty. The men of property, those who own lands and money, are masters of the poor; masters, with none of the feelings, interests or sympathies of masters; they employ them when they please, and for what they please, and may leave them to die in the highway, for it is the only home to which the poor in free countries are entitled.

By contrast, Fitzhugh argued, slavery produced harmony and security:

There is no rivalry, no competition to get employment among slaves, as among free laborers. Nor is there a war between master and slave. The master's interest prevents his reducing the slave's allowance or wages in infancy or sickness, for he might lose the slave by so doing. His feeling for his slave never permits him to stint him in old age. The slaves are all well fed, well clad, have plenty of fuel, and are happy. They have no dread of the future—no fear of want. A state of dependence is the only condition in which reciprocal affection can exist among human beings—the only situation in which the war of competition ceases, and peace, amity and good will arise. A state of independence always begets more or less of jealous rivalry and hostility.

Or as he put it elsewhere: "Nature compels master and slave to be friends; nature makes employers and free laborers enemies."

Many antebellum southern writers published attacks on the treatment of laborers in the North. Indeed, slaveholders produced some of the most scathing criticism of early industrial capitalism in America. But what set George Fitzhugh apart was his willingness to carry such reasoning to what can only be described as its logical conclusion:

Southern thought must justify the slavery principle, justify slavery as natural, normal, and necessitous. He who justifies mere negro slavery, and condemns other forms of slavery, does not think at all—no, not in the least. To prove that such men do not think, we have only to recur to the fact that they always cite the usages of antiquity and the commands of the Bible to prove that negro slavery is right. Now if these usages and commands prove anything, they prove that all kinds of slavery are right.

Eugene Genovese has characterized Fitzhugh's thought as "the logical outcome of the slaveholders' philosophy." Certainly a case can be made that the planters of the Natchez district should have been drawn to a defense of slavery that sanctioned hierarchy among whites. They had consciously cultivated an aristocratic lifestyle, had adopted an "air distingué," to borrow Joseph Holt Ingraham's phrase. And, as John McCallin could attest, they clearly thought of themselves as superior to others less privileged than themselves. It is Genovese's view that the sense of obligation planters in Natchez and elsewhere came to feel for their slaves informed all their relations, those with whites no less than blacks.

Yet, while slaveholders did speak out regularly against the cruelties of free labor in the North, they showed no inclination to argue that all laborers, regardless of race, would be better off as slaves, and while they looked upon less fortunate neighbors with evident disdain, on the whole they remained committed to the principle of equality for whites. Granted, they conceived of equality in narrow terms. Most acknowledged only that every white man must be free to rise as high as his God-given abilities would carry him. (Meaning that they themselves must be men of superior worth.) But they did believe that race mattered, did accept that nonslaveholders were entitled to opportunities denied even exceptional blacks.

And so while, yes, planters would castigate free labor for its inhumanity, contrary to all logic they would retreat to a defense of "mere negro slavery." The inconsistent quality to their reasoning is illustrated best, perhaps, in the famous "mud-sill" speech delivered on the floor of the Senate in 1858 by the South Carolina planter and politician James Hammond:

> In all social systems there must be a class to do the menial duties, to perform the drudgery of life. That is, a class requiring but a low order of intellect and but little skill. Its requisites are vigor, docility, fidelity. Such a class you must have, or you would not have that other class which leads progress, civilization, and refinement. It constitutes the very mud-sill of society and of political government; and you might as well attempt to build a house in the air, as to build either the one or the other, except on this mud-sill. Fortunately for the South, she found a race adapted to that purpose to her hand. A race inferior to her own, but eminently qualified in temper, in vigor, in docility, in capacity to stand the climate, to answer all her purposes. We use them for our purpose, and call them slaves. . . . I will not characterize that class at the North by that term; but you have it; it is there; it is everywhere; it is eternal. . . .
>
> The difference between us is, that our slaves are hired for life and well compensated; there is no starvation, no begging, no want of employment among our people, and not too much employment either. Yours are hired by the day, not cared for, and scantily compensated, which may be proved in the most painful manner, at any hour in any

street in any of your large towns. Why, you meet more beggars in one day, in any single street of the city of New York, than you would meet in a lifetime in the whole South. We do not think that whites should be slaves either by law or necessity. Our slaves are black, of another and inferior race. The *status* in which we have placed them is an elevation. They are elevated from the condition in which God first created them, by being made our slaves. . . . They are happy, content, unaspiring, and utterly incapable, from intellectual weakness, ever to give us any trouble by their aspirations.

"Happy, content, unaspiring." It was ultimately these supposed innate characteristics of blacks, and not the fundamental immorality of free labor, that served as the basis for the claim by planters that slavery was a "positive good." Historians apply the term "Sambo" to the stereotypical image of the slave presented in antebellum southern descriptions of plantation life. "Sambo," says Stanley Elkins, who made the mistake of confusing the stereotype with the reality, was "docile but irresponsible; loyal but lazy; humble but chronically given to lying and stealing; his behavior was full of infantile silliness and his talk inflated with childish exaggeration. His relationship with his master was one of utter dependence and childlike attachment: it was indeed this childlike quality that was the very key to his being." "A northerner looks upon a band of negroes, as upon so many *men*," observed Joseph Holt Ingraham from Natchez in the 1830s. "But the planter . . . views them in a very different light." The planter saw them as children, he meant, in need of care and direction. Dempsey Jackson put the sentiment more crudely. "The niger we Know him the mass of them are stupid and indolent." They "ever will require guardians."

It is tempting to dismiss such statements as mere rhetoric, they sound so self-serving. But consider the following extraordinary passage from a letter written shortly after the Civil War by Joseph Shields, one of the defense attorneys at the trial of Henderson, Reuben, and Anderson:

> Let me describe a scene that has just passed before my door. Mary is sitting backwards in Dades wagon. Cy & Daniel & Caius & Hinds are the mule Team while Walter is the driver—Huntz stands in the house and dictates the track—They are enjoying themselves just as much as though they were not Free.

"Just as much as though they were *not* Free." Because in Shields' mind they were meant to be slaves; because in his mind these children of slaves would never develop mentally or morally into adults and so needed the care and protection that only slavery could provide.

"Sambo" was not unique to the South. The eminent historical sociologist Orlando Patterson calls him "the ideological imperative of all systems of slavery." But why in the South did the stereotype take on a racial connotation? Why did it attach to all blacks and not just those blacks—granted, the great majority—who happened to be slaves? The natural reaction, I think, is simply to say that slaveholders were racists: Their assumptions about blacks were the inevitable result of a history of color prejudice tracing back to Elizabethan England. But the Elizabethans themselves did not assume that black skin indicated a childlike personality and even Thomas Jefferson, who departed from other leading thinkers of the Revolutionary era in believing that blacks were inferior by nature and not because of circumstance, did not conclude that they were therefore meant to be slaves. As well, antislavery advocates in the antebellum North were—most of them, anyway—every bit as devoted to white supremacy as southern planters yet had an entirely different understanding of black character. Recall Ingraham's observation: "A northerner looks upon a band of negroes, as upon so many *men*." Men, not children. The point is, racism by itself did not lead antebellum planters inescapably to the conclusion that blacks were by nature destined for bondage.

Or rather it did, but only after it had been refracted through the prism of class interest. The planters were the chief beneficiaries of an economic order in which certain laborers were slave and others were free. What they needed was some justification for the existing duality, some way to see liberty and slavery as complementary. The position adopted by George Fitzhugh, whatever appeal it might otherwise hold, clearly would not do. It treated the duality as irrational. But a worldview that explained human behavior in terms of race—a worldview that said blacks were by nature suited to be slaves, whites to be free—allowed the planters to reassure themselves that their own elevated status was legitimate and just.

Northern opponents of slavery agreed with Fitzhugh that the status quo was irrational. And while their view of the comparative morality of slavery and free labor was diametrically opposed to his, they nonetheless shared his opinion that American society was at a crossroads. Indeed, it was after reading Fitzhugh that Abraham Lincoln felt inspired to write perhaps his most eloquent statement on the irreconcilability of slavery and free labor. You will recognize the text of his remarks, which were delivered at the state Republican convention for Illinois in 1858:

> "A house divided against itself cannot stand."
> I believe this government cannot endure, permanently half *slave* and half *free*.
> I do not expect the Union to be *dissolved*—I do not expect the house to *fall*—but I *do* expect it will cease to be divided.
> It will become *all* one thing, or *all* the other.

The idea that either slavery or free labor would have to be destroyed seemed the abandonment of all reason to the planters. Different races had different God-given attributes; they needed different systems of labor.

History, it is often said (somewhat misleadingly), is written by the victors. The Civil War and emancipation brought slavery to an end and for that reason secession can appear as a radical, desperate act. But southern planters hardly saw their cause as desperate, and if secession was a radical act, it was a radical act driven by a profoundly conservative agenda: Preserve the existing order. Ensure that the house remained divided.

I earlier wrote about the sense of obligation planters felt toward their slaves. This sense of obligation both promoted and was reinforced by the belief that blacks were childlike by nature. Indeed, the conviction that blacks needed care and guidance allowed the planters to convince themselves they were something more than mere businessmen, allowed them to represent slavery as a "reciprocal" relationship, dictated not by the economics of staple crop production but the inherent needs of their laborers. It was moral, they said. It was divinely ordained.

We can now see why Alexander Farrar and the other planters who investigated the murder of Duncan Skinner were predisposed to implicate a white man in the crime. If blacks were childlike by nature—if they were, as James Hammond maintained, "happy, content, unaspiring, and utterly incapable, from intellectual weakness, ever to give us any trouble by their aspirations"—then there was little likelihood that they would engage in premeditated acts of resistance. Not on their own. Not without some white person putting them up to it.

⁍✛⁌

I seem to have contradicted myself. Perhaps you noticed. Back when I was discussing slave resistance I wrote that the planters "knew that slaves were not reconciled to their fate and that there was always a possibility that any number of them might, without warning, rise in rebellion." Now I appear to be saying—well, okay, I am saying—that they believed slaves were basically content and assumed that premeditated acts of resistance must have been instigated by whites. You no doubt want an explanation.

The planters found themselves in a paradoxical situation. The defense of slavery rested on one interpretation of black character, social reality at times seemed to demand another. Slaves did from time to time murder their overseers or masters, did, even if only on rare occasions, plot insurrection. Of course, you could always tell yourself that treasonous whites were to blame, as the slaveholders typically did. But it would have been risky to assume that blacks were incapable of acting independently. So alongside the image of Sambo—held in reserve by the planters, if you will, for such a day as it might be required—lived a counterimage that John Blassingame has referred to as "Nat":

Revengeful, bloodthirsty, cunning, treacherous, and savage, Nat was the incorrigible runaway, the poisoner of white men, the ravager of white women who defied all the rules of plantation society. Subdued and punished only when overcome by superior numbers or firepower, Nat retaliated when attacked by whites, led guerrilla activities of maroons against isolated plantations, killed overseers and planters, or burned plantation buildings when he was abused.

Let me be clear about what I am saying here. I am not suggesting that planters told themselves that *some* blacks were childlike, *some* blacks were "cunning" and "revengeful." What I mean is, they held to contradictory interpretations of black character and drew on them as circumstances and their own psychological needs dictated. So, for example, the carriage driver who spent his days in loyal and obedient service to his mistress offered them the reassuring presence of "Sambo"; but let that same carriage driver plan a murder described by a local newspaper as "ingenious" and "adroitly concealed" and he suddenly was transformed into "Nat" in their minds.

Most days the planters did not have to deal with threats of murder and insurrection. Slaves by and large went about their business in an orderly if perhaps desultory manner, and while malingering, lying, and theft were common, they could easily be interpreted as proof that blacks were by nature dependent, in need of strict control and moral guidance. Sooner or later, however, someone would report a rumor of a planned insurrection or the body of a murdered overseer would be discovered and the comforting illusion of Sambo would give way to the terrifying specter of Nat. Then, if panic set in, as it sometimes did, the landscape would erupt in a series of bloody reprisals against innocent and guilty blacks alike. Until finally the fear would subside, the demons would be exorcized, and Nat would give way to Sambo once more.

Though clearly meant to represent all blacks, Sambo was a male image. So, obviously, was Nat, "the ravager of white women." But the planters produced contradictory images of black women as well, and for the same reason: because the need to justify slavery favored one interpretation of black character, the reality of life within slavery another. One of those images you likely already know. Usually she's represented in twentieth-century romantic novels about the Old South as a heavy-set woman with a bright bandana and broad, comforting smile. For me "Mammy" brings to mind the picture of "Aunt Jemima" on the boxes of pancake mix when I was a kid. For you maybe it's Hattie McDaniel in *Gone with the Wind*. Mammy had a kind of worldly wisdom; indeed, in many respects she understood the needs of white people better than they did themselves. But she never doubted that the Good Lord intended blacks for slavery, and while she could adopt the manner of a stern disciplinarian with the white children in her care, she was more deeply devoted to her master's family than her own.

But while the image of "Mammy" might serve to reassure planters, it could hardly explain, much less justify, the rape of slave women by masters and their sons. And so slaveholders took refuge in the seductive fantasy of "Jezebel," a product of stereotypes about female black promiscuity going back to the sixteenth century. "Jezebal," writes historian Elizabeth Fox-Genovese, "lived free of the social constraints that surrounded the sexuality of white women. She thus legitimated the wanton behavior of white men by proclaiming black women to be lusty wenches in whom sexual impulse overwhelmed all restraint. The image eased the consciences of white men by suggesting that black women asked for the treatment they received." It eased the consciences of their wives, too, if never so unequivocally, by allowing them to tell themselves that their husbands were not brutish and faithless, merely frail. Dorcas, the house servant on Cedar Grove, would have appeared as Jezebel in the eyes of the planters who interrogated her. Her purported passion for a white man was consistent with the stereotype, and the alleged pleasure she took in his efforts to marry her mistress showed that she was contemptuous of conventional standards of morality.

Jezebel and Nat were mere images, inventions of the white mind. Not so the quarter of a million free blacks in the slave states on the eve of the Civil War. While most lived in Maryland and Virginia, enough made their homes in the major cities of the Deep South that any individual planter would know at least a few by name and reputation. Census takers recorded 225 free blacks in Adams County in 1860, 208 in Natchez. The great majority had menial positions, working as unskilled laborers. There were a handful of privileged families, however, who constituted something of an elite and had cordial, if deferential, relations with the wealthiest of the slaveholders. I mentioned William Johnson earlier. He made a very comfortable living as a barber in town. His doctor was a future governor of Kentucky, his lawyer William T. Martin, the prosecuting attorney at the trial of Henderson, Reuben, and Anderson.

The historians Michael Johnson and James Roark have written a compelling book, *Black Masters*, about a free black man even more successful than William Johnson. William Ellison of South Carolina, though born a slave, was apprenticed to a ginwright at an early age and freed when still only in his twenties. He established himself in the town of Stateburg, building up a profitable trade making and repairing gins. Eventually he acquired a plantation of almost 1,000 acres and more than 60 slaves. Although there was never a question of Ellison being accorded true equality with the slaveholding elite, he was allowed membership in the prestigious Holy Cross Episcopal Church and earned widespread respect for his exceptional craftsmanship.

Ellison, for his part, repaid his white patrons by demonstrating unwavering loyalty to the regime. Some free blacks purchased slaves out of compassion, to provide them with protection. Ellison, however, evidently became a slaveowner to secure his own material interests and enhance his social standing, in other words for the same reasons as his white neighbors. Johnson and Roark speculate that he earned the money to run his operations largely by selling young slave girls.

William Ellison of Stateburg, William Johnson of Natchez, and other representatives of the free black elite in the South consciously sought to establish social distance between themselves and the slaves. Indeed, most of them were mulattoes and viewed themselves as members of a distinct race, superior to pure blacks. So, for example, to secure admission to the prestigious Friendly Moralist Society of Charleston you had to have not only a high social position but proven white ancestry. Nonetheless, the attempt of the mulatto elite to gain recognition as a separate caste never received sanction in the law nor any appreciable measure of support from the planters. How could it, since just about every large slaveholder included at least some mulattoes among his slaves? And when crackdowns took place against free blacks in the community, as they did with increasing frequency as the Civil War approached, it was not the color of your skin that determined whether you would be protected but your ability to secure the patronage of a wealthy white. In 1831 the legislature of Mississippi passed a law that, at least on paper, required every free black to leave the state. To secure an exemption you had to appear before your local board of police with a petition signed by respectable whites attesting to your good standing. In the minds of most planters, free black barbers and tradesmen were more responsible and trustworthy than working-class whites. But that only makes the commitment of the planters to a defense of slavery based on race all that much more paradoxical.

One of the most influential books ever written on American slavery is *The Peculiar Institution*, by Kenneth Stampp, published in 1956. Perhaps more than any other historian Stampp documented the depth of cruelty and injustice on southern plantations. And because of that cruelty and injustice, he concluded, the slaveholders must have had tortured souls: "The pathos in the life of every master lay in the fact that slavery had no philosophical defense worthy of the name—that it had nothing to commend it to posterity, except that it paid."

No one has seriously challenged Stampp's view that slavery was a harsh and exploitative institution, not even those of us who believe, as Stampp did not, that planters felt a genuine sense of obligation toward their laborers. But most historians today would deny that the slaveholders were inwardly distressed about holding human beings as property. True, if you look long enough you can find a letter here, a journal entry there that suggests its author had a troubled conscience. The relevant passages are rarely un-ambiguous, however. It is much easier to argue that planters felt remorse about their failure to fulfill their responsibilities to their slaves than that they had doubts about the morality of slavery itself.

All the same, the thought of the planters *was* marked by glaring incon-sistencies. They told themselves that blacks were intellectually deficient yet associated with wealthy free blacks who owned the works of Shakespeare. They told themselves that slaves were childlike yet justified rape on the grounds that black women were lascivious, told themselves that slaves were content yet justified brute repression on the grounds that black men were "revengeful, bloodthirsty, cunning, treacherous, and savage." The planters who investigated the death of Duncan Skinner showed their predisposition to believe that blacks were incapable of the clever, premeditated murder of an overseer by passing blame on to a white carpenter. But they also took the precaution to see that the three slaves who committed the crime were executed in public as an example to other slaves of the futility of rebellion.

Southern slaveholders undoubtedly recognized at some level that they were trafficking in contradictions. Whether that indicates they had a sense of guilt depends, I suppose, on what I mean by "at some level" (I was delib-erately vague) and what you think of as guilt (a "feeling," my dictionary re-minds me, and therefore difficult to recover from records left by men not known for their introspection). Still, the main problem I have with Stampp is not that he thinks the planters were tormented by guilt but that he seems to believe they were unique among antebellum elites in having *cause* to be tormented by guilt: "When, at last, they lost the profits and conveniences of slavery, they won the chance to live in peace with themselves and with their age." As if wealthy cotton manufacturers in the North who preached liberty and equality but employed impoverished immigrant laborers under hazardous working conditions at miserly wages were not trafficking in con-tradictions of their own. And here, really, was the saving grace for the plant-ers. Because while they were able to develop a certain blindness to the contradictions within their own lives, they showed themselves acutely aware of the contradictions within the lives of northern capitalists. Hypocrisy, no less than beauty, lies in the eye of the beholder.

But, then, why limit these observations to the nineteenth century, why limit them to the United States? In what society do privileged elites not embrace a view of the world designed to justify their status, and in what society does the distance between that view of the world and social reality not create contradictions? And, to return to the starting point of this whole exercise, in what society does the attempt to resolve those contradictions not lead to a search for scapegoats? The scapegoats are not invariably male, they're not invariably white, they're not invariably Irish immigrant carpen-ters named John McCallin. But they all serve the same purpose.

⊰ 7 ⊱

Democracy and Justice

As late as the beginning of the nineteenth century, most Americans considered "democracy" a pejorative term; it suggested mob rule. In 1800, Noah Webster—yes, the author of the first American dictionary, although that was a number of years later—defined a "democrat" as someone who attempted to exert "an undue opposition to or influence over government by means of private clubs, secret intrigues, or by public popular meetings which are extraneous to the Constitution." Many property holders had the vote, but only a privileged few were thought to be qualified to occupy office. In the southern states this meant wealthy planters. Political campaigns reflected the prevailing skepticism about the ability of the electorate to understand matters of public policy. A candidate for office would not make speeches outlining his views on the pressing issues of the day nor pledge himself to specific initiatives. Rather, his friends would testify to his sterling character and he would prove his generous nature by providing lavish "treats" of food and, more important, liquor, at picnics and barbecues held in his honor.

During the following decades, however, the South, along with the rest of the nation, underwent what amounted to a democratic revolution. The franchise was broadened, with voting restrictions for white males being reduced or, especially in the more western states, eliminated altogether. Requirements for officeholding also were lowered and many more positions were made elective. Mississippi, in particular, was swept up in the call for reform, becoming, by its constitution of 1832, "the most democratic state in the whole South" according to the historian Charles S. Sydnor:

> Universal manhood suffrage was established, property qualifications for voting were abolished, the state treasurer and the state auditor became elective officers, and the undemocratic county courts were

replaced by boards of police whose five members, together with nearly all other county officers, were elected for two-year terms. Mississippi went farther into democracy than any Southern state by granting to the people the right to elect all their judges, even the three members of the High Court of Errors and Appeals, for limited terms of office.

The "other county officers" who had to stand for office at regular intervals included tax assessors, sheriffs, coroners, treasurers, surveyors, rangers, justices of the peace, constables, and district attorneys, such as Henry S. Van Eaton, who, nominally anyway, was responsible for the prosecution of Henderson, Reuben, and Anderson. Of course, when Sydnor speaks of "universal manhood suffrage" and refers to "the people" as having the right to elect their judges, he is, at the very least, choosing his words carelessly. Only men had the franchise, and white supremacy being the order of the day, even prominent free blacks such as William Johnson were excluded from the ballot box.

But it was not only the extension of voting rights and other institutional changes that marked the democratic revolution of the early nineteenth century. There was a transformation in attitude as well. To get elected now it was not enough to provide liberal quantities of alcohol to the voters, although that remained a prominent feature of any campaign. You also had to demonstrate a willingness to be guided by the views of the electorate. Some planters, such as Alexander Farrar, accommodated themselves to the changed political conditions and acquired powerful positions as party leaders. But during the decades leading up to the Civil War, most offices were filled by men drawn from the middle class.

Historians speak of this era as the "age of the common man" and mark its symbolic arrival with the election of Andrew Jackson to the presidency in 1828. Jackson was by this time a wealthy Tennessee cotton planter, but never mind. He was of humble origin and in the eyes of the public stood as the antithesis of aristocratic privilege. The new democratic order effectively received its christening when some of his supporters—variously described by witnesses as a "rabble" or "mob"—crashed a reception at the White House following his inauguration. In their scramble to get a glimpse of him they tracked mud across the carpet and onto the damask furniture and knocked over valuable china and crystal, until finally someone got the idea to drag the ice cream and barrels of punch out into the garden. Jackson named his political party the "Democratic Republicans," later shortened to "Democrats," a clear sign that for most Americans the idea of democracy had been purged of its derogatory connotations.

In view of the leveling tendencies within southern politics, it should come as no surprise that the historical record contains evidence of scorn among small slaveholders and nonslaveholders for the pretensions of wealthy planters. On his way to Natchez from Woodville, 30 miles to the South, Frederick Olmsted encountered a farmer who dismissed the children of the elite as nothing more than "young swell-heads!"

> You'll take note of 'em in Natchez. You can tell them by their walk. I noticed it yesterday at the Mansion House. They sort o' throw out their legs as if they hadn't got strength enough to lift 'em and put them down in any particular place. They do want so bad to look as if they weren't made of the same clay as the rest of God's creation.

The *Mississippi Free Trader*, which included members of the elite among its subscribers, complained some years earlier:

> The large planters—the one-thousand-bale planters—do not contribute most to the prosperity of Natchez. They, for the most part, sell their cotton in Liverpool; buy their wines in London or Havre; their negro clothing in Boston; their plantation implements and supplies in Cincinnati; and their groceries and fancy articles in New Orleans.

But if the conspicuous consumption of the planting elite aroused feelings of envy, and their pretensions to gentility provoked resentment, it is nonetheless the case that they held significant influence within the Natchez district. Notwithstanding the editorial in the *Free Trader*, many planters provided valuable services for less privileged whites, patronizing the stores of local merchants, hiring the services of craftsmen such as John McCallin, and ginning and marketing the cotton of small farmers.

Moreover, the planting elite represented the ideal for most nonslaveholders and small slaveholders. "Cotton and negroes are the constant theme—the ever harped upon, never worn out subject of conversation among all classes," commented Joseph Holt Ingraham. Earlier I quoted his more evocative statement on the same subject: "A plantation well stocked with hands is the ne plus ultra of every man's ambition who resides in the South." The mere fact that wealthy planters owned so much more land and so many more slaves than anyone else earned them a certain esteem, fostered the suspicion in the minds of other whites that they were men of superior worth. We can assume that there were artisans and laborers who spent their evenings over drinks at the Hibernian Society in Natchez making derisive comments about "aristocrats" and "swell-heads," yet removed their hats, directed their eyes groundward, and adopted a deferential tone in the presence of an Alexander Farrar.

But ultimately the influence of the planters rested on something more fundamental than the services they provided for other whites or their impressive wealth. It rested on the commitment of all members of society to the sacrosanct nature of private property. Property included slaves, of course, which is why the law of the plantation regularly took precedence over the law of the state.

In the Old South, then, the white population placed great value on the principal of democracy, but they established a form of democracy that accorded planters wide latitude to act independently in matters relating to slavery. Both factors—the commitment to democracy in principle and the reality of planter influence—played a significant role in determining the manner in which first John McCallin and later Henderson, Reuben, and Anderson were brought to justice.

⊨✛⊨

During the early 1850s, Jesse Skinner served as overseer on Commencement for Alexander Farrar. They had a sufficiently close relationship that when Skinner's two-year-old daughter, Mary Eliza, died in February 1853, she was buried in the Farrar family cemetery. Later that same year, however, the two men had a falling out when he decided to acquire the lease to a ferry and tavern on the Homochitto River. He subsequently took a job as an overseer on another plantation in the neighborhood, but a year later he signed an agreement allowing Farrar free passage on the ferry, so seemingly they had resolved their differences (if, perhaps, at Skinner's expense). And it was apparently to his former employer that Jesse Skinner turned in May of 1857 when a coroner's jury ruled that his brother Duncan had died as a result of a fall from his horse.

The mere fact that he would bring his doubts about the verdict to Farrar, a private citizen, and not Oren Metcalfe, the sheriff of Adams County, is revealing. It demonstrates where authority was presumed to lie in such cases. Equally revealing is what Farrar did next. Rather than take his concerns to Metcalfe or some other public official, he approached another wealthy planter, David P. Williams, and the two of them organized the party—"posse" might be a more accurate term for it—that conducted the inquiry into Duncan Skinner's death. Though never given formal authority by the state, the investigators collected the evidence later used by the prosecution to convict Henderson, Reuben, and Anderson of murder. Indeed, according to Giles Hillyer, they "received a warm acknowledgment from Mr. Martin in his eloquent speech at the conclusion of the trial."

The decision by Farrar and Williams to operate outside the law—or perhaps I should say to assume the mantle of the law—was entirely in keeping with accepted practice in the Old South. Planters had unwritten authority to investigate suspected criminal activities by slaves. But during their interrogation, the slaves on Cedar Grove made an apparently unexpected allegation. They claimed that they had been acting under orders from the carpenter John McCallin. And this had significant implications for the course of the investigation, because the authority planters had to monitor the activities of slaves did not translate into the right to pass judgment on whites. Nonetheless, if Farrar and Williams had second thoughts about proceeding against McCallin, they set them aside. And so we got the following notice in the local newspapers:

> WE, THE UNDERSIGNED, having examined the negroes on Mrs. Clarissa Sharp's plantation, in reference to the murder of Mr. Duncan B. Skinner, find, upon examination, that he was without the least shadow of doubt murdered; and from the confessions of the negroes, made separately and apart from each other, without their having any possible chance of knowing what each had confessed, that the conduct of MR. JOHN McCALLIN has been such, that we hereby warn him not again to make his appearance among us; and we, the undersigned do hereby pledge ourselves to enforce the warning herein given:

Because they signed their names to the warning, we can identify the eighteen men who served, in effect, as McCallin's judge and jury. Table 1 provides the relevant information. If we follow conventional practice and designate anyone who owned at least 20 slaves as a planter and those with at least 50 slaves as large planters, twelve men belonged to the planting class,

Table 1. Investigating Party

Name	Occupation	Birthplace	Age	Slaveholding
Daniel F. Ashford*	Planter	Mississippi	20	107
James P. Ashford*	Planter	Mississippi	22	107
John W. Baird	Planter	Unknown	44	Unknown
Charles P. Calvit	Planter	Mississippi	35	75
Alexander K. Farrar	Planter	Mississippi	42	229
Caleb F. Farrar	Physician	Mississippi	35	4
Fountain W. Ford	Farmer	Mississippi	26	15
William G. Foules	Engineer	Mississippi	22	50
William Griffin	Farmer	Mississippi	41	15
Lansford O. Ireson	Planter	Mississippi	39	37
Joseph W. Sessions	Planter	Mississippi	40	66
Benjamin Skinner	Overseer	South Carolina	30	Unknown
Jesse Skinner	Overseer	South Carolina	47	Unknown
Absalom H. Sojourner**	Planter	Mississippi	24	33
William Sojourner**	Planter	Mississippi	26	33
Henry Clay Swayze	Planter	Mississippi	27	45
Joshua Thorn***	Planter	Mississippi	27	68
David P. Williams	Planter	Mississippi	43	219

*James and Daniel Ashford both lived in the home of their mother, Clarissa Ashford. The figures on slaveholding come from her entry in the census.
**William and Absalom Sojourner both lived in the home of their aunt, Eliza Sojourner. The figures on slaveholding come from her entry in the census.
***Joshua Thorn lived in the home of his father, James Thorn. The figure on slaveholding comes from James Thorn's entry in the census.

with eight ranking as members of the elite. Of the remaining six, no information is available on the holdings of John W. Baird, but he was a brother-in-law of Absalom and William Sojourner, who also participated in the investigation and were themselves planters (in addition to being nephews of Clarissa Sharpe). Caleb Farrar was a wealthy doctor and the brother of Alexander Farrar. Fountain W. Ford was a former overseer for Clarissa Sharpe on Bonne Ridge plantation, now a farmer, who in the fall would be elected to the Board of Police. And Jesse and Benjamin Skinner were, of course, brothers of the murdered man. That leaves only William Griffin, with 15 slaves, as someone without an identifiable connection to the planting class, and he hardly qualifies as a man of modest circumstances. Clearly John McCallin was tried and convicted by a very select element of the society.

But Farrar and Williams must have feared that, once they resolved to take action against someone who was white, there might be accusations that they had overreached their authority, because they decided to publish, along with the warning, a declaration of support from seventeen men not involved in the investigation:

> We, the undersigned, believe the foregoing statement, and hereby pledge ourselves to co operate in any course that the foregoing signers may deem necessary.

As Table 2 shows, of the seventeen individuals who signed the document, at least thirteen would qualify as large planters. No clear information is available on Robert Dunbar, but the family name—Dunbar—belonged to one of

Table 2. Group Supporting the Findings of the Investigating Party

Name	Occupation	Birthplace	Age	Slaveholding
Edwin R. Bennett	Planter	Delaware	45	190
Henry L. Bennett	Planter	Delaware	56	67
Thomas F. Davis	Planter	Mississippi	55	35
Robert Dunbar	Unknown	Unknown	Unknown	Unknown
William B. Foules	Planter	New York	57	50
James A. Gillespie	Planter	Tennessee	62	191
John Holmes	Planter	Mississippi	66	237
Thomas McCouen	Planter	Mississippi	39	60
Henry L. Metcalfe	Planter	Mississippi	27	108
James W. Metcalfe	Planter	Mississippi	37	317
James H. Mitchell	Planter	Virginia	57	50
Routh Henry Phipps	Planter	Mississippi	40	40
Lewis Pipes	Planter	Mississippi	56	188
Robert Pipes	Planter	Mississippi	27	22
A. D. Rawlings	Planter	Mississippi	37	66
J. T. Rawlings	Planter	Maryland	40	62
Daniel Smith	Planter	Mississippi	58	321

the oldest and most successful planting clans in the lower Mississippi Valley. If we except Robert Pipes, a son of Lewis Pipes, who also signed the statement and owned 188 slaves, only Thomas F. Davis, and Routh H. Phipps fall below the usual designation for members of the elite, and with 35 and 40 slaves respectively, they clearly qualify as wealthy men. In other words, in seeking to secure support for their actions, the members of the investigating party turned not to individuals who might have represented a broad cross-section of the community, but to planters, men like themselves. Or, rather, men like themselves but on average older and more affluent, what we should probably think of as senior spokesmen for the slaveholding elite. Whether this represented an accurate reading of how best to persuade the community that a nonslaveholding carpenter was responsible for the murder is open to debate. It does suggest that Farrar and Williams were operating under the assumption that less privileged whites would defer to the judgment of wealthy planters like themselves.

Of course, as we know, McCallin was not intimidated by the accumulation of respectability mounted against him:

> I HAVE LATELY SEEN A NOTICE in the Natchez Courier, signed by A. K. Farrar, David P. Williams, and numerous others, the tendency of which is to charge me, upon the statements of negroes, with being implicated in the murder of my *friend* Mr. Duncan B. Skinner, and which also threatens me with personal violence. The charge so contained is utterly false, and as I believe maliciously prompted by the negroes, as in due time will be made to appear. As to the threats against me, although I also may be murdered, I shall entirely disregard them.

In his refusal to be intimidated, McCallin created a considerable dilemma for Farrar, Williams, and the other members of the investigating party. If they elected to ignore his declaration and follow through with their threat to drive him from the community, they risked offending the democratic sensibilities of most white residents of Adams County. On the other hand, they had little interest in giving him a platform to defend himself. I doubt they were afraid he would be able to produce proof of his innocence. To their mind the evidence against him was "irresistible." It was, rather, a question of their honor. Here was a mere carpenter, a nonslaveholder, challenging their truthfulness, accusing them of unprincipled behavior. And who knows? By exploiting class resentment he might have been able to raise difficult questions about their right to speak for the community as a whole.

What they chose to do, as we have seen, was arrange for a "public" meeting in Kingston. But that meeting was democratic in form only, not substance. No advance announcement was published in the local newspapers, and, as the following letter to Alexander Farrar suggests, it is quite possible that many if not all of the forty or so men in attendance were there at the personal invitation of members of the investigating committee. The letter was written by the wealthy planter Nathaniel Hoggatt Jr.

> I this moment received your very acceptable note and in reply thereto I would certainly go to Kingston to day was it not in consequence of business engagements. There will to day be a large crowd of gentlemen at my house by agreement and promise. There is to be shooting for beef cattle, horse racing, and various other amusing things to take down here to day. Was it convenient I certainly would comply with your request.

There is no way of determining whether nonslaveholders were present in Kingston, but the decision to hold the meeting outside Natchez would undoubtedly have discouraged McCallin's workingmen friends and acquaintances from attending, assuming they even knew a meeting was to take place. Some unnamed person—Alexander Farrar, most likely—appointed the chairman, Dempsey Jackson. Jackson was a close personal friend of Farrar who owned over 3,000 acres and more than 100 slaves. The man chosen as secretary, Charles Pipes, was a young lawyer, son of the wealthy slaveholder Lewis Pipes and brother of the planter Robert Pipes, both of whom had signed the statement in the papers supporting the findings against McCallin. When Jackson asked if anyone doubted that McCallin was guilty or had evidence to offer on his behalf, no one spoke up. He then appointed a committee made up of William J. Gillespie, D. M. Hayden, Orrick Metcalfe, Israel S. Scott, and John Thorn to "draft resolutions expressive of the sense of the meeting." Thorn, Metcalfe, Gillespie, and Hayden were all large slaveholders. Scott was listed in the Adams County tax rolls as having 1,440 acres but only eight slaves, a figure that seems far too low, especially in view of the assessment made of him by the local representative of the R. G. Dun & Co. Agency: a "fine high toned man [of] wealthy parentage." In the resolutions brought forward by the committee, the planters made every effort to establish that they were involved in a democratic forum and that they therefore could legitimately speak for the white population as a whole. "[W]e citizens of the county of Adams, in public meeting assembled" is how they referred to themselves. Furthermore, they took pains to show that McCallin had committed a crime not simply against Duncan Skinner, but against everyone in the community. McCallin concealed the facts from "the public." The killing "led to the subsequent murder of McBride, on a neighboring place, and the general restless state of the slaves in that vicinity." His "presence . . . is alike detrimental to the slave, and dangerous to the master." And they specifically endorsed the actions of the investigating party, stating that they were "entirely approving the course pursued by our fellow citizens" and resolving "That the thanks of this community are due to Messrs. Farrar and Williams, and the other gentlemen who aided them, for their efforts and success in the discovery of the murderers of Mr. Dun-

Table 3. Public Meeting at Kingston, August 8, 1857

Name	Role at Meeting	Occupation	Birthplace	Age	Slaveholding
William J. Gillespie	Committee Member	Planter	Mississippi	25	59
D. M. Hayden	Committee Member	Planter	Unknown	Unknown	61
Dempsey P. Jackson	Chairman	Planter	Kentucky	61	108
Orrick Metcalfe	Committee Member	Planter	Mississippi	33	76
Charles A. Pipes	Secretary	Lawyer	Mississippi	21	0
Israel S. Scott	Committee Member	Unknown	Unknown	Unknown	8
John H. Thorn	Committee Member	Planter	Indiana	58	68

can B. Skinner, and of the tampering of said McCallin with the slaves upon the Sharp Plantation, and his suggestions to said slaves . . . " It was a small step from assuming the authority to speak for the community to obligating other whites to assist in the enforcement of their ruling: "we esteem it the duty of all good citizens to aid in ridding the country of such characters."

The story does not end here, as you no doubt recall. Evidently someone of standing in Tensas Parish was prepared to help McCallin get a hearing back home in Waterproof. Two names suggest themselves from the historical record. Zenas Preston, a native of Ohio and one of the three men chosen to examine the evidence in the case, had been among the early settlers in the parish. Now an influential and respected planter, he had served as witness to a notarized document that McCallin was required to sign upon receipt of the deed for his house in December 1856. Individual planters and artisans in the Old South often formed what amounted to patron-client relationships. McCallin was a successful carpenter and ginwright. It is possible that Preston regularly called on his services and felt a sense of responsibility toward him, just as it seems likely that McCallin found a protector in Absalom Sharpe when he first came to Adams County.

The other possibility is Hamilton McCullough, who acted as chairman at the hearing in Waterproof. We know from notices in the newspapers that he was a member of the Democratic Party executive in Tensas Parish. It always seemed to me that McCallin must have had some ulterior motive for charging he was a victim of "political persecution." Prominent figures in the American Party may have organized the meeting in Kingston, but he could hardly have been unaware that Democrats were present and approved the resolutions passed against him. But suppose his allegation was just a ploy to gain the support of Democratic leaders in Waterproof? Certainly his complaint that the elite of Adams County were prejudiced against him because of his humble birth was unlikely to win him sympathy from the wealthy planters of Tensas Parish. Aristocratic pretensions were not confined to the Mississippi side of the river.

Whoever arranged for a review of the evidence, one thing is clear. Although the hearing in Waterproof was referred to as a "meeting of the citizens of Tensas parish," it, too, like the hearing in Kingston, was controlled by planters. McCullough was the owner of more than 80 slaves on his exotically named plantations, Bombay and Bengal. No information is available on William Gordon, who was appointed secretary, but he was probably an heir of James Gordon, who at his death in the 1850s left 1,490 acres and 124 slaves. Preston had 91 slaves on his plantation, Burn Place, while the other two men appointed to the investigating committee, Robert Bowman and Henry Drake, owned 39 and 15 slaves respectively; Drake would increase his slaveholding by 20 over the next three years. Planters had convicted McCallin. It would apparently be left to planters to decide whether the guilty verdict should be overturned.

McCallin could hardly have considered his prospects promising. At least two of the men involved in the hearing had close personal ties with Alexander Farrar. Drake knew him through his father, Benjamin M. Drake, a prominent Methodist preacher who rode a circuit in Mississippi that included the church attended by Farrar and his family. The deferential tone of the letter Henry Drake sent to Farrar on behalf of the committee reveals the nature of their relationship: "Excuse me for troubling you. I would not have done so, except under a sense of duty." We do not know the connection between Farrar and Bowman but the two must have been more than casual acquaintances because Bowman sent Farrar the following letter prior to the hearing:

> Your [illegible word] form of the 16th inst came to hand this moment & I reply only to let you know that we had already made our arrangements, & will be there. I shall gather all the papers with all the evidence connected with it. I suppose for such a purpose we will have to quietly hear all that is said about you. Which I had thought of replying to.
>
> We have had a great deal of Chill & fever, & I do not know now whether I am a doctor or overseer. Ruby is at the well. My respects to Mrs. F. & the rest of the family—

The committee apparently gave some credence to McCallin's charge that he had been prevented from acquiring evidence that would exonerate him. So they agreed to grant him two weeks' grace and "guarantee to him his personal safety while in search of said evidence, and furnish him with an escort of protection." But in what was surely carefully chosen language, they reaffirmed that the resolutions produced at Kingston reflected the public will across the river. And they added a chilling declaration of their own: "being called upon to endorse the character of John McCallin, in con-

Table 4. Public Meeting at Waterproof, September 19, 1857

Name	Role at Meeting	Occupation	Birthplace	Age	Slaveholding
Robert J. Bowman	Committee Member	Planter	Unknown	Unknown	39
Henry W. Drake	Committee Member	Farmer	Mississippi	28	15
William Gordon	Secretary	Unknown	Unknown	Unknown	Unknown
Hamilton McCullough	Chairman	Planter	Mississippi	40	83
Zenas Preston	Committee Member	Planter	Ohio	49	91

travention of certain imputations made against him by certain citizens of Adams county, Miss.; and said McCallin having failed to offer anything before this meeting, in explanation of the circumstances connecting him with said charges, and having heard the evidence in support of them, we see no reason to differ from said citizens of Adams county, in opinion." Should he prove unsuccessful in securing the evidence he sought, they warned, they would "regard him as he is regarded by the citizens of Adams county, as dangerous and unworthy to remain in any community, and advise him to leave forthwith."

There is no mention in the newspapers of any further public attention that may have been given to the case in Waterproof. Indeed, aside from the affidavit signed by Alexander Farrar and the other two planters who interviewed Clarissa Sharpe less than two weeks after the meeting, no additional evidence exists regarding McCallin's role in the crime. The next time he appears in the historical record it is the summer of 1860. He is living in Waterproof, although whether he has been there continuously since the fall of 1857 or has left and returned, whether he has cleared his name or is held in disgrace, our source, the census schedules, do not say. All we know for sure is that he was sharing a residence with a 45-year-old Irish carpenter named Frank McCafferty.

☗✛☖

Like whites, slaves charged with capital crimes in Mississippi were arraigned before a grand jury of white male property holders between the ages of 21 and 60 chosen by the county board of police. There was no requirement that any of the men be slaveholders. If indicted, the slaves were then bound over for a trial in the circuit court. Responsibility for drawing the panel from which the jury they faced would be picked was in the hands of the sheriff. He, too, was restricted to white male property owners but had to ensure that at least 12 slaveholders were included among the 24 men selected.

The five men who made up the Adams County Board of Police at the time of the November 1857 session of the circuit court were Eli Montgomery, William B. Foules, Thomas Galtney, Fountain W. Ford, and George M. Marshall. Montgomery was an elderly farmer who owned eleven slaves.

Ford, much younger at 26, was the former overseer for Clarissa Sharpe who had served on the investigating committee. The other three were wealthy planters, a clear indication of the ability of the elite to win election to important local offices.

Thanks to a list provided in the *Mississippi Free Trader* we know the names of the property holders the board appointed to the grand jury. As Table 5 indicates, more than half were planters, with four—James McCaleb, Richard W. Phillips, A. D. Rawlings, and James H. Rowan—ranking as members of the elite. Planters, it should be noted, made up less than 20 percent of the males eligible for service. Of the remaining eight men, five owned seven slaves or more, while there is no record of a J. S. Scott in either the 1857 tax rolls or the 1860 census. That leaves just James W. Alexander, a merchant, and Richard Mason, a bookkeeper, as nonslaveholders. Alexander likely relied on planters for his business. Certainly that was true of the grand jury foreman, E. B. Baker, who was listed in a city directory as dealing in "plantation goods." Incidentally, two of the planters—Henry Clay Swayze and William Sojourner—had taken part in the original interrogation of the slaves, while two more—Routh Henry Phipps and A. D. Rawlings—had signed the declaration in the papers supporting the findings of the investigating party.

Some of the background information on the men who were involved in the trial of Henderson, Reuben, and Anderson you have already heard. The

Table 5. Grand Jury

Name	Occupation	Birthplace	Age	Slaveholding
James W. Alexander	Merchant	Virginia	34	0
E. B. Baker	Merchant	Connecticut	45	9
Hilary Bell	Farmer	Mississippi	37	14
James H. Blanchard	Planter	Mississippi	43	40
Richard R. Brown	Farmer	Mississippi	43	7
Richard D. Chotard	Planter	Mississippi	31	28
James S. Gillespie	Farmer	Pennsylvania	41	12
Richard Mason	Bookkeeper	Pennsylvania	45	0
James F. McCaleb	Planter	Mississippi	45	81
John McCollum	Planter	Scotland	59	29
H. H. Middleton	Planter	Mississippi	39	42
Richard W. Phillips	Planter	Maryland	Unknown	60
Routh Henry Phipps	Planter	Mississippi	40	40
Levi Pipes	Farmer	Mississippi	57	10
A. D. Rawlings	Planter	Mississippi	37	66
John Robson	Planter	Mississippi	31	45
James H. Rowan	Planter	Mississippi	29	51
J. S. Scott	Unknown	Unknown	Unknown	Unknown
William Sojourner*	Planter	Mississippi	26	33
Henry C. Swayze	Planter	Mississippi	27	45

*William Sojourner lived in the home of his aunt, Eliza Sojourner. The figure on slaveholding comes from her entry in the census.

presiding judge was Stanhope Posey, a successful planter, with almost 60 slaves on his estate in Wilkinson County. The district attorney, elected only a month earlier, was Henry S. Van Eaton, northern-born and a nonslaveholder. In theory, he might have brought a somewhat different perspective to the proceedings. However, he had received his legal training from Posey and, in any case, turned conduct of the prosecution over to William T. Martin, who was married to a daughter of William C. Conner, an influential member of the elite who owned a plantation bordering Cedar Grove. We have it from the *Courier* that Martin had been working on the case since the summer, several months before Van Eaton took office, so perhaps his role at the trial was merely a matter of courtesy or expediency. Still, it is highly unlikely that the district attorney would have felt the need to defer to someone with links to the planting class if the defendants had been nonslaveholding whites. The two lawyers appointed by the court as counsel for the slaves, Joseph D. Shields and Douglas Walworth, were sons of prominent planters. Both owned slaves themselves, with Shields holding a half-interest in a large estate in Tensas Parish. Walworth, like Martin, had married a daughter of William C. Conner.

There is an influential school of thought that sees juries as a crucial element of American democracy. In that sense it is noteworthy that none of the 12 men picked to be on the jury ranked among the local elite. On the other hand, there seems good reason to doubt Bertram Wyatt-Brown's assertion that jury service represented the "poor man's ballot" in the South. Not only were sheriffs legally required to restrict jury membership to landowners, but as Table 6 indicates, only three of the men who sat in judgment on Henderson, Reuben, and Anderson—the ginwright Amasa Davis, the carpenter Charles Stietenroth, and the bookkeeper W. C. Wade—appear as nonslaveholders in the 1857 tax rolls. Davis depended on planters for his livelihood. So did the slaveholding merchants Esau Foulk, Charles Green, and John B. Quegles, as well as the carriage builder Robert Clark and the seedsman Alexander L. Wilson. Indeed, while the absence of large slaveholders may indicate an attempt on the part of the sheriff, Oren Metcalfe, who himself owned more than 30 slaves, to involve ordinary citizens in the proceedings, no doubt members of the elite were content to escape public service generally regarded as onerous.

The trial was completed in a single day, November 17. So was the trial the following day of the three slaves charged with the murder of Y. W. McBride, the overseer on Mandamus. "It is a humane provision of our Statutes," wrote Giles Hillyer in the *Courier*, "that whenever a slave, degraded as he may be in social position, or in intellect, is charged with an offence involving life, the same aegis of protection is thrown around him, as around the white man. He is shielded by the same laws, tried by the same rules, entitled to the same guarantees, and favored by the same chances and

Table 6. Jury

Name	Occupation	Birthplace	Age	Slaveholding
John Botto	Confectioner	Italy	46	1
Robert Clark	Carriage Builder	England	48	2
Amasa Davis	Ginwright	Maine	55	0
Larkin C. Field	Butcher	Mississippi	36	10
O. K. Field	Brick Mason	Kentucky	45	5
Esau S. Foulk	Merchant	Unknown	31	8
Charles Green	Merchant	England	31	7
H. Polkinghorne	Marble Yard	England	40	1
John B. Quegles	Merchant	Mississippi	39	1
Charles Stietenroth	Master Carpenter	Hanover	48	0
W. C. Wade	Bookkeeper	New Hampshire	46	0
Alexander L. Wilson	Seedsman	Scotland	37	5

presumptions, that protect his master and his superiors." Southerners insisted that slaves received impartial treatment before the courts, and if you take a sufficiently narrow view of things, you can find some apparent support for their claims. A number of influential jurists wrote opinions stressing the need to ensure due process in all criminal cases regardless of the color of the defendant. And statistics collected from the records of superior and state supreme courts indicate that conviction rates were comparable for blacks and whites charged with the same serious crimes. Writes Edward Ayers, a respected authority on justice in the nineteenth-century South, "It was true that blacks accused of major offenses could expect procedural fairness; once slaves entered the higher levels of the judicial machinery, in particular, they were treated much like whites."

Ayers is not arguing that there was a broad commitment to justice for blacks but rather that by following "procedural fairness" in court cases involving slaves, masters "strengthened their sense of moral legitimacy." Nonetheless, it may trouble you to see the terms "slaves" and "fairness" juxtaposed. It troubles me. Keep in mind, for slaves the courts represented only a minor component of the "judicial machinery" of the South. It was the master who dealt with most suspected criminal acts by his laborers, and he ordinarily answered to no one but his own conscience.

Nor is it entirely accurate to suggest that blacks and whites were subject to the same penalties for "major offenses." In Mississippi, homicide committed without "express malice" was manslaughter, not murder. But a white convicted of manslaughter faced a term in the penitentiary; for blacks the punishment was hanging. Indeed, even the attempted murder of a white person by a slave was a capital offense. Furthermore, many illegal acts by slaves were perfectly lawful when carried out by whites. If a house servant removed a ham from her owner's larder, that was stealing. But if her owner seized the collard greens she had grown during her free hours, well, that was entirely within his prerogative. And the inequity was hardly confined to cases of petty theft. In *Celia, A Slave*, the historian Melton McLaurin tells the tragic story of a 19-year-old woman who bludgeoned her master to death after five years of repeated sexual abuse. At her trial, her court-appointed attorney attempted to argue that she had the right, as did any woman, to defend herself from rape. But the presiding judge correctly ruled that sexual assault of a slave was not a criminal offense under the law, and so Celia was made to pay with her life. The fact that, in a technical sense, she may have received "procedural fairness" would seem to be beside the point.

But even if we confine our attention strictly to how court proceedings were conducted, it is difficult to make the case that slaves were treated much like whites. For one thing—or is the point too obvious to make?—blacks had no opportunity to sit as judges or practice the law or serve on juries. Beyond that, and as the following exchange between James McDonald, editor of the *Mississippi Free Trader*, and Giles Hillyer, editor of the Natchez *Courier*, makes clear, other considerations besides demonstrating the "moral legitimacy" of the system influenced the outcome of any court case involving slavery.

The point of dispute between the two editors arose over the trial of the slaves charged with killing Y. W. McBride. The jury found all three of the accused guilty even though two, Tom and John, swore they had acted alone, and witnesses placed the third, Reuben (a different Reuben than the carpenter implicated in the death of Duncan Skinner), in his cabin playing with his children at the time of the murder. "Better that ninety-nine guilty men should escape punishment, than that one innocent man, though a slave, should be unjustly executed," wrote McDonald, supporting Judge Posey's decision to order a retrial for Reuben and lending substance to the claim that blacks could expect impartial treatment in the courts.

But Hillyer objected, and it is clear from the tenor of his remarks that he was less concerned with whether or not Reuben was guilty than the possible repercussions of overturning his conviction:

> All the negroes in that section of the county have heard of these proceedings. They have all pointed to Reuben as guilty, and as the guiltiest. They find him virtually acquitted. In his case, the awful punishment that his presumed rebellion and murder have deserved, will not have been enacted; and with perfect deference to the opinion of the Court and the highest respect to Judge Posey, and full acknowledgment of his conscientious discharge of duty, we dread the consequences. There will, we fear, be a growing spirit prompting to an immediate meting out of justice, when it is found that the law's delay is inadequate. Terms of Court, and Grand Juries, and forms of pleading, in their application to slaves, will grow unpopular, and speedier justice will be demanded.

McDonald replied in the *Free Trader* that Hillyer's arguments "must shock every calm and unprejudiced mind and should cause the writer to blush crimson, if there is crimsoning in him." But Hillyer was unrepentant:

> As to the order of the Court granting a new trial, we remain of the opinion that it will exert a baneful influence. So believing, a sense of duty requires us to state it; and we do not shrink from doing so. We think it will operate badly on the negro; badly on the community. The former will see a guilty murderer virtually remain unpunished, while the latter will believe that our laws as applied to these cases are insufficient; that a summary "black code" will have to take their place; or if this is not done, the temptation will be strong in such flagrant cases, to an immediate meeting out of justice.

When he was retried the following May, Reuben was acquitted, but no doubt mindful of the concerns Hillyer had raised, the grand jury immediately brought down a new indictment against him for being an accessory to the murder.

From the circuit court records and coverage in the *Courier* we know the defense Joseph Shields and Douglas Walworth presented at the trial of Henderson, Reuben, and Anderson. Their principal contention was that the "manner of death" was in doubt. If Duncan Skinner was indeed murdered, they told the court, then in all probability the blacks who testified for the state were to blame. Very likely, however, he died after falling from his horse or suffering a heart attack, as the coroner's jury had originally ruled. The lawyers also made two motions—one at the trial, one at the sentencing— that, on the face of it, would seem to demonstrate a genuine commitment to the interests of their clients. At the trial they attempted to have Henderson's confession ruled inadmissible, presumably because it had been secured at the end of a whip. And at the sentencing they petitioned for a retrial on the grounds that the official indictment had omitted the name of the prosecutor.

The request for a new trial was, in fact, no more than an empty gesture. Attorneys were required to raise any complaints about the drafting of an indictment before the jury handed down its verdict. However, the move to have Henderson's confession excluded was solidly based on judicial precedent. Only a year earlier the Mississippi High Court of Errors and Appeals had taken up the case of a runaway slave convicted of stabbing another slave to death. Among the witnesses at his trial had been two white men, private citizens, who had threatened him into disclosing where he had hidden the murder weapon. The appeals court ruled that the judge in the case had erred in allowing their testimony to be heard:

> By the tenth section of the first article of the Constitution of the State, it is provided that no person shall be compelled to give evidence

against himself. This protection extends as well against violence used by private individuals, as to compulsion exercised by the officers of the government, in order to obtain a confession of guilt; and evidence obtained by such means, cannot be used against the prisoner, *under any circumstances or for any purpose whatever.* . . . It is no answer to say that the confession was true—the question, and the only question which can be considered is, whether the confession was voluntary, extorted by threats or violence, or induced by the hope of reward, or immunity from punishment.

Henderson had been whipped, perhaps after being staked down, so Shields and Walworth had a legitimate reason for asking that his confession be excluded. Had Judge Posey ruled favorably on their motion, the trial would no doubt have followed a somewhat different course. Nonetheless, the verdict presumably would have been the same. While the court records and newspaper accounts do not reveal the testimony that members of the coroner's jury gave on the witness stand, we can safely assume that most if not all of them repudiated their original finding of accidental death. In his letter to Henry Drake, Alexander Farrar wrote that several men who had been on the coroner's jury later served in the investigating party (we can identify them as Absalom Sojourner, his brother William, and Fountain W. Ford) and, after taking part in the interrogation of the slaves, expressed themselves "fully satisfied that Reuben Henderson and Anderson had murdered Skinner." As for the suggestion that Dorcas, Jane, and the other blacks who testified for the state might have committed the crime, the defense attorneys could hardly have imagined anyone would take it seriously. Not when two of the witnesses were from Magnolia, and not in light of the circumstantial evidence against their clients—the scars on Henderson's neck, most obviously—and the (apparently) uncoerced and, therefore, admissible confessions made by Anderson and Reuben.

Of course, Shields and Walworth were severely constrained in choosing a defense. Because manslaughter was a capital crime for slaves accused of killing whites, they really had only two options. They could argue, as they did, that Henderson, Reuben, and Anderson had nothing to do with Skinner's death. Or they could claim that the three slaves had killed their overseer in "self-defense." Suppose, for a moment, they had chosen the second option. According to the high court, an act of homicide could be excused only in cases where the individual responsible had faced an "immediate, pressing, and unavoidable" threat to life. In other words, Shields and Walworth could not have asked for an acquittal on the grounds that Skinner was sadistic and his brutal treatment of laborers was bound to lead to deaths on the plantation. Indeed, any admission that the killing had been premeditated would have ensured a guilty verdict. Rather, they would have had to convince the jury that Henderson, Reuben, and Anderson had gone to see

Skinner on the morning of May 14 for some reason other than to kill him. Consider how differently the trial might have unfolded if they had presented the following explanation for the crime:

Skinner was a cruel overseer who repeatedly subjected the slaves to abusive treatment. After an evening in which he had wielded the whip with unusual ferocity, Henderson, Reuben, and Anderson decided to approach him with a plea for leniency. When they went to his cabin, however, and told him why they had come, he exploded in a rage, grabbed Henderson by the throat, and began to strangle him. Finally, in desperation, Reuben wrestled Skinner away and snapped his neck, inadvertently killing him. In panic the slaves dragged the body into the woods and attempted to make it look as if he had died by accident.

Arguing that their clients had committed justifiable homicide would have offered a number of obvious advantages to Shields and Walworth. It would have rendered the testimony by the members of the coroner's jury irrelevant, since the slaves would have admitted to the murder. It also would have explained the scars on Henderson's neck. It may even have allowed the lawyers to introduce evidence about Skinner's abusive behavior, although judges were ordinarily reluctant to admit testimony regarding the character of a murder victim. The key problem they would have faced was spelled out in a ruling handed down by the high court two years earlier:

> Every killing is presumed to be malicious, and amounts to murder, until the contrary appears from circumstances of alleviation, excuse, or justification; and it is incumbent upon the defendant to make out such circumstances to the satisfaction of the jury, unless they arise out of the evidence produced against him.

Since any statements made by Henderson, Reuben, and Anderson would inevitably have been seen as self-serving, Shields and Walworth would have faced the difficult task of finding slaves from Cedar Grove willing to swear that, so far as they knew, the defendants had not intended to harm Skinner when they went to see him on the morning he died. Still, *if* the two attorneys had chosen to claim their clients had acted in self-defense, and *if* they had somehow been able to provide credible witnesses, Martin would have been under pressure to prove that the killing had been premeditated. In and of itself, that might not have been difficult. The *Courier* tells us that one or more witnesses at the trial spoke of "threats made previous to the murder." But threats are made for a reason, and the question of motive represented something of a Pandora's box for the prosecution. Martin would have been reluctant to acknowledge that Skinner had a history of brutality since, at the very least, that would have suggested that Clarissa Sharpe and Alexander Farrar had been negligent in controlling him. But he could hardly offer the explanation for the murder arrived at by the investigating party, that a white carpenter who protested his innocence was responsible. Indeed, Judge Posey almost certainly would have prohibited testimony implicating John McCallin in the crime.

I am not suggesting that Shields and Walworth deliberately chose a defense designed to make it easier for the prosecution to secure a conviction. Not consciously, anyway. But it seems doubtful to me that they saw their purpose as saving Henderson, Reuben, and Anderson from the gallows. Indeed, their role looks more like that of actors in a stage production than participants in a legal proceeding. Think of the trial as a play—a morality play—produced and directed by members of the planting elite and performed for the benefit of other whites in the community and the local slave population.

Actually, the slaves were only invited in for the final act, when Reuben, Henderson, and Anderson were executed "as a warning spectacle to others of their class." It is clear that considerable thought went into the staging of this climactic moment. For one thing, we have the letter Farrar wrote to William Foules expressing concerns about what the slaves might say from the gallows. In addition, an article in the *Free Trader* noted that the site for the execution, across the road from where Reuben and Anderson had dumped Skinner's body, was selected as "the most proper, where the slaves on all the neighboring plantations can witness the certain vengeance of the law."

However, it is really the white audience that is of principal concern to me here. One obvious purpose of the trial was to reinforce the belief that white supremacy and slavery were inextricably linked and divinely ordained. Henderson, Reuben, and Anderson had been "moved and seduced by the instigation of the Devil," stated the indictment brought down by the grand jury. To Giles Hillyer, writing in the *Courier*, their crime was not merely murder but "social treason." And he went on to pay the following tribute to the prosecuting attorney, William T. Martin:

> He has a right to congratulate himself, the sorrowing friends of the murdered man, and the community, upon the laws being vindicated, truth elicited, murder brought to light, the guilty punished, rebellion made an example of, our social institutions rendered more safe, and the negro taught that God has made him in subjection to the white race, and that so he must remain, submissively and cheerfully performing his duty in that situation of life in which it has pleased God to place him.

Read that passage again. The "negro" has been made "in subjection," not to his master alone, but to the entire "white race." Slavery ("that situation of life in which it has pleased God to place him") is the indispensable foundation for southern liberty and democracy.

Still, fostering the view that blacks were divinely ordained for subservience to all whites carried dangers for planters. In one of his columns attacking the decision to grant a retrial to the slave Reuben convicted of murdering Y. W. McBride, Gilles Hillyer warned that if the "community" grew disillusioned with the existing system of justice, it might feel compelled to impose "a summary 'black code.'" Planters were well aware that to ensure protection of their slave property they had to take care that nonslaveholders were satisfied whenever blacks appeared before the courts. Perhaps, as a result, slaves from time to time received something we might call "procedural fairness." But it was largely fortuitous, a byproduct of the effort by the elite to secure the trust of less privileged whites. Joseph Shields and Douglas Walworth obviously understood what was at stake. Wrote Hillyer in the *Courier* following the trial: "As one of the prisoners' counsel himself remarked, there was one bright spot in the black drama, and that was that no summary vengeance was executed." Shields and Walworth had done their job. They had helped prevent a lynching.

⊰✛⊱

In June of 1857, the same month that the investigating party came to Cedar Grove to interrogate the slaves, a book was published in New York entitled *The Impending Crisis of the South: How to Meet It*. Written by a North Carolina native named Hinton Rowan Helper and dedicated to the three-quarters of southern whites who were nonslaveholders, it sought to prove through more than 400 densely written pages filled with statistics that the South had fallen far behind the North in almost every important aspect of material and cultural life, indeed had become "subservient to the North." And why, Helper asked, had southern economic development been retarded? Why, in comparison with the free states, did the South "contribute nothing to the literature, polite arts and inventions of the age"? The answer seemed inescapable:

> In our opinion, an opinion which has been formed from data obtained by assiduous researches, and comparisons, from laborious investigation, logical reasoning, and earnest reflection, the causes which have impeded the progress and prosperity of the South, which have dwindled our commerce, and other similar pursuits, into the most contemptible insignificance; sunk a large majority of our people in galling poverty and ignorance, rendered a small minority conceited and tyrannical, and driven the rest away from their homes; entailed upon us a humiliating dependence on the Free States; disgraced us in the recesses of our own souls, and brought us under reproach in the eyes of all civilized and enlightened nations—may all be traced to one common source, and there find solution in the most hateful and horrible word, that was ever incorporated into the vocabulary of human economy—*Slavery!*"

Planters had deceived the electorate into supporting an institution destructive to the interests of white society as a whole. It was imperative that nonslaveholders "rescue the generous soil of the South from the usurped and desolating control of these political vampires."

Helper, I should point out, was not motivated by a desire to benefit the slaves themselves. Quite the contrary, he was a vicious racist who believed all blacks should be shipped off to Africa or Central America or some unwanted corner of the United States. Their emancipation was merely a means to a much more needful emancipation: emancipation of nonslaveholders from the exploitative power of the planting elite.

Helper's impassioned appeal produced an equally impassioned response in the South, though not of the kind he had sought. He was vilified everywhere, and by slaveholder and nonslaveholder alike. Should he return to the region, one newspaper caustically promised, North Carolina would be glad to "make a home for him in the bosom of his native soil." And Helper, then living in the North, did not return, not until after the Civil War, anyway. Meanwhile, his book was ruthlessly suppressed wherever it appeared in the slave states. In North Carolina anyone caught distributing it was guilty of a felony. Convicted twice, you could face the death penalty.

The reaction that greeted *The Impending Crisis* in the South highlights perhaps the most striking irony in the history of a region known for its ironies: The willingness to tolerate criticism of slavery ended around the same time as those whites who seemingly had most to gain from elimination of the institution acquired the political voice to determine its fate. Not that all nonslaveholders would necessarily have benefitted from the abolition of slavery. Some, such as John McCallin, depended on planters for their livelihood. But in the Cotton South, 10 percent of the slaveholders owned well over half of the agricultural wealth, the nonslaveholding majority under 10 percent. And slave prices were rising rapidly during the 1850s, leaving men of limited means reduced opportunities to enter the slaveowning class. Furthermore, slavery inhibited the growth of a domestic market for manufactured goods while consuming capital that might have been used to create a more diversified economy and increase job opportunities for white laborers. The point is, there were good reasons for nonslaveholders to ask whether slavery served their economic interests. Yet no significant public consideration was given to abolition in the years before the Civil War.

Of course, you could always argue that the benefits nonslaveholders sought are not to be measured in material terms. W. E. B. Du Bois spoke of the "public and psychological wage" that whites have historically enjoyed in America, what historian David Roediger has referred to as "the wages of whiteness." Slavery gave nonslaveholders a sense of heightened self-esteem, whatever it may have meant for the distribution of wealth in the society. But slavery is not the only means of securing white supremacy, arguably not even the most effective means. Just read accounts of life in the Deep South during the first half of the twentieth century. And keep in mind, there were more than a quarter of a million free blacks in the slave states in the 1850s. A small number owned slaves themselves. In other words, a commitment to white supremacy does not lead inescapably to support for slavery.

So we are left with a perplexing problem: Why did the nonslaveholding majority, with seemingly so much to gain from an open debate over slavery, repeatedly elect men to office who ruthlessly suppressed criticism of the institution? Here we might find some guidance in the events described in these pages. They suggest that the authority available to planters within the confines of the South's democratic order allowed them to influence how slavery was perceived by other members of the white population.

Think back to the trial. From the indictment handed down by the grand jury against Henderson, Reuben, and Anderson through the summation presented by William T. Martin to the sentence imposed by Judge Posey, the message conveyed was simple and clear: blacks are meant by God to be slaves; black slavery is the foundation for a just and civilized society. Or consider the actions taken by Alexander Farrar and the other members of the investigating party. Presumably when they first came to Cedar Grove they had no purpose other than ensuring that those responsible for the death of Duncan Skinner were brought to justice. But the effect of their finding against John McCallin was to validate the "positive good" argument and reinforce the view that blacks only represented a danger to society when they were deluded into denying their own nature by false-hearted whites.

Given the heavy-handed efforts of the elite to control public discussion of the allegations against McCallin and their very careful management of the trial and hanging of the slaves, it would be easy to conclude that their goal was to subvert truth, not expose it. But that, I believe, would be to misread the depth of class prejudice in the Old South. Whatever concessions planters were prepared to make in terms of rhetoric, they remained deeply suspicious of democratic processes. Left to determine the fate of slavery, less privileged whites might arrive at the mistaken conclusion that the institution was harmful to the interests of society. Left to determine the fate of John McCallin, they might arrive at the mistaken conclusion he was innocent.

≈ 8 ≈

In Search of John McCallin

Writing a work of history is inevitably a humbling experience. Sooner or later someone comes along to point out mistakes you've made or challenge your interpretation. In December of 1990 I published an article on the murder of Duncan Skinner in the *Journal of American History*. Since then, I have come to learn that it contains a number of factual errors. That I was the one who discovered them provides not the slightest bit of solace.

For the most part the mistakes are small and inconsequential. I stated that Clarissa Sharpe was 56 at the time of the murder, taking the figure given for her age in the 1860 census and subtracting three years. A genealogical work listing her date of birth establishes that she was 55. But two of the errors are more conspicuous and worth some attention for what they reveal about historical research.

The article included a table claiming to show the panel from which the jury was drawn at the trial of Henderson, Reuben, and Anderson. My source was a notice in the *Mississippi Free Trader* naming the men selected for jury duty the week of the trial. Later, when I had a chance to examine the Adams County Circuit Court records, I learned to my dismay that seven members of the jury were not mentioned in the list reproduced in the newspaper. That sent me scrambling to the laws on criminal proceedings, where I discovered that, in capital cases, the sheriff was required to summon a "special *venire*," a separate panel of potential jurors. Recourse was made to the regular panel only once the special *venire* was exhausted.

On reflection, I should have done a thorough survey of the statutes before I reached any conclusions about the trial. However, knowing the provisions of the law would not have told me who served on the jury. For that information I needed the circuit court records, and the circuit court records were not salvaged from the courthouse until after my article was published. That brings me to the first point I wanted to make: Although history deals with events in the past—in some cases, the very distant past—the body of historical evidence is still accumulating. New sources regularly come to light, old sources become more accessible. In the last thirty years the study of slavery in the Old South has been enriched by the publication of the W.P.A. narratives, by the microfilming and distribution of a substantial quantity of archival material, by the recovery of state, county, and municipal records, by archaeological work on plantations, by the recording of songs and tales passed down by slaves to their descendants, and by the sale and donation of numerous collections of private papers to public institutions. I could point to similar developments in other areas of history. Those torn and fading letters in your basement, the ones written by your great-grandmother before she was married. Deposited in a state archives or university library, they will one day help scholars describe the role of women a century ago—the education they received, the work they did, the clothes they wore, their social life, their views on childbirth, their relations with their parents, and much more.

I have little doubt that sooner or later someone will come across new evidence on the murder of Duncan Skinner. A total of 18 men were involved in the investigation at Cedar Grove and 17 others signed the statement in the newspapers supporting the findings against John McCallin. We can assume that between 60 and 100 people took part in the meetings in Kingston and Waterproof, and perhaps a similar number attended the trial of the slaves. Surely some of these men and women—possibly John McCallin himself—wrote to friends or relatives about what they had heard or seen. A few letters would have survived in places I never dreamed of looking. Perhaps in a collection of papers deposited at a state historical society in the North or in a library at one of the Ivy League schools. Or maybe in an attic in Natchez, or Philadelphia, or Londonderry. I like to think that the new evidence, when it surfaces, will tend to confirm what I have written. But inevitably it will show me to be wrong in at least some particulars. I made the point before: It is history that has the last word, not any individual historian.

Now to the second error in my article. After discussing the decision of the committee in Waterproof to give John McCallin fifteen additional days to come up with evidence, I wrote: "Here the thread of the story pertaining to McCallin disappears from the historical record. All we know is that by 1860 he was gone from the area." But as I subsequently discovered, and you have already learned, in 1860 the census enumerator found him living in Waterproof with an Irish carpenter named Frank McCafferty.

At the time I did my original research, no index had yet been produced for the Louisiana census records. The only way to determine whether John McCallin was still in Waterproof was to look through the schedules for Tensas Parish myself. I did and failed to find him. I also examined tax registers in the parish courthouse in St. Joseph. McCallin is included in the 1857 roll, but not in the next surviving roll, for 1866. Nor does he appear in an index for the Mississippi census schedules of 1860. And so I concluded he had been run out of the district. In my more creative moments I speculated he had been murdered.

As it turns out, an index for the 1860 Louisiana census was completed shortly after I finished collecting evidence for my article. However, I didn't come across a copy until some years later, while on a trip to New Orleans. Thinking that John McCallin might have remained in Louisiana after he left Tensas Parish, I looked up his name. He was in Louisiana all right, but the index directed me to the same Tensas schedules I had examined years before. I was flabbergasted. Embarrassed, too, considering what I had written. I got out the schedules and went to the page specified and, yes, there he was, in Waterproof. Somehow I had missed him first time around.

There are excuses I could offer. The schedules for the parish include almost 1,500 names, the handwriting is unfamiliar, the spelling of the last name is entered "McAllen." Anyone who has worked with the manuscript census knows the difficulties. And yet the truth is, his name was there; I should have found it. I can only conclude that I was careless, which, if you remember, was what I said about the planters who investigated the murder: They were careless when they looked at the evidence. Only then I went on to attribute their carelessness to a predisposition—the predisposition to find someone white responsible for the crime. And so I asked myself, might I have been misled by a predisposition of my own?

Much as I would rather not admit it, I have to say that probably I was. Consider the full text of the resolutions passed at the September 19 meeting in Waterproof:

> *Resolved,* That being called upon to endorse the character of John McCallin, in contravention of certain imputations made against him by certain citizens of Adams county, Miss.; and said McCallin having failed to offer anything before this meeting, in explanation of the circumstances connecting him with said charges, and having heard the evidence in support of them, we see no reason to differ from said citizens of Adams county, in opinion.
>
> *Resolved,* That whereas the said McCallin has stated that he could not procure evidence in his behalf, from danger of personal violence, we will guarantee to him his personal safety while in search of said evidence, and furnish him with an escort of protection.
>
> *Resolved,* That if said McCallin fails to take any steps to procure any of said evidence in his behalf in fifteen days, we will regard it as conclusive against his innocence, and regard him as he is regarded by the citizens of Adams county, as dangerous and unworthy to remain in any community, and advise him to leave forthwith.

The tone is ominous. There is little to suggest that anyone at the meeting imagined McCallin would be able to produce the evidence he promised. Even if he did, at least two of the three men on the committee responsible for evaluating it were friends of Alexander Farrar. Keep in mind as well, the planters of Tensas Parish, like the planters of Adams County, subscribed to the "positive good" defense of slavery and were predisposed to accept testimony implicating whites in premeditated acts of resistance by slaves. No notice was printed in the newspapers of the deliberations that must have taken place in Waterproof after the deadline given McCallin was up, but I felt sure I knew his fate: He was found guilty and run out of town. I did not seriously entertain the possibility that he might have been exonerated. Or that, in the event of a guilty verdict, he might have chosen to remain in the district in defiance of community sentiment. Or that, if forced to flee, he might have returned some months later, after the incident had begun to recede from public memory. And so when I examined the census schedules I did not expect to find him. And so I was careless. And so I did not find him.

I am still strongly inclined to believe that McCallin failed to establish his innocence. The entry on him in the census indicates he no longer owned any real estate in Tensas Parish in 1860, meaning he had lost his home and part interest in a store. But the outcome of the proceedings in Waterproof aside, my real concern here is the lesson to be taken from the error I committed. Historians, no less than southern planters, sometimes are betrayed by their own expectations. Another reason why the process of historical reconstruction is never ending.

⊭✛⊯

The discovery that John McCallin was living in Waterproof in 1860 led me to wonder if I could trace him in later years. The obvious place to begin was the census of 1870. An index for the Mississippi schedules revealed that he had moved back across the river, to Jefferson County. I went to the indicated page and found that he was living in the town of Rodney, about 25 miles north of Natchez, with a 21-year-old black woman from Virginia, a farm laborer named F. Robertson. To say I was taken by surprise would be a substantial understatement. She could be a hired hand, I thought. In the same household were three girls: Mary Randolph, age 7, Udoxie Robertson, 5, and a nine-month-old identified only by the first name Margaret. The census of 1870, unlike the census a decade later, did not record information on family relationships. However, it seemed almost certain that the three girls were daughters of F. Robertson. Udoxie and Margaret were listed as mulatto, and naturally I wondered whether John McCallin (or McAllen, as his name was again spelled) might be their father.

In hopes of finding an answer I turned to the census of 1880. The existing index for the Mississippi schedules includes no listing for John McCallin with any of the variant spellings of his last name, but it's incomplete, so I decided to examine the microfilm for Jefferson County myself. I like to think I was more conscientious this time, mindful of my earlier lapse. In any case, I did find him, at least in a manner of speaking. What I mean is, I found his widow: F. McAllen, a black field hand from Virginia. Her age is given as 35, but she was living in Rodney and there could be no doubt it was the same F. Robertson mentioned in the census of 1870. Her household included four children: three daughters and a son, all with the last name McAllen. The oldest child—16, black, and identified only by the initial M.—was presumably the Mary Randolph of the preceding census. I concluded that John McCallin was her stepfather. The others—Udoxie, 14, Maggie, 11, and Frank, 9—were almost certainly his children. The enumerator entered them as mulattoes and wrote "Ireland" in the space provided for the birthplace of their father. As I pointed out previously, I originally rejected the claim that McCallin and Dorcas had been lovers but then, when I was nearing the end of my research, happened across a piece of evidence that caused me to suspect I had been wrong. The 1880 census entry on F. McAllen, who, though much younger than Dorcas, had almost certainly been born a slave, was that piece of evidence.

The common-law marriage of John McCallin and Frances Robertson (or Roberson or Robinson, as the name appears in other documents) is confirmed in the following petition presented before the Jefferson County Chancery Court in September of 1876:

> The Petition of Francis [sic] Roberson shows that John McAllen departed this life on the 19th day of March A.D. 1876 leaving a Last Will and Testament. . . . That said decedent died seized and possessed of a small real estate where he lived in his mansion house in said county of Jefferson with a small amount of personal property worth about One Hundred Dollars. Your Petitioner avers and charges that for many years prior and up to the time of the last sickness of said decedent your petitioner and said decedent lived together and cohabited together as husband and wife and that by the law of the land they were virtually husband and wife. The premises considered your Petitioner prays that said Paper Writing purporting to be the last Will and Testament of said deceased may be admitted to Probate and that your Petitioner as his widow may have letters of Administration with said Will annexed granted to her on her entering into Bond according to Law and for such other and different relief as shall be in accordance with Equity and good conscience and as in duty bound shall ever pray.

The document was signed by Frances Robertson with her mark. The Court acknowledged her claims and granted her petition. She lived another 66 years, until 1942, but never married again.

A few weeks after I found the entry in the 1880 census, a genealogist assisting me tracked down baptismal records for the four children. They established that John McCallin was, indeed, the stepfather of Mary Randolph and the father of Udoxie, Maggie, and Frank. The baptisms were performed at the Sacred Heart Catholic Church in Rodney less than two weeks before he died. Whether they were carried out under his instructions or at the request of his wife, the source does not say.

The children of John McCallin grew up to be respectable and productive members of the black community in Rodney. Udoxie found a teaching position in the local public school. She later married a farm worker named John Thomas. Maggie became the wife of Richard Smith, a laborer. She took in laundry to help support the family and see that her children—the census of 1900 lists three boys and three girls—were free to acquire an education. Like many blacks, the Smiths migrated north in the early twentieth century, eventually settling in Flint, Michigan. Frank McAllen became a barber. His wife, Ada, like his sister, served as a teacher in the public school in Rodney. Frank and Ada had two children. The older, a girl, they called Udoxie. The younger was a boy born in 1911, 35 years after the death of his grandfather. They gave him the name John.

What are we to make of the union of John McCallin and Frances Robertson? A sign, perhaps, that McCallin's reputation in the white community had been irreparably damaged by the charges against him, further evidence he had become an outcast. Patrick Murphy, a fellow Irish Catholic immigrant and a builder who gave him work after the Civil War, noted cryptically but tellingly in his diary in the summer of 1867, "Poor McCallan his has been a hard lot." But consider what ostracism would have represented for a man of John McCallin's background. As a number of scholars have recently shown, when the first wave of Irish Catholics arrived in the United States, they were not immediately treated as whites. That may be hard to grasp, that there was a time when the "whiteness" of Irish immigrants was in question. But racial definitions have always been much more mutable than most Americans seem to realize. Native-born Protestants called Irish Catholics "niggers turned inside out," and some small number even speculated that they belonged to a separate "dark" race that had its origins in Africa. "How the Irish became white," to quote the title of a book by Noel Ignatiev, is an important chapter in the history of nineteenth century America. In that sense the personal odyssey of John McCallin may appear to us metaphorically, if not perhaps literally, as a story of whiteness won and then lost.

⊭✢⊯

Every year I ask the students in my course on the history of the Old South to write a book review on some scholarly study dealing with slavery. And every year, when I go over the reviews, I find that three or four of the students seem to think that the book in question is a "novel." I dutifully write in the margin that a work of history is not a work of fiction. But, of course, as should by now be more than apparent, all works of history involve considerable imagination. The difficulty of capturing feelings and private thoughts from the kinds of records that survive, the gaps in evidence, so many other obstacles to interpreting the human experience in earlier times necessitate that historians be extraordinarily resourceful and creative. But if the writing of history is to a significant extent an act of imagination, it is an act of imagination written according to carefully defined rules. Historians are not allowed to introduce fictional places or characters or events into their accounts. Nor may they use invented dialogue. A historian cannot, for example, fabricate a conversation between a carriage driver and house servant involved in the murder of an overseer, no matter how confident he may feel about his ability to interpret their actions.

These restrictions are the price historians believe they must pay to help ensure that illusion does not overtake reality in their attempts to reconstruct the past. But the rules have an ironic side effect. Because of the constraints under which they operate, historians rarely are able to produce narratives as fully realized or richly textured as those dreamed up by skilled novelists. Call it an occupational hazard. It's true that a scholar who is a truly gifted writer—C. Vann Woodward comes most readily to mind among historians of the South—can to some extent transcend the limitations imposed by the dictates of the craft. But no historian, not even a C. Vann Woodward, can hope to breathe life into characters the way, say, Charles Frazier has done in *Cold Mountain*, his haunting novel of the Civil War South.

That can be frustrating, to be so dependent on surviving records. There can hardly be a historian alive who has not reached the end of a project without musing about documents and artifacts lost in the course of time— letters casually tossed away, diaries deliberately destroyed, government records incinerated, untitled portraits auctioned off at garage sales. At the conclusion of my research I would have sacrificed a great deal for just one piece of evidence, beyond the brief notice published in the newspapers, allowing me to see the events discussed in these pages through the eyes of John McCallin. I even dragged two friends, Ed Ayers and Joe Reidy, off from a conference in Natchez one afternoon to search for clues in an overgrown cemetery on a hill above Rodney, itself now little more than a ghost town. But we found nothing.

Given some minimal evidence, a historian is allowed to engage in informed speculation. But we have no sources documenting how John McCallin viewed the remarkable trajectory of his life and any opinion I could offer would amount to nothing more than blind guesswork. The only alternative is silence. Silence or fiction. My professional training dictates silence. So, arguably, does prudence. But after years of struggling to solve the riddle of John McCallin, I seek the kind of closure very commonly denied to historians. And so this chapter ends with a fictional document, a letter from John McCallin to his son. Let me be perfectly clear about this: I have absolutely no evidence that John McCallin wrote such a letter, and even if he did, he would hardly have used the words and phrases of a late twentieth century scholar born and raised in Canada and trained in New England. Furthermore, there is every possibility he would have explained his personal history in an entirely different way than I do. Treat the letter, then, as I intend it, as sheer fantasy. But when you're through, you might ask yourself this: Does my reading of John McCallin conform to the picture of him you have formed over the course of this book?

⊨✛⊭

John McCallin to his son, Frank, February 13, 1876
(To be given to Frank when his mother
believes he is old enough to understand.)

My dear son,

I'm dying now. Your mother tells me I'll recover but she knows it isn't true. I'm not frightened. Death holds few terrors for me after life in this forsaken land. All that saddens me is the thought I must be separated for a time from those I love. With the money your mother earns and the property I've left, it should be possible for your sisters to continue in school and you to begin classes in the fall. If all goes as I hope, by the time you read this letter you will have used your education to make something of yourself and developed the strength of character you undoubtedly have needed and will continue to need for dealing with the whites who cross your path.

My purpose in writing is to let you know something of the flawed man who was your father. Every life has a turning point. Mine came almost twenty years ago when I was accused of conspiring with some slaves to murder their overseer. You yourself may have heard the charge from some of my enemies. It is a base fabrication and I want you to know the true story. Even more, I want you to see how the injustice I suffered awakened me to my own wrongdoing and provided the inspiration I needed to find my way back to God.

I grew up in a small Catholic community in the north of Ireland. We knew very little about Negroes or slavery, but we understood oppression because we were oppressed ourselves. It was why I came to America, to gain freedom from oppression. However, in Philadelphia, where I first settled, life turned out to be little better than at home. I had a hard time getting steady work and Protestant gangs used to storm through my neighborhood at night looking for Catholic blood. Philadelphia was different from Ireland in one respect, though. In Philadelphia there were people even more despised than we were. I didn't realize that at first. The Protestants used to shout at us, "You're no better than niggers." But I learned quickly that anyone with skin the color of mine, even Catholic immigrants with little money, had opportunities not available to Negroes.

I moved to Mississippi in 1837 because I heard there were more opportunities for an Irishman in Natchez than in Philadelphia. Buildings were going up everywhere and I had no trouble getting work. One of my first jobs was down near the town of Kingston. I was hired as part of a crew to build a home for a plantation owner named Absalom Sharpe. Sharpe saw that I was reliable and helped me find other work in the neighborhood. He also loaned me money to buy tools and spoke to the sheriff on my behalf the one time I had some trouble with the law. Power was in the hands of the men who owned plantations and slaves. So I did my best to win their confidence and dreamed of owning plantations and slaves myself.

The plantation Absalom Sharpe owned in Adams County was called Cedar Grove. He also had another place over in Catahoula Parish. All together he owned more than 100 slaves. When he spoke about Negroes he sounded much the same as other planters. They're like children, he said. You have to beat them now and then but if you see they're well fed and clothed and given proper religion, God will make sure they do the work He intended for them. And compared to most slaveowners, Absalom Sharpe was a decent master. His slaves ate better than many people I knew in Ireland. He brought in doctors to take care of them when they got sick and gave them time off from work and regular holidays. I also never saw him sell a child away from its mother. Still, I got to know some of the slaves on Cedar Grove well (too well, it was later said), and they never seemed like children to me. I kept my opinions to myself, though. Slavery was a part of life in the South and I was determined to get ahead. So I called the slaves "niggers" and said the things men in my position were supposed to say. I was making a pact with the Devil, only I didn't realize it at the time.

I lived down in Adams County for more than a decade. However, after Absalom Sharpe died, I found it more and more difficult to get jobs. The man who managed his estate, Alexander Farrar, took a disliking to me. Politics might have been part of it. I did a lot of organizing for the Democrats among the Irish in Natchez. Farrar was a powerful planter and an important official in the old American Party. However, his main objection to me was my relationship with Absalom Sharpe's widow, Clara.

Clara and I had always gotten along well, and after her husband died she had me out to Cedar Grove to complete some work on the house. Eventually I moved up to Waterproof, where I acquired a home and a part interest in a general store. However, I knew Clara enjoyed my company and made a point of visiting her whenever I could. The truth is, I had formed it in my mind she might agree to marry me. In the eyes of most planters in the neighborhood, an immigrant carpenter was not a suitable husband for the widow of one of their friends. However, in Farrar's case something more was involved. From what Clara had told me, he was making a lot of money from managing her husband's estate. I did not love Clara. I have only ever loved one other woman beside your mother, and she was a slave. However, Clara was kind and gentle and if she had consented to marry me I would have fulfilled all the proper obligations of a husband to his wife and treated her with the respect she deserved.

The overseer on Cedar Grove was a man named Duncan Skinner. A more vicious individual I have never known in my life. He had come to work for Clara shortly after her husband died, hired by Alexander Farrar, who employed his brother. Duncan Skinner abused the female servants and beat the field hands without mercy. The slaves often complained to me about him, and I passed on what they said to Clara. However, he was good at producing profits, and for Farrar little else mattered.

It was probably inevitable that he would come to a violent end, but on the day I received a note from Clara saying he had gone missing, my first thought was that he was probably at his brother's place sleeping off a night of drinking. Clara said she was concerned, though, so I left immediately for Cedar Grove. By the time I arrived, his body had been found and a coroner's jury had ruled he'd died accidentally after a fall from his horse. I suppose I should have guessed the slaves had killed him, but I didn't. Even if I had, it wouldn't have made much difference to me. Skinner was a brute. He got what he deserved.

I spent over a week with Clara. She was obviously relieved to have me around, and by the time I left for home I felt that my prospects for marrying her were considerably improved. On the way to Waterproof, however, I stopped at the Hibernian Society in Natchez, where I learned there had been an article in the newspaper a few days earlier reporting Skinner had been murdered. I also heard a rumor that Farrar was making plans for an investigation. So I rode right back to Cedar Grove to tell Clara.

Naturally she was shocked by the news and it took me hours to calm her down. I knew that Farrar would never take either of us into his confidence, and so I told her I would make some inquiries of my own. She was concerned about what Farrar would say, but I went ahead and talked to several of the slaves anyway. They admitted nothing, although Henderson, the carriage driver, declared he was glad Skinner was dead. The rest of the slaves, you could see the guilt in their eyes. I felt sorry for them. I knew Farrar would use the whip to get at the truth and reminded Clara how cruel Skinner had been. Then I left, promising to return in two or three weeks. It was the last time I ever saw her. Not long after that, she sent back the trunk I kept at Cedar Grove with a note saying I was no longer welcome on the plantation.

I wrote her immediately asking for an explanation but received no answer. It was not until more than a week later that I learned what had happened. Under interrogation three slaves had admitted to murdering Skinner. The ringleader was Henderson, the carriage driver. After being whipped, Henderson swore that he and the other slaves had been acting on my orders. A number of the slaves also claimed that, after I learned in Natchez that their attempts to conceal the murder had been unsuccessful, I returned to the plantation to warn them.

I rode to Natchez. There was no doubt in my mind why the slaves had told lies about me. It was Farrar. He'd whipped them into doing it. I went to the Hibernian Society, had too much to drink, swore in a loud enough voice for everyone to hear that I was being framed, and accused Farrar of swindling Clara out of her husband's plantation in Louisiana. It was a reckless thing to do, and the next day some of his friends came looking for me. I was lucky to escape with my life. A few days later Farrar and the other planters involved in the investigation took out a notice in the Natchez papers blaming me for the murder. Someone cut out a copy and sent it to me, although I never found out who. They warned me not to show my face in Adams County again. I knew if I did I could expect to be shot.

I never was a man to be easily intimidated, your mother will tell you that. I had a notice of my own placed in the papers saying I was being framed and would prove it. I'm not sure what I thought would happen next. Maybe I imagined Clara would speak out in my defense. Certainly back then I still believed that I could expect to receive a fair and open hearing. Instead I got anonymous death threats in the mail. Meanwhile Farrar organized a meeting in Kingston to consider the two notices. He called it a "public" meeting but, so far as I was able to learn, the only people there were planters he knew. It was becoming hard for me to get information. Clara did not answer any of my letters, and the few friends in Natchez who continued to write said they'd been threatened themselves.

It was obvious I needed the support of someone important. Ham McCullough was on the Democratic Party executive in Tensas Parish. He'd had me out to repair his gin a couple of times and I decided to ask him for help. I told him the meeting in Kingston had been organized by the American Party and that I was being persecuted because of my work for the Democrats in Natchez. I knew it wasn't true, but by now I was getting desperate. People in Waterproof were starting to say if I wasn't fit to show my face in Adams County I wasn't fit to live in Tensas Parish. McCullough called a public meeting in Waterproof, where I was allowed to speak briefly. I charged that the slaves had been beaten into implicating me and repeated what I had told him about the meeting in Kingston. After a heated debate, it was agreed a committee would be appointed to investigate my allegations. However, although I was unaware of it at the time, two of the three men selected were friends of Alexander Farrar.

I wrote to everyone I knew in Adams County asking them to testify on my behalf. No one responded. I believe the only evidence the committee considered was written by Farrar himself. At the meeting where they made their report, all three committee members came out in support of the findings against me and recommended I be ordered to leave the parish. I passed around a few of the letters I had received threatening my life and protested it had been impossible for me to obtain testimony that would prove my innocence. The committee had indicated that they regarded my unexpected return to Cedar Grove after the murder as the single most important piece of evidence against me. I was satisfied that if I could just meet with some of my friends in the Hibernian Society I could at least get them to say I was taken completely by surprise when I heard that Skinner had been murdered. I even held out hope Clara might yet be persuaded to speak on my behalf.

A few Democrats at the meeting were disturbed enough by the threats against me to argue I should be given some additional time to collect evidence in Adams County and a guarantee of safe-conduct. The committee reluctantly went along, allowing me two more weeks and arranging to have a farmer from the parish accompany me to Natchez. However, he showed little enthusiasm for his assignment, and none of the workingmen who consented to meet with us would swear that I had returned to the plantation for the reason I claimed or even that they knew me to be an honorable man. This included men I had believed were my friends, some who had come to me for money when they were down on their luck!

I wanted to go out to Cedar Grove but was told the committee had been informed that Clara would not agree to see me under any circumstances. Eventually Farrar produced an affidavit stating she had said the only possible explanation for my reappearance at the plantation was to threaten the slaves into silence. However, by then I was already back in Waterproof, having given up any hope of proving my innocence. I transferred title to my property to Frank McCafferty, a trusted friend, with instructions for him to get whatever price he could for it. Then, just as the two-week deadline was up, I gathered my things together and headed downriver to New Orleans. Frank is one of the few truly trustworthy white men I have ever known. It is a matter of pride for me that my only son is named in his honor.

With the money I got from the sale of my home, I was able to live comfortably in New Orleans. However, after I'd been away for two years I decided to return. Somehow I imagined everything would be forgotten. Frank and I rented a house together in Waterproof and I went out looking for work, but with little luck. Most of the whites treated me as if I no longer existed, and a few complained to Frank that I was "no better than a nigger." So I figured I'd come full circle.

A year later the war broke out. I was too old to be conscripted and had no desire to fight. I stayed in Waterproof until the Yankees captured Vicksburg, then moved over here to Rodney, where I met your mother and built the home we live in today. I thought for a while I had finally escaped all the false accusations, but even here and even now I hear it whispered that I am a murderer. Such slander no longer has the power to do damage to me, but it may yet cause pain for you. At least now you know the truth.

But I fear that in recounting these dark events I have said things that must hurt you much more deeply than any slander against me ever could. Because now you know that your father was guilty of something far worse than murder. Although born into oppression, I gave my loyalty to oppressors. I consorted with slaveholders and dreamed of owning slaves myself. For many years after I was cast out of white society, I allowed my bitterness to blind me to my transgressions. But I find that the approach of death has restored my vision and allowed me to see what I knew when I was a young man in Ireland but had long since forgotten: The independence of one people cannot be built on the oppression of another.

It has also allowed me to see that, for all that I was a victim of the treachery of others, I have no one but myself to blame for the trials I suffered. I acted contrary to the law of God and so He decreed that I must be brought low. But the Lord is ever compassionate, and in His tender mercy He chose to raise me up again. He gave me the companionship of those who had been the victims of oppression, He gave me the love of a woman who waited patiently for me to see the light of His truth, and He gave me two beautiful daughters. Then, when surely it must be thought I had reached the limits of His forgiveness, He gave me a son to carry on my name.

God has now purged the South of slavery, but white Americans have not yet renounced all false belief. I pray you may live to see a time when Negroes in this country can escape the cruel shadow of injustice and enjoy the fruits of their own labor fully and without fear. And I comfort myself with the certainty that one day we will meet again in a far better place. May the love of God always be with you.

I am your devoted father,
John McCallin

An Epitaph for Duncan Skinner

The plantation house that John McCallin helped build still stands at Cedar Grove. Because it has a number of unique architectural features, and not for anything having to do with the murder of Duncan Skinner, it has recently been added to the National Register of Historic Places. To get to the house, you take Route 61 south out of Natchez toward Baton Rouge, then head east along the Kingston road. You'll pass the Kingston Fire Department on your right after 10 to 15 minutes. Cedar Grove lies half a mile farther, on your left.

Clarissa Sharpe remained in possession of the plantation until her death in 1875, after which it was sold to a local planter, John Neely, who acquired it for his granddaughter. During the twentieth century the property passed through several more hands, but in the kind of ironic twist that, as we have seen, seems to define southern history, it has recently been purchased by a distant relative of Absalom Sharpe. He is currently operating the residence as a bed-and-breakfast.

A short distance still farther along the Kingston road, in the cemetery of the Jersey settlement, stands one last piece of evidence. It's an obelisk marking the grave of Duncan Skinner. Although Skinner had a modest station in life, his tombstone is large and impressive, as large and impressive as those of some of the prominent slaveholders who were laid to rest on the same site. Still, he was buried a distance apart, as if in testimony to the singular circumstances of his death. Who paid for his tombstone is unknown, but on it the following epitaph appears:

IN
memory
of
D. B. SKINNER,
Born
the 29th of
Jan. 1820,
Died
on the 14th
of May,
1857.
Be ye also ready,
for in such an hour,
as ye think not, the
son of man cometh.

IN
memory
of
D.F. SKINNER
Born
the 29th of
Jan. 1820.
Died
on the 14th
of May.
1857.

Be ye also ready,
for in such an hour.
as ye think not. the
son of man cometh.

Appendix 1

First Draft and Fragment of a Second Draft of the Letter from Alexander Farrar to Henry Drake

Passages that Farrar deleted in editing have lines marked through them; passages that he added are enclosed in square brackets. The first draft is dated September 4:

Dear Sir: Yours of the 27th August, relating to John McAllin, and requesting a full history of his case, came to hand by the last mail, and I now proceed to reply: The overseer of Mrs. Sharp, Duncan B. Skinner was found dead in the woods. A coroners inquest was held, and a verdict from the jury, that he came to his death, by a fall from his horse. His brother Jesse Skinner was not satisfied with the verdict, and called upon the neighbors to assist him, in an investigation. Caution was observed to prevent the design from becoming public. Mrs. Sharp was not apprised of the intention until the morning of the investigation. Her overseer went out to the field brought all the negroes to the house and placed them upon a line before the company assembled. He permitted no conversation among them, nor was there any permitted during the investigation. Several of the negro men were handcuffed, and tied to trees, sufficiently far apart to prevent the hearing of conversation. The cook of Mr. Skinner was taken aside, and told that something badly had happened upon the place,—that it could not happen without her knowing it,—and that she had better tell all about it. She disclosed the murder,—those who participated in it, and the manner in which it was done. But one of the murderers (Reuben) was then in custody. Anderson being runaway, and Henderson the carriage driver at Mrs. Sharps house. After getting through with Jane the cook, we went to Reuben making a similar statement to him as was made to Jane, and he disclosed the whole transaction, agreeing precisely with Jane's statement. He told us how they went to the house a little before daylight, struck Skinner with a club while in his bed—how he jumped out of the bed, on the opposite

197

side to them, and ran into an adjoining room—how they pursued him,—got him down, and killed him in the corner of the room, then carried him off in his night clothes into the woods, and because of his occasionally manifesting symptoms of life, they took him by the head, and twisted it around, thereby breaking his neck,—how they laid him down and Anderson returning to get his clothes, watch, gun, horse & c—how they dressed him, took the bloody shirt to Jane and she burned it—how Anderson got on the horse—took Skinner up also, rode around through the woods, and around a beech tree, jumping the horse about the tree and upon the roots, skinning them, and throwing the body upon them—turning the horse loose, with the saddle turned on his side,—firing one barrel of the gun off—laying it down within a few paces of the body, and also his whip, and cap, arranging every thing so as to bear the appearance of the horse being frightened and having thrown his rider.—how they took his key to the house and unlocked his trunk, and divided out a portion of his money, and then took the key back to where he was laying in the woods, and put it in his pocket.^x—Jane and her husband took us to their hen house and dug up a tin box containing something over 18 dollars, which they said was Skinners money. Reuben had deposited a 20 dollar gold piece with Dorcas which he said was Skinners. Dorcas being a house servant we went to house and asked for the money Reuben had given her to keep, she took us up stairs over the Hospital, and produced the 20 dollar gold piece, and protested that she knew of no other money.

^xWe then went into the house and found the blood where we were told the murder was done. We then examined a number of the other negroes, ~~all of whom confessed~~ their confessions all agreeing and corroborating each other [as well as Jane & Reubens]. Henderson was sent for and tied off from the others. At first he denied knowing [of] anything [that had been done] wrong on the place, his conversation and looks however clearly indicated guilt. Reuben had previously told us that in the struggle Skinner had caught Henderson by the throat, and that the mark or print of his finger nails were still to be seen. We examined, and the scars were plainly imprinted upon his throat. Several of those who composed the coroners jury were present, and they as well as the whole crowd assembled expressed themselves as being fully satisfied that Reuben, Anderson and Henderson had murdered Skinner. ~~Jane and her husband knew of it.~~ [and that nearly all the negroes on the plantation] knew of it. Jane and her husband took us to their hen house and dug up a tin box containing something over 18 dollars in gold, and silver, which they said was Skinners money. Reuben said that he had a 20 dollar gold piece and had given it to Dorcas to take care of. Dorcas being a house servant, we went over to the house and demanded her to give up the money Reuben had given her to keep. She took us up stairs over the hospital and got the money, saying that Reuben gave it to her, and that she knew of no other money. Henderson still denied knowing of any thing wrong, or that he

had any money belonging to any one. [x]~~At the same consultation we came to the conclusion that in as much as there were a number of negroes who had participated in the murder, who could not be reached by law, and also as Henderson put on such a bold and _____ [brief missing passage] that we would put them under the lash. Accordingly a committee was formed, who waited upon Mrs. Sharp, and obtained her consent. Henderson was taken off by one party and staked down. While other parties of four and five, took other negroes off and staked them down, seperate and apart so that there was no possible chance for them to hear what each other said. Henderson received but a few stripes.~~ [x]His brother Lem was implicated by the negroes [as going as far as the door to assist in the murder but that his heart failed then, and he turned back] and for a long time he held out but finally confessed. After some consultation we concluded that both Lem and Henderson ought to be whipped, consequently we formed a committee who waited upon Mrs. Sharp and obtained her consent. [Up to this point we had not inflicted any punishment.] We formed two companies and took them off so they would not hear each other talk. ~~Lem was whipped~~ Henderson received but a few stripes before he made his confession agreeing precisely with what the others stated. [he also told that he had thrown the Powder & shot flasks off Skinner in the horse pond for which we searched and found—] Upon being asked where his portion of the money was he said that it was in Mr. McAllin's trunk. ~~How did it get there~~ that he gave it to Dorcas to put there, and she said she had done so. We then consulted together to know what to do, some of us concluded to go over to the house and see Dorcas. While we were on the gallery talking to Mrs. Sharp, Dorcas walked up, and hearing us speak of Hendersons saying that his money was in McAllin's trunk, she spoke out, and said Hendersons money ain't in Mr. McAllins trunk, it is up stairs over the ironing room. So we went with her and she produced four ten dollar, and one five dollar gold pieces, such as Henderson described. By this time it was growing late in the evening, we had found out from the negroes, that Anderson was harbored in the gin on the Magnolia plantation, the Estate of Stephen C. Smith. Also that he was there waiting for Reuben to get ready to go off with him, as he [had told that he] had a good place to go to. So we concluded to place the principal and leading men upon the place in confinement, with a guard over them, to prevent communication [until morning], which was done, while some went home, and others in pursuit of Anderson. We were fortunate in capturing Anderson in the gin to which we had been directed, who at once confessed the murder. Next morning we met again. And we concluded that in as much as there was a number of negroes on the place who had participated in the murder, and could not be punished at law, that we would put them under the lash, and in the mean time we would find out more about the money, as there was much yet that could not be accounted for, we having a clue to the amount that had been taken. Companies formed of four or five to a negro, and took them off and began whipping them. It was soon discovered that some two or three more spoke of money being in McAllin's trunk, put there by Dorcas. She was sent for, but denied ~~there being~~ [putting] any money in his trunk, and that she did not have the key. We however took her to the house to her Misstress, who showed us up stairs and pointed out the trunk to us. We then ordered Dorcas to get the key and unlock the trunk. She stepped to an armour and pulled a small box from underneath, and took from it a key and unlocked the trunk in the presence of her Misstress and the crowd. In the trunk were several pairs of shoes, and other articles, which Dorcas claimed to be hers. There was also a lot of fine shirts, and other mens clothing which Mrs. Sharp and Dorcas said was McAllins. his dgeureotype was also in the trunk. and three purses each containing money, in gold and silver. We made a Memorandum of the description of each purse and the contents thereof, signed our names to it, and placed it along with the purses of money for safekeeping. There was something over $60 in the purses. We then returned to the quarter, to pursue our investigations for the money, and likewise scourge the negroes for committing the murder. We asked ~~how it happened that~~ what made them think of hiding their money in Mr. McAllins trunk, and why they called his name. Which led to the following disclosures. To wit: That Dorcas was, and had been the "Sweet Heart" of McAllin's for some 15 years or more—that she told them (the negroes), that McAllin [said, he] was trying to marry her Misstress, and that, for some time past he had not been making such good "headway", which was on account of Skinner—that it seemed like Mrs. Sharp had more confidence in Skinner than any body else—that she went by every thing he said, and that the only chance he (McAllin) had was for the negroes to put Skinner out of the way—that if they would do that, he (McAllin) could then marry their Misstress and then, there should be no overseer, and they (the negroes) should have better times. Also that when McAllin returned to the place after Skinners death,—(which he did and staid 8 or 10 days) that ~~McAllin~~ Dorcas came out to them, and told, that McAllin said, "now you have got Skinner out of the way, and the white folks have been here and they couldn't find it out, all you have got to do is keep your mouths shut—" Also that he said he didn't know much about McBride—that he had seen him a few times, and knew his face very well. That he was a "through going man (meaning we supposed <u>thorough</u>) _____ [brief missing passage] to take him up one side and down t'other, that he was a full match for Skinner, and that he had got what he deserved. It was also stated that McAllin himself passed along by the horsepen and said "I don't know whither you boys killed ~~Mr.~~ Skinner or not, but if you did, you had better keep your mouths shut."*

It looks as if Farrar abandoned the letter at this point. The undated fragment of a second draft goes as follows:

[missing section] of McAllin for some 15 years, or more. That she told them that McAllin was trying to marry their Misstress—it seemed [he said] that he was not [now] making as good "headway" [as he once did, and that it was] on account of Mr. Skinner—that she (Mrs. Sharp) went by everything he (Skinner) said,—and that if the boys would put him out of the way he then could marry Mrs. Sharp,—and [then would] turn off all the overseers and they would have better times—And that when McAllin came to Mrs. Sharps after Skinners death, Dorcas came to the quarters and told them that "Mr. Mac says, that, now you have got Mr. Skinner out of the way, and the white folks have been here and couldn't find it out, all you have got to do is keep your mouths shut— This is the statement of several negroes made seperate and apart, without any prompting, or without the lash, so far as McAllin was concerned. The whipping was given the negroes to make them produce the money, and besides, all on the plantation were more or less implicated and it was thought that in as much as all could not be reached by the law, that they deserved and the safety of the community required that they should be severely scourged, with the exception of Henderson—It was also stated that McAllin [when at Mrs. Sharps] went to the horsepen and told them that he did not "I don't know whether you boys killed Mr. Skinner or not, but if you did you had better keep your mouths shut—"* Henderson the carriage driver states that he went up stairs one night to get McAllins boots to black, that McAllin was standing by a window looking out towards the quarter, listening to a noise in the quarter occasioned by Mr. Skinners whipping some of the negroes, that he said, Hen' there is quite a fuss in the quarter to night, and that he (Hen) replied yes, but that's a common thing here. To which McAllin replied, Well if I was you boys I would put that man out of the get rid of that man. How, says Henderson? Why I would put him out of the way. After some further talk Henderson went down stairs with the boots, and in the morning when he returned with them, McAllin rose up in his bed, and said Hen, how long did that fuss last, last night in the quarter.—I don't know sir, it is such a common thing here, I didn't pay much attention to it—Well (says McAllin) you boys are a cowardly chicken hearted set, or you wouldn't stand this man's whipping and beating you so—you would put him out of the way. If you were to do so, then I could marry the widow and then there would be no overseer, and you would all have better times. He further states that this conversation took place the last time McAllin was at the place before the death of Skinner,—that he (Henderson) went [among the negroes] over to the horsepen one noon while the plough boys was feeding and told them about it, and they formed the plan to kill him.—that his plan, was to have thrown Skinner and his horse off, of a high bridge, that there is on the place but the other boys. He further states that when McAllin returned after Skinners death that Dorcas bore [all] the messages from McAllin to the negroes, that McAllin left to go up the river where he lived, and that ~~in a day or two~~ the next day he returned that he, (McAllin) [then] came [out] to the carriage house where he (Henderson) was cleaning his harness and rubbing the brasses on the carriage, and said Hen' do you know what Jesse Skinner is riding about here so much for.— I don't know sir.—Well I can tell you he is trying to find out who murdered his brother, and if you boys don't mind he will find it out, for there is a great deal of talk that he was murdered. I have been up to Natches and have heard a good deal of talk there that he was murdered, and its even in the newspaper that he was murdered. And I have come all the way back to put you on your guard: Now Jesse Skinner had been riding about, he had staid at Mrs. Sharps a night or two previous to Mr. McAllins departure for Waterproof. Mrs. Sharp says that McAllin left her house for Waterproof, that she requested him, to stop on his way up, and examine the jails at Natches and ~~Waterproof~~ Vidalia for Anderson (the runaway) and if he was in jail to leave a letter for her at Mrs. Holden's in Natches, and as there was constantly passing, Mrs. Holden could send it out to her.—That she did not know that McAllin was going to come back, that he never told her what he come back for, and she did not know what brought him back unless it was for what Henderson said. *[Besides it was in the Natches Courier that it was, supposed that Skinner was murdered. And there was likewise a good deal of talk in Natches that he was murdered. Also we were informed that McAllin did know something of McBride, and we all know that he was an entire stranger in the neighborhood.] A few days after the investigation at Mrs. Sharps a number of us met at Mr. Foules's, who had his negroes who murdered McBride, his overseer, brought from jail in order to give them an opportunity of producing corroborating testimony—They produced the watch, hat, shoes & c & c, [of McBride and made a clear confession of every thing.] From their statements we were satisfied that they knew the Sharp negroes had murdered their overseer, and as the "white folks" didn't find it out, they were induced to make a similar experiment.—A few days after this, we met at the Magnolia plantation, the Estate of Stephen C. Smith. There the negroes were likewise examined seperate and apart. They confessed to having harbored Anderson, that he told them all about the murder of Skinner. They confessed to having visited the Sharp place, and through Henderson & Anderson they had learned all about the murder. They confirmed every thing that *the Sharp negroes said about McAllin's wanting to marry Mrs. Sharp, and what Dorcas had said to the negroes as coming from McAllin. They went a little further than the Sharp negroes. They told that Henderson had told them, that Dorcas told him that McAllin said to her, that when he married Mrs. Sharp, she (Dorcas) must not take it to heart and let it frustrate her feeling, and make her make a fuss—but that she must behave herself and act as if there never ~~was~~ [had been] any thing between them—that when he married her Misstress he could do more for her [Dorcas] than he now could: Henderson has been asked, since, what it was, that he told the negroes at Magnolia, that Dorcas said, McAllin said to her that she must do [when he married her Misstress]. He studied a moment and broke into a laugh and said Oh, I will tell you. And then repeated [precisely] what I have written above as coming from the Magnolia negroes. The negroes on the Sharp place says that Skinner told them, that if he ever caught one of them talking with McAllin that he would whip them—, that McAllin knew it, and never stopped to talk with them, if there was any chance for Skinner to see, or hear of it. That all the chance McAllin had for communicating with them was through Dorcas & Henderson. Mrs. Sharp says that ~~she did not know any thing about~~ when Skinner and McAllin met in her presence they spoke, that McAllin confined himself _____ [brief missing passage] to the house and yard, that he _____ [brief missing passage] a week or two and go off without going where Skinner was; or seeing him.ˣ The negroes were put under the lash in order to find out where the balance of the money had gone to, and also to show those that the law could not operate upon that they would not be permitted to go unpunished. No one dreamed of putting them under the lash to find out concerning McAllins complicity in the murder, for there were men present, and those too, who took an active part in the investigation who did not until the negroes called McAllins name know of such a man, and those who knew him never thought ~~once~~ of his being concerned until, the negroes made their statements. One of the gentlemen [who took an active part in the investigation] to whom the confessions were being made, cried out, who is this McAllin? And where is he? What does he follow & c & c. Up to the calling of his name by the negroes he knew of no such man as McAllin—The idea of the proceedings against McAllin growing out of political prosecution is ridiculous. There are names of several democrats to the first notice to McAllin, & At the last meeting at which D. P. Jackson presided, there was more democrats attended, and took part in the meeting than usually vote at the Kingston Precinct. Mr. Alex. Boyd one of our oldest citizens, and a democrat attended both meetings. He did not sign the first notice to McAllin, but announced publickly that his reason for not signing the notice, was that he _____ [brief missing passage] man and did not wish to pledge himself to anything that might lead to violence, but that he believed ~~what the negroes said~~ that McAllin was guilty of what the negroes charged—He also attended the meeting over which Mr. Jackson presided and made the same statement. There is no evidence here of friendship existing between McAllin & Skinner, on the contrary it is against their friendship. McAllin has been known in this neighborhood since about the year AD 1838, at which time he began to work for Mr. Sharp. ~~So far as I have ever heard he has been~~ It has been talked of from that time to the present that he made a Misstress of the girl Dorcas, and I presume that he ~~could~~ will not deny it. There is also a rumor that when he first took up with Dorcas she became pregnant, and that he was instrumental in producing an abortion, which rumor I am informed emenated from Mrs. Sharp. He has been in the habit of visiting Mrs. Sharp and remaining with her 8 or 10 days at a time. He staid with her during the epidemic of 1853. He has always been a still quiet man here, would come, and leave Mrs. Sharps without it hardly being known in the neighborhood. ~~The Native Americans of the County must surely consider their work finished, if they can find nothing more to do than~~ It would be too tedious for me to undertake to enter into the minutiae and all the details of this matter. I have now however sketched down the principal portions of the testimony. The marked attention of McAllin to Mrs. Sharp, as well as his dressing finer than he formerly had done, had for some time attracted attention, and caused some _____ [brief missing passage] that he was after marrying her. It has been reported here that he has stated somewhere in the neighborhood of Waterproof or St. Joseph, that he was going to marry a rich widow down here. We were satisfied that Dorcas had talked to the negroes, as they reported. We could not see any motive she had for putting into circulation a wrong report concerning McAllins. Every thing induced the belief that she ~~was anxious for McAllin~~ had made the reports, and that McAllin and her must have had such conversations. One thing is certain the conversation concerning McBride must have taken place, as McBride was an entire stranger and no one knew him but McAllin. Dorcas's manner clearly indicates guilt. She has confessed to knowing the morning Skinner was murdered that it was done. In short she has confessed to every thing the negroes has stated, but that which refers to McAllin. McAllins leaving the place and returning as he did, after having been at Mrs. Sharps for 8 or 10 days, is with us irresistable. I have heard of various reports which it is said, have emenated from McAllin—Such as the negroes being prompted to accuse him—that they were put under the lash and compelled to do it—that it was political persecution. In one place I learn he has charged me with being the cause of all the difficulty, that I wanted to drive him out of the country, because I knew, that he was knowing, to my ~~wanting to~~ cheating Mrs. Sharp out of some property—In another place I learn he says the plot was to kill him, as well as Skinner, that I did not like either him or Skinner because they prevented me from getting certain property from Mrs. Sharp leaving it to be infered that I had produced the murder—In another place I learn that he says that the negroes were instigated to do the murder by me, through a negro of mine. I have lived to but little purpose in this life, if where I am known, that it is even rendered necessary for me to deny such vile and infamous charges. Could I get at all that McAllin has said concerning the matter I am satisfied I could commit him with his own words. If talk be true he has already convicted himself for if the plot was to kill him as well as Skinner, why did he not disclose that plot, he must have been informed of it previous to the finding out about the murder [as he has not been here since]. May I ask of the committee, to collect what evidence they can with what, they may already possess, relating to what McAllin says concerning the murder, and particularly what he says in reference to me [and forward to me]. I disclaim [having had] any feeling towards McAllin, that would have induced me to injure him in any manner. And as for the charge of my taking advantage of Mrs. Sharp I am prepared to show that it is wholly false.

Appendix 2

Court Records from the Trial of
Henderson, Reuben, and Anderson

The surviving documents from the trial can be found in the records of the
Adams County Circuit Court, housed at the Historic Natchez Foundation.
Some are located in a Minute Book containing information on all matters
before the court, and the rest are in a separate case file relating specifically
to the proceedings against Henderson, Reuben, and Anderson.

The first mention of their trial comes from an entry in the Minute Book
made Wednesday, November 11:

> This day comes the said State by her District Attorney and the said
> prisoner [sic] being brought to the bar of the Court in the custody of
> the Sheriff of Adams County and arraigned upon the Indictment herein,
> plead and say that they are not Guilty in manner and form as charged
> in said Indictment, and for trial put themselves upon the County; and
> the said State by her District Attorney doth the like.
>
> The Court appointed Douglas Walworth and Joseph D. Shields to
> defend said Prisoners.

The following summons appears in the case file:

The State of Mississippi,
To the Sheriff of Adams County,—— Greeting:
    You are hereby Commanded to Summon
A. K. Farrar
that all business being laid aside he do in his proper person appear on
the 8th day of the present Term, before the Judges of the State aforesaid, at a Circuit Court now holden at the Courthouse of said county,
then and there to testify the truth, in a case now pending in said Court,
between The State, Plaintiff, and Reuben Henderson & Anderson,

Defendant, on the part and behalf of the said Dfts and this he shall by no means omit, under the penalty and forfeiture of one hundred dollars, as well as the consequences that may fall thereon.

WITNESS, The Honorable Stanhope Posey Presiding Judge of the First Judicial District of the State aforesaid, at the Courthouse of the said county, on the 2 Monday in November 1857.

Issued the 16th day of Nov 1857.

Three additional summonses can also be found in the case file: One naming R. W. Wood, the coroner, who was ordered to produce the verdict of the coroner's jury; one naming an additional twelve individuals—the coroner's jury, presumably—most of whom were residents of Natchez but including three men who had served in the investigating party, A. H. Sojourner, his brother William, and Fountain W. Ford; and one naming ten slaves: two from Magnolia and eight from Cedar Grove, including Jane, her husband Burrell, Dorcas, and Henderson's brother Lem.

The case file also contains notes given by the defense attorneys Joseph Shields and Douglas Walworth to Judge Posey:

> The Court is requested to instruct the jury
> That if there is a reasonable doubt as to the guilt of the prisoners they will acquit.
> 2nd If the jury believe from the testimony that Duncan Skinner's death <u>may have</u> been produced by a fall from his horse while hunting—or from disease, they will acquit.
> 3rd If the jury believe from the evidence that the defendant Henderson is not guilty, or if they believe there is a reasonable doubt as to his guilt, they will acquit him.
> 4th No testimony in the form of a confession when under a fear or hope of favor is admissible.
> 5th All the material allegations of the indictment must be proved & the manner of the death is a material allegation.

The Minute Book from the circuit court includes the following entry for the trial:

> This day comes the said State by her District Attorney and the prisoners being brought again to the bar of the Court in the custody of the Sheriff of Adams County and having been arraigned at a previous day of this present term upon the Indictment herein and plead "Not Guilty" and thereupon the following Jurors, being freeholders or householders of said County of Adams, were drawn from the Special Venire in this case to wit:

Charles Stietenroth	Amasa Davis	
Alexander L. Wilson	H. Polkinghorne	Robert Clark
John B. Quegles	W. C. Wade	

And after said Special Venire had been exhausted
O. K. Field, Charles Green, L. C. Field, E. S. Foulk, John Botto were drawn as Jurors in said cause from the regular Venire for this week being also freeholders or householders of said County of Adams, and said Jurors to wit

1 Charles Stietenroth	5 H. Polkinghorne	9 Charles Green
2 Alex L. Wilson	6 W. C. Wade	10 L. C. Field
3 John B. Quegles	7 Robert Clark	11 E. S. Foulk
4 Amasa Davis	8 O. K. Field	12 John Botto

Who being elected empanelled, tried and sworn the issue joined to try, upon their Oaths do say, We the Jury find that the said Defendants Reuben, Henderson & Anderson are Guilty in manner and form as charged against them in the Indictment herein. Thereupon the Court adjourned until to morrow morning at Nine O'clock.

On Saturday, November 21, the following deposition, which can be found in the case file, was presented before the court. It was signed by J. S. Scott, L. B. Field, W. J. Gillespie, J. A. J. Foster, and James Carradine. Scott had served on the grand jury; his occupation is unknown. Levi Field was a butcher, James Carradine a merchant, and William Gillespie and James Foster planters. Gillespie had been a member of the committee that drew up the resolutions at the Kingston meeting:

We the undersigned slave holders of the County of Adams state of Mississippi summoned by the sheriff of said County to be and appear in open Court to find the value of Reuben Henderson & Anderson, slaves convicted at the present Term of the Court of Murder do hereby assess the value of said Reuben to be Two Thousand Dollars and the said Henderson to be Fifteen Hundred Dollars and the said Anderson to be Fourteen Hundred Dollars. And we further certify that the said Reuben, Henderson & Anderson, are the property of Mrs. Clarissa Sharpe a citizen of this state.

The sentencing of the slaves is recorded in an entry in the Minute Book, also dated November 21:

This day comes the said State by her District Attorney, and the said prisoners being now at the bar of the Court in the custody of the Sheriff of Adams County, and this cause coming on to be heard on the motion of Defendants for a new trial, Because there is no prosecutors name marked on the Indictment, It is ordered by the Court that said motion be overruled: and the said Reuben Henderson and Anderson being thereupon asked if they have anything to say why the Court should not proceed to pass the sentence of the law upon them offer nothing.

Whereupon all and Singular the premises being seen and fully understood by the Court: It is considered by the Court that the said Reuben,
Henderson and Anderson be taken to the Jail of said County of Adams
from whence they came, and from thence to the place of execution on
Friday the 11th day of December now next ensuing to wit: the 11th day
of December in the year 1857: and then and there be hanged by the
neck until they are <u>dead</u>.

It is further ordered that the Sheriff of said County carry this Sentence into execution.

Another entry in the Minute Book, made the same day, deals with compensation for the defense counsel:

It is ordered by the Court that Joseph D. Shields Esqr and Douglas
Walworth Esqr be allowed the sum of Three Hundred Dollars for De-
fending said Reuben Henderson & Anderson slaves of Mrs. Clarissa
Sharp, she the said Clarissa Sharp having failed to provide counsel to
defend said Slaves, and they the said Shields and Walworth, having been
appointed by the Court for that purpose:

Formal notification of the sentence from Judge Posey to the sheriff,
Oren Metcalfe, can be found in a warrant included in the case file:

Whereas at the present November Term 1857 of the Circuit Court of
said County - Reuben, Anderson and Henderson slaves were severally
convicted of the crime of murder - and on the 21st instant, sentenced by
said court (the undersigned presiding Judge) to the punishment of death -

Now therefore you are hereby required to carry said sentence into
execution by hanging said convicts and each of them by the neck until
they and each of them be dead, on the eleventh day of December now
next ensuing - and at the place of execution.

On the back of the warrant are two sworn statements, both dated December 11. The first was signed by Oren Metcalfe:

In pursuance & by virtue of the within death Warrant to me directed by
the Judge of the 1st Judicial District of Mississippi I have this day executed
the within named convicts to wit: Reuben Henderson & Anderson, by
hanging said convicts by the neck until they were dead as directed herein
& at the place designated by the Board of Police of said County.

The second statement was signed by Alexander Farrar, Giles Hillyer,
R. H. Phipps, Caleb Farrar, and William Foules:

We the undersigned citizens of Adams County Miss. do hereby certify
that we were present and witnessed the execution of Reuben Henderson
& Anderson the within named convicts for murder, by the sheriff of
said County as the law directs.

Appendix 3

Additional Material in the Newspapers Relating to the Trial and Execution of Henderson, Reuben, and Anderson

Earlier I presented the resolutions passed at the meeting in Kingston. The full report of that meeting appeared in the Natchez *Courier* from August 11–14 and August 20–23 and in the *Mississippi Free Trader* from August 14–18. Relevant copies of the *Concordia Intelligencer*, which was published in Louisiana, have not survived.

> At a meeting of the citizens of Adams county, held at Kingston, August 8, 1857, on motion of Dr. Orrick Medcalfe, the meeting came to order, and Dempsey P. Jackson appointed Chairman, and, on motion of D. M. Hayden, Chas. A. Pipes was appointed Secretary. The Chairman stated that the object of the meeting was to take in consideration the testimony upon which was based a notice given to JOHN McCALLIN, through the Natchez Courier, Free Trader and Concordia Intelligencer; and in reply thereto, also a card, published in the same papers, by John McCallin. After full hearing, discussing and considering the testimony, and the card of McCallin, the Chairman called upon the meeting to know if there was present, any one who doubted the guilt of McCallin; if so, they were invited to show upon what grounds they believed him innocent. No one answering, Dr. Medcalfe moved that a Committee of five persons, who were not engaged in giving the "Notice" to McCallin, be appointed by the Chair to draft resolutions, expressive of the sense of the meeting; whereupon, the following persons were appointed: Dr. Orrick Medcalfe, D. M. Hayden, John H. Thorn, Israel S. Scott and William Gillespie, who reported the following resolutions, which were received and unanimously adopted:
>
> Whereas, Many prominent, well-known citizens of this county, upon full investigation, published a card, warning the public against one John McCallin, and notifying him not to make his appearance again among them, because of his complicity in the murder of the late Duncan B. Skinner; and, where, the said McCallin has since made a publication,

reflecting upon the motives and conduct of the authors of the first mentioned card: now, we citizens of the county of Adams, in public meeting assembled, having investigated the facts upon which the original card was based, and entirely approving the course pursued by our fellow citizens, do, therefore, *resolve*,

1st. That the thanks of this community are due to Messrs. Farrar and Williams, and the other gentlemen who aided them, for their efforts and success in the discovery of the murderers of Mr. Duncan B. Skinner, and of the tampering of said McCallin with the slaves upon the Sharp Plantation, and his suggestions to said slaves, which, if not the prime cause of said murder, were instrumental in producing it.

2nd. From the evidence before us, we are satisfied that said McCallin, in his card, has falsely styled himself the friend of Mr. Skinner. That on the contrary, Skinner distrusted him—and said McCallin, though cognizant of the murder, and knowing those who perpetrated it, concealed the facts from the public, and advised the murderers of the efforts making to discover them.

3rd. That the intimation of said McCallin, that the negroes were prompted to accuse him, is wholly false; and that the slaves, on the Sharp and Smith estates, under circumstances which precluded any concert between them, when examined separately, and apart, without suggestion or prompting, established a clear, consistent and convincing case of guilt against said McCallin; and that there is no reasonable ground to doubt that said McCallin did suggest to the slaves, upon the former estate, the possibility, and propriety of their "putting Skinner out of the way," to use McCallin's own language, or more plainly, advised them to murder their overseer, and that this crime led to the subsequent murder of McBride, on a neighboring place, and the general restless state of the slaves in that vicinity.

4th. That said McCallin's presence in a slave community, is alike detrimental to the slave, and dangerous to the master.

5th. That we esteem it the duty of all good citizens to aid in ridding the country of such characters.

6th. That the warning heretofore given to said McCallin, is now here repeated, let the consequences be what they may.

On motion it was resolved, that the proceedings of this meeting be published in the Natchez Courier, Free Trader and Concordia Intelligencer, and on motion the meeting adjourned.

The report on the Waterproof meeting was carried in the *Courier* on September 27 and in the *Mississippi Free Trader* on October 2. It was signed by the investigating committee, made up of Henry W. Drake, Robert J. Bowman, and Zenas Preston:

At a meeting of the citizens of Tensas parish, La., held at Waterproof, Sept. 19th, inst., Major McCollough was called to the chair and Wm.

Gordon appointed Secretary. After hearing the evidence against J. McCallin, in reference to his complicity in the murder of Mr. D. B. Skinner, the meeting unanimously adopted the following resolutions:

Resolved, That being called upon to endorse the character of John McCallin, in contravention of certain imputations made against him by certain citizens of Adams county, Miss.; and said McCallin having failed to offer anything before this meeting, in explanation of the circumstances connecting him with said charges, and having heard the evidence in support of them, we see no reason to differ from said citizens of Adams county, in opinion.

Resolved, That whereas the said McCallin has stated that he could not procure evidence in his behalf, from danger of personal violence, we will guarantee to him his personal safety while in search of said evidence, and furnish him with an escort of protection.

Resolved, That if said McCallin fails to take any steps to procure any of said evidence in his behalf in fifteen days, we will regard it as conclusive against his innocence, and regard him as he is regarded by the citizens of Adams county, as dangerous and unworthy to remain in any community, and advise him to leave forthwith.

On November 17 the Natchez *Courier* printed the criminal docket of the circuit court for the coming week:

Reuben, Henderson and Anderson, slaves of Mrs. Sharpe—charged with the killing of Duncan Skinner; trial set for Tuesday, Nov. 17, at nine o'clock, A.M.

Reuben, Tom and John, slaves of Wm. B. Foules—charged with killing Y. W. McBride; trial set for Wednesday, November 18, at nine o'clock, A.M.

Peter, slave of Robson—charged with assaulting a white person with intent to kill; set for trial on Friday, Nov. 20, at 9 o'clock, A.M.

On November 24 the *Courier* gave the following report on the sentencing:

On Saturday last, Reuben, Henderson and Anderson, the slaves who murdered Mr. Duncan B. Skinner, were brought out of jail, for sentence. When asked if they had any statement to make, they replied "nothing." Judge Posey than addressed them, stating that they had been indicted for the crime of wilful murder; that this was an offence for which, on conviction, the law imposed capital punishment. The prisoners had had a fair and impartial trial. The Court had employed able counsel for them, who gave them every opportunity to free themselves of the charge. But there had been no possibility of an acquittal. They were clearly guilty, having taken human life with premeditation and malice. There had been no excuse, no palliation in the circumstances attending the commission of the crime. It was proved beyond all question to have been a cold-blooded, deliberate and ferocious murder. There was no possibility of a pardon. No human mercy could be now shown them. Their death was inevitable; and their only business in this life, was to look to God for mercy in the next.

The sentence of the Court was then pronounced, that the prisoners should be conducted back to jail; thence on Friday, the eleventh day of December next, to be taken to the place of execution, and there to be hung by the neck, until they were dead.

On December 8 the *Courier* carried the following notice:

THE COMING EXECUTIONS. The Board of Police, at its session yesterday, appointed the place for the execution of the Negroes convicted at the recent Circuit Court of the crime of murder. The three negroes belonging to the Sharp estate, who murdered Mr. Skinner, are to be hung near the scene of the tragedy, on land adjoining Mrs. Sharp's plantation; and the boys who murdered Mr. McBride, are to be hung on Mr. Foules' plantation, at the spot where they are to suffer. The former execution will take place next Friday, the 11th inst; the latter the Friday after.

The following day the *Courier* ran a clarification: "The types made us say yesterday that the negroes who killed McBride 'were to be hung on the spot where they are to suffer.' The location the types gave was certainly remarkably precise, but unfortunately not very communicative of the information we meant to give. We wrote 'to be hung on the spot where they committed the awful crime for which they are to suffer.'"

On December 11 the *Mississippi Free Trader* ran an announcement about the imminent hanging of the slaves:

To-day, Reuben, Henderson and Anderson, slaves of Mrs. Clarissa Sharp, will be executed near the spot where they deposited Mr. Skinner after the murder.

The Board of Police selected that place as being the most proper, where the slaves on all the neighboring plantations can witness the certain vengeance of the law.

On the same date the *Free Trader*, as it did under contract every Friday, published a notice summarizing the recent work of the board of police. Included was the following passage:

Whereas at the November Term, 1857, of the Circuit Court of Adams county, Miss., the following named slaves of Clarissa Sharp, to wit: Reuben, Henderson and Anderson, were duly convicted of the murder of Duncan B. Skinner, and were by said Court sentenced to be hung according to law on the 11th day of this present month, and this Board being satisfied that the interest of the public requires that said execution should be public, it is therefore ordered and adjudged that said sentence be carried into effect on the day and in the manner specified in said sentence by the Sheriff of said county, at the following described place, to wit: About fifty yards west of the Natchez road passing to Kingston and Woodville, on the Rose Hill plantation of Mrs. Ashford, and near where said plantation corners with James G. Lessleys land, and nearly opposite the place where said culprits deposited the body of said Skinner.

On December 15 the *Courier* reported on the hangings in an article entitled "The Execution of Friday":

We mentioned briefly on Saturday the fact of the murder of Mr. Duncan B. Skinner. They were hung some thirteen miles from the city, at a point overlooking the spot where the murderers had placed the body of their mangled victim. Their last earthly gaze caught sight of the old beech roots which they had employed for their hellish purposes. It was retributive justice, and well calculated to produce a lasting impression.

We recur to the subject only to pass upon Mr. Sheriff Metcalfe, and his excellent Deputy, Mr. Richard W. Samuel, the credit they deserve for the perfectness of their arrangements, and the calm, solemn, but merciful manner in which their duty was performed. There was no mere display of the law's vengeance. There was no skulking; no turning over to a hireling, as an unpleasant job, the duty that the law imposed on the Sheriff and his Deputy. The solemn business was performed by those to whom the law entrusted it; and the manner of its performance showed that they were equal to their task. At the appointed hour the culprits commenced their long journey from the jail, arriving at the scene of execution within a few minutes of the appointed hour. While upon the gallows, although allowed the privilege, they said nothing to the assembled multitude. Quietly and calmly, the signal was given; the murderers fell dead, in the presence of a large gathering of witnesses; and the curtain dropped on the awful drama of social treason and of murder.

The Adams Light Guard, commanded by Lieut. Lindsay, attended on the occasion—a fine body of men—parading thirty muskets, lending their presence and efficient services.

The report of the execution in the *Free Trader* was much briefer:

On last Friday, the slaves Reuben, Henderson and Anderson, expiated their crime of murder, near and in the sight of Mrs. Sharp's plantation, on the gallows, in the presence of some 250 spectators.

The Adams Light Guard, under command of Lieut. Lindsley, were taken out in vehicles, as escort, and attended the execution of the slaves.
Why cannot the wealthy county of Adams keep up a Horse Company.

On December 18 the *Free Trader* ran a notice listing the expenditures approved by the board of police during its weekly session. Herbert Bixby was a 50-year-old native of New Hampshire who managed a plantation belonging to his uncle, Dr. Benjamin Chase. John McCaffrey was a 21-year-old carpenter. What testimony they gave at the trial is unknown:

The following accounts against the County were presented, examined and allowed, and warrants ordered to be issued for the same:
O. Metcalfe, assignee for Edward G. Brewerton, for lumber furnished for, and making gallows, and hauling same to Kingston. $38.77
O. Metcalfe, for expenses incurred in executing slaves Reuben, Henderson and Anderson. $114.17
O. Metcalfe, for jail fees of prisoners, & c. $263.35
H. Bixby, for fee as witness in case, State *vs.* Reuben, Henderson and Anderson, slaves. $2.50
John McCaffrey, for fee as witness in same case. $1.50

Appendix 4

Additional Archival Material

Jesse Skinner served as overseer for Alexander Farrar in the early 1850s. The Farrar Papers include the following three letters from late September 1853 indicating why their relationship came to an end. (The letters written by Skinner do not include punctuation. For convenience I have added commas and periods where they seem appropriate.):

Dear Sir your conversation & treatement to wardes me the otherday, the rune of your converstion, Sounded to me as if you wood Like to get Rid of me, or in other words it Seames that you Have vary Littel confidence in me. if Such is the case I wood Like to Know So I can make arngements for Bisness Sum whare else. after Sevrel Days Reflection I can think of nuthing I Have Done in violation to the Rules of the place except the accommodation of Mr Samuels & Family. I Have all ways Held my Selfe in rediness to Leve a place when my employier thought I was not profitable to Him. if thare ar eney things that you Have Heard that are the case of your treatement to wards me I am able to give it Justce if not Satisfaction. I feel vary much Hurte So much so that I Shall make sum arangements for a nother y case I think I can get a Home without going to the Ferry.

yours very Respcly,
Jesse Skinner

Dear Sir: Your note of to day has just been handed to me by Clinton, and as I had just parted with you, and you made no reference to it, I presume you are still under the same influence that prompted you to write me such a bold, independent, and I might add insulting letter. Your allusion to Samuels and his family was for no other purpose than to provoke me. Your knowledge of me forbids the intimation you have made. Could you find in your conscience a feeling that would allow you to undertake to make Mr. Samuels, or any one else believe that I was dissatisfied about him and his family being with you, in the face of, not only my conduct, and treatment toward you, but every one. I view your allusion to the matter as an effort to <u>provoke</u> & <u>insult</u> me. And I hereby inform you that you have accomplished your purpose. In my conversation with you the other day, I gave it as my opinion that you could not make a ferry and house of entertainment profitable without living on the premises, which it seems has insulted you, and caused you to inform me that "you should make arrangements for another year, and that you could get a home without going to the ferry". You have my best wishes wherever you go. I have always taken an interest in you and desire that you may prosper. Prepare your account and to morrow morning I will settle with you.

Yours Respectfully
A. K. Farrar

Dear Sir

you Rote to me that you thout I in tended to insult you. you are missstaken in that I nevery intended it. My in tenshon was to noty fie you So you night pane for another yeare as well as my Selfe for I a Shour you that I thout I Saw Dissatsfaction on yor Side. you call for a Setlement if it is yor wish go a hed.

yours,
Jesse Skinner

The following letter from Richard Samuel, deputy sheriff of Adams County, to Alexander Farrar, dated July 16, can be found in the Farrar Papers. Census records for 1860 list James Norman as a 27-year-old laborer in Natchez. He was the head of a household that included, in addition to his own wife and three children, two white laborers from the North and two artisans born in Ireland: a carpenter named Patrick McCabe, and a brick mason, James Conner. "Mr. Dobbins" may have been B. F. Dobyns, the jailer in Vidalia, Louisiana.

I called on Mr. Dobbins according to promise and he stated the conversation that occurred between himself and McAllen which was not of a positive nature. But from inference it was of a vile insinuating nature of which I will deffer giving untill I see you. Dobbins refers to James Norman for particulars as they at the same time & place had a long conversation in relation to the matter. I think it will be well to see him and I am satisfied he will not conceal any thing.

The diary of Douglas Walworth, who served as defense attorney at the trial of Henderson, Reuben, and Anderson, is in the collection of his papers at Louisiana State University. It includes the following entries for 1857:

November 11—Attended the Circuit Court all day—Was appointed by the Court to defend the Sharpe negroes—Father came home in the evening.

November 17—The three negroes of Mrs. Sharpe were tried all day— Shields & I in the defence—were found guilty.

November 21—Attended Court all day—Uncle Horace left in the afternoon on the H. R. W. Hill. [This is the date on which Henderson, Reuben, and Anderson were sentenced to death.]

December 11—Rebecca came home in the forenoon—Was at my office all day—In the evening went to the concert with the girls. [This is the date on which Henderson, Reuben, and Anderson were executed.]

The diary of Reverend Joseph B. Stratton, minister of the First Presbyterian Church of Natchez, is also at Louisiana State University. It includes the following entry for December 9, 1857:

Attended prayer meetings at night
Visited yesterday in prison three negro men under sentence of death for murder. They are to be hung on Friday. Talked & prayed with them.

Essay on Sources and Suggestions for Further Reading

You've already seen the evidence I was able to locate dealing directly with the murder. We can begin, then, with the steps I took to acquire information on the individuals involved in the case, from the principals themselves to the men who presided over the meetings in Waterproof and Kingston to the jury at the trial of Henderson, Reuben, and Anderson. My starting point was the manuscript census of 1860 (the schedules filled in by enumerators), available on microfilm from the National Archives. The population schedules contain information on the age, occupation, color (white, black, or mulatto), and birthplace of each person. The government made no provision for the collection of data on family relations, but enumerators were required to list individuals according to household, so kinship can often be inferred. Separate slave schedules include information on the names of all slaveowners and the size of their holdings. Of course, not all people connected to the case were entered in the 1860 census. Some, like Duncan Skinner, were dead; others had moved. So to fill in the gaps I turned to the population and slave schedules compiled a decade earlier, in 1850.

Although the manuscript census includes estimates on wealth, the numbers are not thought to be reliable. By a fortunate coincidence, however, tax assessment rolls have survived for both Adams County and Tensas Parish for the year of the murder. They include entries on some forms of personal property—it was the Tensas assessment roll that told me John McCallin owned two horses—but their main benefit lies in the information they contain on landholding: the amount of real estate each individual owned and its value. The Tensas Parish assessment rolls are located at the parish courthouse in St. Joseph, Louisiana. The Adams County rolls are housed at the Mississippi Department of Archives and History in Jackson.

The Tensas Parish Notarial Records are also available in St. Joseph (and on microfilm at the New Orleans Public Library). They're especially useful for evidence on land transactions—deeds, mortgages, leases, and so forth. Two deeds in the Tensas Notarial Records told me when John McCallin acquired his home and part interest in a store. The Adams County Deed Record, available at the courthouse in Natchez as well as on microfilm at the Mississippi Department of Archives and History, is similarly useful. It was through the deed record I learned that Giles Hillyer, editor of the *Courier*, was indebted to Alexander Farrar for almost $4,000.

The deed record is also an important source for information on the business affairs of Alexander Farrar, including, most notably, his dealings with Clarissa Sharpe. However, most of my evidence on his management of her husband's estate came from probate records in the Adams County courthouse, and the records of the Catahoula Parish District Court, at the courthouse in Harrisonburg, Louisiana. As mentioned earlier, the Catahoula District Court records also provided me with the noteworthy detail that Reuben was a carpenter.

Most of the evidence on John McCallin's history after 1860 comes from the deed record and chancery court record for Jefferson County, both found at the courthouse in Fayette, Mississippi. The baptismal records for Sacred Heart Catholic Church are also in Fayette. They told me (very late in my research) that McCallin was a Catholic, a fact arguably of great significance for interpretation of his life. A document in the minutes of the circuit court for Warren County, at the courthouse in Vicksburg, revealed that McCallin became an American citizen in 1840. It also directed me to a declaration he'd filed a number of years earlier in Pennsylvania indicating his intention to take out citizenship. That declaration, located in the records of the quarter sessions court at the Philadelphia city archives, mentions his date and place of birth and when he immigrated to the United States.

The R. G. Dun & Co. Agency kept credit ratings on many merchants in the district as well as some planters and professional men. Its records are housed in the Baker Library at the Harvard Business School, in Boston. It was in the ledger for Adams County that I found evidence of the precipitous decline in Alexander Farrar's reputation following the Civil War.

Like many historians, I have benefited greatly from the work of genealogists. *The History of the Descendants of the Jersey Settlers of Adams County, Mississippi* (2 vols.; Jackson, 1981), by Frances Preston Mills, is an invaluable source for the area around Kingston. It not only lists family trees but also contains letters and photographs, among them a reproduction of a daguerreotype of Alexander Farrar. I found details on the family histories of Absalom and Clarissa Sharpe in *Henry Sharp of Sussex County, New Jersey and Fayette County, Pennsylvania and His Wife Lydia Morgan and Some of Their Descendants* (Cleveland, 1975), by Elizabeth Cobb Stewart Eastwood and Helen Sharp Wickliffe, while material relating to the Skinner family is located at the Darlington County Historical Commission, Darlington, South Carolina. *Goodspeed's Biographical and Historical Memoirs of Mississippi, Embracing an Authentic and Comprehensive Account of the Chief Events of the State and a Record of the Lives of Many of the Most Worthy and Illustrious Families and Individuals* (2 vols.; Chicago, 1891) is basically a historical *Who's Who*. There are a couple of volumes for Louisiana as well, published a year later, but I'll spare you the title.

⊰✠⊱

Going beyond evidence on individuals to sources dealing with the character of life in the Natchez district, two volumes of the published census (as opposed to the enumerators' schedules) provide basic statistical data: *Agriculture of the United States in 1860* and *Population of the United States in 1860*, both published in 1864 in Washington. *Report on the Agriculture and Geology of Mississippi* (Jackson, 1854), by Benjamin L. C. Wailes, also contains useful information. *A. Mygatt & Co.'s New Orleans Business Directory with a Map* (New Orleans, 1858) has a section on Natchez. Like any antebellum business directory, it devotes most of its attention to merchants, among them E. B. Baker, foreman of the grand jury that indicted Henderson, Reuben, and Anderson.

Local newspapers are an extremely valuable source for information on politics and real or imagined criminal activities, but presumably you've already gathered that. They're revealing in other ways as well. The Natchez *Courier*, *Mississippi Free Trader*, and Concordia *Intelligencer*, which was produced across the river from Natchez in Vidalia, contain, among other things, advertisements for runaway slaves, articles on social events, daily reports on the cotton market, notices of estate sales, and announcements by local storekeepers. It was in the two Natchez newspapers that I found the advertisement in which John Botto "assures those ladies who patronize him that they shall have a private and quiet entertainment."

Then there are the travel accounts. Joseph Holt Ingraham, of Portland, Maine, came to Natchez about 1830 and took a job as instructor of languages at nearby Jefferson College. In 1833 he published a series of articles in the *Courier* entitled "Letters from Louisiana and Mississippi by a Yankee" which later were collected into the two-volume *The South-West; by a Yankee*, published in 1835. Its success drew him into a career in writing, and he subsequently gained popularity as the author of historical romances. His observations of the Natchez district elite also tended to the romantic, painting the planters in chivalrous tones. He said little about the slaves that we would consider complimentary, however. You may recall a passage I quoted from *The South-West; by a Yankee* in which two carriage drivers brag about their relative monetary worth.

Frederick Law Olmsted, a native of Connecticut known today principally for his work in the late nineteenth century as a landscape architect (he designed Central Park in New York), had already made trips to China and across Europe and England when he decided to journey to the South in the 1850s to witness slavery firsthand. He traveled extensively, producing three books about his experiences: *A Journey in the Seaboard Slave States with Remarks on Their Economy* (New York, 1856), *A Journey through Texas: Or, a Saddle-Trip on the Southwestern Frontier* (New York, 1857), and *A Journey in the Back Country in the Winter of 1853–4* (New York, 1860), which included a description of conditions in the lower Mississippi Valley. The antagonism he felt toward slavery only deepened during his travels. He was particularly critical of the planters in and around Natchez, calling them, as we have seen, "ignorant newly-rich." During the secession crisis, Olmsted's English publisher proposed he produce a single abridged volume bringing together all three of his accounts. The result was *The Cotton Kingdom: A Traveller's Observations on Cotton and Slavery in the American Slave States*. It's still available today, in an edition published by Da Capo Press and edited by Arthur Schlesinger, Jr.

Natchez also attracted other observers, although none who had as much to say about the town and its surroundings as either Olmsted or, especially, Ingraham. James Silk Buckingham, a British politician, world traveler, and prominent reformer, came to Natchez in 1839, where he delivered a public lecture at the First Presbyterian Church and expressed himself much impressed with his planter audience. He recorded his opinions in *The Slave States of America* (2 vols.; London, 1842). The well-known British naturalist Robert Russell, who passed through Natchez almost twenty years later, offered a similarly flattering assessment of the slaveholding elite. For his observations, see *North America, Its Agriculture and Climate: Containing Observations on the Agriculture and Climate of Canada, the United States, and the Island of Cuba*, published in Edinburgh in 1857.

H. S. Fulkerson, a factory worker in the district before the Civil War, left us his memories in *Random Recollections of Early Days in Mississippi* (Vicksburg, 1885). Practical details of the life of the most famous black resident of antebellum Natchez, the slaveholding barber William Johnson, are contained in his diary, which was edited by William R. Hogan and Edwin A. Davis and published by Louisiana State University Press in 1951 under the title *William Johnson's Natchez: The Ante-Bellum Diary of a Free Negro*.

During the 1930s the Works Progress Administration (W.P.A.) employed writers across the United States to gather material on local history. The boxes and boxes of files produced in Mississippi, located at the Department of Archives and History in Jackson, include a large number of articles on Adams County. Some of the articles make claims of doubtful validity, but a judicious researcher can come up with a great many usable facts on religious organizations, schools, plantation homes, and so forth. The W.P.A. materials for Louisiana, which contain only limited information on the Natchez district, are housed at the Louisiana State Library in Baton Rouge.

Also in the Mississippi W.P.A. files are interviews with former slaves, some small number of whom were born and raised in Adams County. For reasons I have already discussed, these "slave narratives" have to be interpreted carefully. Several drafts exist for some of the Mississippi narratives, evidence that the editors made revisions to suit their own purposes. Still, for a rare glimpse into the perspective of the slaves, the interviews are invaluable. Published versions of the final drafts of all the Mississippi narratives can be found in George Rawick, Jan Hillegas, and Ken Lawrence (eds.), *The American Slave: A Composite Autobiography*, Supplement, Series 1, Vols. 6–10 (Westport, Conn.: Greenwood, 1977). Ira Berlin, Steven F. Miller, and Marc Favreau have included a rare and very affecting tape recording of interviews with former slaves in their edited collection, *Remembering Slavery: African Americans Talk about Their Personal Experiences of Slavery and Emancipation* (New York: New Press, 1998).

However, by far my main source was private papers on deposit at archives and libraries across the South, mainly the papers of planter families. The sheer volume of documents relating to routine financial matters—consignments of cotton, receipts from merchants, that sort of thing—can be overwhelming. But in diaries, journals, and personal correspondence you can find substantial evidence on social, cultural, and economic developments, not to mention politics. There are five major repositories for materials from the Natchez district: the Louisiana and Lower Mississippi Valley Collections, L.S.U. Libraries, Louisiana State University, Baton Rouge; the Mississippi Department of Archives and History, in Jackson; the Southern Historical Collection, Manuscripts Department, Louis Round Wilson Library, the University of North Carolina at Chapel Hill; the Natchez Trace Collection, Center for American History, University of Texas at Austin; and the Rare Book, Manuscript, and Special Collections Library, Duke University, Durham, North Carolina. Fortunately for researchers, University Publications of America has now made many collections available on microfilm in a series edited by Kenneth M. Stampp entitled "Records of Ante-Bellum Southern Plantations from the Revolution through the Civil War."

There would be little point in trying to enumerate all the sets of family papers from the Natchez district deposited at the archives I mentioned. They number in the hundreds. Instead, I offer you a sample. The Louisiana and Lower Mississippi Valley Collections at Louisiana State University contain the richest body of material. As you already are aware, much of the evidence on the murder of Duncan Skinner can be found in the papers of Alexander Farrar. The same source also provides valuable details on the social life of Adams County planters and, to a lesser extent, their political activities. The

Joseph B. Stratton Papers include the very informative journal of the Presbyterian minister who prayed with Henderson, Reuben, and Anderson before they were hanged, while the Douglas Walworth and Family Papers include the diary of Douglas Walworth, who served as one of the defense attorneys at their trial. The papers of Joseph D. Shields, the other defense attorney, are also at L.S.U. While they contain no evidence on the murder, they do offer testimony on the character of the planting elite. Other prominent men whose papers can be found at L.S.U. include Stephen Duncan, one of the richest men in antebellum America; William J. Minor, third generation of a clan whose extensive holdings included both sugar and cotton plantations; William N. Mercer, owner of four plantations with more than 450 slaves in Adams County; and the respected planter John Carmichael Jenkins. The James Foster and Family Papers are especially useful for relations between planters and their sons, while the diary of Eliza L. Magruder recounts the experiences of a teenage girl who lived on the plantation of her uncle. A unique source is the William T. Johnson Memorial Collection, which contains the papers of the free black barber whose diary I mentioned earlier. The Patrick Murphy Papers document the life of an Irish Catholic immigrant who became a prominent builder in Natchez. Murphy knew John McCallin well, gave him work after the Civil War, and referred to him from time to time in his diary. The account books of Robert H. Stewart, an undertaker in Natchez, are helpful for learning about burial practices. I refer to them here principally for an entry dated May 15, 1857, which notes that Clarissa Sharpe was billed $60 for a "coffin covered lined & trimmed" as well as a hearse to transport the body of Duncan Skinner to the cemetery.

Among the sources at the Mississippi Department of Archives and History are valuable journals from two plantations: Fonsylvania near Vicksburg, owned by Benjamin Wailes, and Aventine, only a couple of miles from Cedar Grove. The Aventine journal told me, among other things, that it was clear and cold the morning Henderson, Reuben, and Anderson were executed. Anyone interested in plantation life should also have a look at the papers of Joseph E. Davis, older brother of Jefferson Davis; the Charles D. Hamilton and Family Papers; the Trask-Ventress Family Papers; and the papers of George W. Humphreys, who became governor of Mississippi after the Civil War. The Darden Family Papers include the diary of Susan Sillers Darden, which offers a revealing look into of the experiences of the wife of a Jefferson County planter who, incidentally, also happened to be related by marriage to Jesse Skinner. The diary contains no mention of the murder, however. Jefferson College was located in Washington, Mississippi, a few miles from Natchez. A private academy for young men from the district, it included Alexander Farrar on its board of governors. The papers from the college provide information on the education of the slaveholding elite.

Probably the most valuable collection at the University of North Carolina is the Quitman Family Papers. It contains not only evidence about John Quitman, the charismatic planter, politician, and military leader, but many letters to and from his wife and daughters. Another politician whose papers are at Chapel Hill is John Perkins of Louisiana, a U.S. congressman in the 1850s and a member of the Confederate Congress a decade later. George W. Sargent was son of the first territorial governor of Mississippi. He kept notebooks, also housed at Chapel Hill, containing copies of letters he wrote to his wife, merchants, and business associates. The diaries of Charles Whitmore and John Nevitt, planters with estates near Natchez, and the papers of James Allen, a wealthy slaveowner in Warren County, shed light on plantation operations. The Minor Family Papers complement the William J. Minor Papers at L.S.U., while the Douglas Papers contain the correspondence of an Episcopalian minister and his wife. The diaries of Mahala Roach (in the Roach and Eggleston Family Papers) and Mary S. Ker provide much worthwhile testimony on the circumstances of women in the Old South, although arguably their main value is for the postbellum period.

The Natchez Trace Collection at the University of Texas at Austin is made up of more than seventy separate sets of papers, some just a handful of items, others massive. If you go through the collection as I did, on microfilm, and watch as frame after frame after frame of bills and receipts roll by, your brain, like your eyes, can start to swirl. Still, show patience and your efforts will be rewarded. The records of the Bank of the State of Mississippi, which had its headquarters in Natchez, contain substantial evidence on the operation of the regional economy, especially in the early part of the nineteenth century. So do the papers of James Campbell Wilkins, a banker and planter. The Winchester Family Papers include letters and legal documents of Josiah Winchester, a prominent attorney who had dealings with some of the richest slaveowners in the lower Mississippi Valley. A section of the Natchez Trace Collection entitled "Crime and Punishment" includes an interesting set of records from the Warren County Circuit Court, while the Richard Thompson Archer Family Papers and Basil Kiger Papers are extensive holdings of two planters from Claiborne County and Warren County, respectively. Among the papers of F. H. and Thomas P. Farrar, lawyers in Point Coupee Parish, I found letters from one of their clients, Susan Conner of Berkeley plantation near Cedar Grove. You may remember her as the friend of Clarissa Sharpe who brought suit in the courts of Louisiana to try and recover a plantation owned by her late husband.

There are two collections at Duke of special interest. The Letters and Papers of B. L. C. Wailes include twenty-eight volumes of his remarkable diary. (The other eight volumes are at the Mississippi Department of Archives and History.) The diary offers abundant insight into the mind of a man who, though uncommonly learned for his day, was in many respects a representative member of the planting class. I quoted his very candid remarks about the circumstances that led him to fire the overseer Rogillio. Haller Nutt, whose papers are also at Duke, is best known for his vast wealth—he owned more than 800 slaves on various plantations scattered across Mississippi and Louisiana—and for Longwood, the six-story home he was building on the outskirts of Natchez when the Civil War broke out. Only the ground floor was ever finished. The Philadelphia workmen he had hired fled north when fighting began, leaving behind tools and cans of paint to intrigue later generations of tourists. Octagonal shaped, topped by a tower with a dome, Longwood stands as a baroque monument to the dreams of antebellum planters.

Taken together, these collections include substantial evidence on life in the Natchez district before the war. But they also provided me with the occasional unexpected detail. In the Natchez Trace Collection I discovered a notebook listing slaves designated for road duty in Adams County during the 1850s. It indicated that all five slaves implicated in the murder of Duncan Skinner—Henderson, Reuben, Anderson, Jane, and Dorcas—were among the laborers called to work on the roads in February 1856. Or another example: While going through the papers of Joseph Shields at L.S.U. I came across a letter written by a young woman who described him as "an indefatiguable dancer." I couldn't find any way to work her comment into my discussion of his role at the trial. But of such fascinating small discoveries is historical research made.

One thing more deserves mention before I get to the secondary sources. To write this book I needed to ensure I had a good grasp of the laws—laws on slavery; laws on homicide; laws on the property rights of women. By coincidence, and to my good fortune, in the year Duncan Skinner was murdered the state of Mississippi published a compendium of all its legislation under the title *The Revised Code of the Statute Laws of the State of Mississippi* (Jackson, 1857). The many volumes of *Reports of Cases Argued and Determined in the High Court of Errors and Appeals for the State of Mississippi*, published in Boston, offer evidence on how superior court justices expected the lower courts to interpret the law. Whether judges such as Stanhope Posey paid attention is an interesting question.

Writings by Historians

It would be a daunting task to attempt to put together a summary of all the studies that have shaped my views on the many issues raised by the murder. What I have chosen to do instead is provide a frankly idiosyncratic survey of some of the more important books on slavery, the Old South, and racial ideology, with special attention to recent works, many of which promise to take historical inquiry in new directions. I have largely, though not exclusively, confined myself to books still in print and endeavored to include the latest, rather than the original, date of publication.

Over the past century there have been three major studies of slavery in the Old South: *American Negro Slavery* (Gloucester, Mass.: Peter Smith, 1980) by Ulrich B. Phillips, first published in 1918, which depicted the institution as largely benign; *The Peculiar Institution: Slavery in the Ante-Bellum South* (New York: Random, 1990) by Kenneth M. Stampp, published in 1956, which depicted it as almost unreservedly cruel; and *Roll, Jordan, Roll: The World the Slaves Made* (New York: Random, 1976) by Eugene D. Genovese, published in 1974, which acknowledged that slavery was harsh and exploitative but borrowed insights from Phillips to argue that masters and slaves were tightly bound in a "paternalistic" relationship. Although there has been no significant reinterpretation of antebellum slavery since *Roll, Jordan, Roll*, two notable works covering the colonial and Revolutionary periods have recently been published: *Many Thousands Gone: The First Two Centuries of Slavery in North America* (Cambridge, Mass.: Harvard University Press, 1998) by Ira Berlin, and *Slave Counterpoint: Black Culture in the Eighteenth-Century Chesapeake and Low Country* (Chapel Hill: University of North Carolina Press, 1998) by Philip D. Morgan, in my opinion the most textured, most carefully crafted study of American slavery yet produced. Both Berlin and Morgan stress that slavery varied across time and place, because different crops produced different labor demands and because different labor demands produced different patterns of demography. *American Slavery, 1619–1877* (New York: Hill & Wang, 1993), by Peter Kolchin, is a very fine synthesis. The bibliographical essay he includes should serve as a model for anyone interested in providing a truly useful guide to readers.

Orlando Patterson's *Slavery and Social Death: A Comparative Study* (Cambridge, Mass.: Harvard University Press, 1985) examines slavery throughout the course of human history, concluding that "natal alienation" was the common thread linking slaves in different times and different places. Another comparative study, *Unfree Labor: American Slavery and Russian Serfdom* (Cambridge, Mass.: Harvard University Press, 1990), by Peter Kolchin, sheds light on specific tendencies within the southern experience. The problems created by slavery in the urban centers of the Old South, Natchez among them, are examined by Richard C. Wade in *Slavery in the Cities: The South, 1820–1860* (New York: Oxford University Press, 1967).

Time on the Cross: The Economics of American Negro Slavery (New York: Norton, 1995) by the Nobel Laureate Robert William Fogel and Stanley L. Engerman attracted widespread public attention when it was first published in 1974 because of claims by its authors to scientific exactitude. The book contains findings that are interesting but in the end it delivered much less, and had a much less enduring impact, than its public relations machinery promised. Ironically, Fogel's more recent econometric study, *Without Consent or Contract: The Rise and Fall of American Slavery* (New York: Norton, 1994), though arguably more valuable, has created less of a stir. Gavin Wright has also produced an important work on the Old South economy, *The Political Economy of the Cotton South: Households, Markets, and Wealth in the Nineteenth Century* (New York: Norton, 1978). Michael Tadman, *Speculators and Slaves: Masters, Traders, and Slaves in the Old South* (Madison: University of Wisconsin Press, 1996) is the best study we have of the domestic slave trade, while Walter Johnson's *Soul by Soul: Life Inside the Antebellum Slave Market* (Cambridge, Mass.: Harvard University Press, 1999) provides a detailed look into the workings of the country's largest slave market, in New Orleans. The most thorough treatment of the role performed by overseers is still William Kauffman Scarborough, *The Overseer: Plantation Management in the Old South*, now out of print.

Two works that would be very helpful for anyone specifically interested in Mississippi are John Hebron Moore, *The Emergence of the Cotton Kingdom in the Old Southwest: Mississippi, 1770–1860* (Baton Rouge: Louisiana State University Press, 1988), and Charles S. Sydnor, *Slavery in Mississippi*, now out of print. D. Clayton James, *Antebellum Natchez* (Baton Rouge: Louisiana State University Press, 1968), is the best source on life in the community where Henderson, Reuben, and Anderson were put on trial for murder.

Southern Slavery and the Law, 1619–1860 (Chapel Hill: University of North Carolina Press, 1996), by Thomas D. Morris, is comprehensive and indispensable. An older work on the same subject, by A. Leon Higginbotham, *In the Matter of Color: Race and the American Legal Process, the Colonial Period* (New York: Oxford University Press, 1980), remains useful for the seventeenth and eighteenth centuries. Jenny Bourne Wahl, *The Bondsman's Burden: An Economic Analysis of the Common Law of Southern Slavery* (New York: Cambridge University Press, 1998), examines how legal attempts to define property rights in human beings had broad implications for southern society as a whole. Philip J. Schwarz, *Twice Condemned: Slaves and the Criminal Laws of Virginia, 1705–1865* (Union, N.J.: Lawbook Exchange, 1998), and Edward L. Ayers, *Vengeance and Justice: Crime and Punishment in the 19th-Century American South* (New York: Oxford University Press, 1985), look at the response of the legal system whenever slaves such as Henderson, Reuben, and Anderson were suspected of criminal behavior. However, no study makes more painfully clear how vulnerable slaves were before the courts than Melton A. McLaurin's riveting *Celia, A Slave* (New York: Avon, 1993).

With one notable exception, the most influential interpretations of the Old South produced in the past thirty years give central attention to slavery. In *The Political Economy of Slavery: Studies in the Economy and Society of the Old South* (Middletown, Conn.: Wesleyan University Press, 1989), Eugene Genovese contends that the existence of the institution restricted the development of capitalism in the region. James Oakes has directly challenged this view in *The Ruling Race: A History of American Slaveholders* (New York: Norton, 1998), arguing that slaveowners were driven by the desire to maximize profits and little else. In a later book, *Slavery and Freedom: An Interpretation of the Old South* (New York: Norton, 1998), Oakes seemingly revised this view somewhat, exploring the tension between slavery and liberal capitalism. The "one notable exception" I mentioned above is *Southern Honor: Ethics and Behavior in the Old South* (New York: Oxford University Press, 1983), by Bertram Wyatt-Brown, which regards slavery as almost incidental in the formation of southern character. Far more important, in Wyatt-Brown's view, is a culture of "honor" that existed long before Englishmen arrived in North America and traced its origins back to the mist-ridden forests of prehistoric Germany. Let's just say I'm dubious.

Two books on the early years of slavery in the South have dominated discussion on the subject for the better part of a generation. Edmund S. Morgan, *American Slavery, American Freedom: The Ordeal of Colonial Virginia* (New York: Norton, 1995), describes the transformation of slavery from a system of labor not all that dissimilar to indentured servitude to a rigid form of race control. Peter H. Wood, in *Black Majority: Negroes in Colonial South Carolina from 1670 through the Stono Rebellion* (New York: Norton, 1996), to some degree anticipated Ira Berlin and Philip Morgan by drawing out the links between the structure of American slavery and staple crop production. A brief but helpful introduction is Betty Wood, *The Origins of American Slavery: Freedom and Bondage in the English Colonies* (New York: Hill & Wang, 1997). Recently Kathleen M. Brown, in *Good Wives, Nasty Wenches, and Anxious Patriarchs: Gender, Race, and Power in Colonial Virginia* (Chapel Hill: University of North Carolina Press, 1996), has given a new turn to the debate by showing how English ideas about women influenced policies adopted toward slaves.

No work has had greater influence on the study of American racial ideology than Winthrop D. Jordan's *White over Black: American Attitudes toward the Negro, 1550–1812* (Chapel Hill: University of North Carolina Press, 1995), first published in 1968. Jordan and Edmund Morgan, in *American Slavery, American Freedom*, take somewhat different positions on how deeply ingrained color prejudice was at the time the English first settled North America. To judge for yourself look at James Walvin's *The Black Presence: A Documentary History of the Negro in England, 1555–1860*, now out of print. A perceptive and important survey of white attitudes toward blacks during the nineteenth century is George M. Frederickson's *The Black Image in the White Mind: The Debate on Afro-American Character and Destiny, 1817–1914* (Middleton, Conn.: Wesleyan University Press, 1987). That can be supplemented by William Stanton, *The Leopard's Spots: Scientific Attitudes toward Race in America, 1815–1859,* which, unfortunately, is out of print. To get Thomas Jefferson's views on race, it is best to go to his *Notes on the State of Virginia* (New York: Viking Penguin, 1998), which was originally published in 1785. Mia Bay, *The White Image in the Black Mind: African-American Ideas About White People, 1830–1925* (New York: Oxford University Press, 1999) is an important look at perceptions from the other side of the racial divide.

The most insightful, not to mention absorbing, study we have of the life of a southern planter is *James Henry Hammond and the Old South: A Design for Mastery* (Baton Rouge: Louisiana State University Press, 1982), by Drew Gilpin Faust. Faust is particularly adept at drawing out Hammond's relations with his family and slaves. Charles S. Sydnor's *A Gentleman of the Old Natchez Region, Benjamin L.C. Wailes* (Westport, Conn.: Greenwood, 1970) is more modest in scale but worth noting here because it deals with a man from the same social circle as the planters who investigated the murder of Duncan Skinner. Joan E. Cashin, *A Family Venture: Men and Women on the Southern Frontier* (Baltimore: Johns Hopkins Press, 1994) purports to find a decline in paternalism and a rise in materialism as planters moved from the eastern seaboard to western states like Mississippi. I'm not sure my findings for the Natchez district support her conclusions.

The Southern Lady: From Pedestal to Politics, 1830–1930 (Charlottesville, Va.: University of Virginia Press, 1995) by Anne Firor Scott, first published in 1970, proved a pioneering work, arguing that there was a vast distance between the popular image of the Southern Belle and the reality of life for most white women. Catherine Clinton developed this theme in much greater depth in her authoritative *The Plantation Mistress: Woman's World in the Old South* (New York: Pantheon, 1984). Scott also argued that a sense of identification with slaves led many women to become "private abolitionists." However, in *Within the Plantation Household: Black and White Women of the Old South* (Chapel Hill: University of North Carolina Press, 1988), Elizabeth Fox-Genovese vehemently disagreed, maintaining that planters' wives valued the privileges of class too much to question the legitimacy of slavery. A more recent statement on relations between white and black women can be found in Marli F. Weiner, *Mistresses and Slaves: Plantation Women in South Carolina, 1830–1880* (Urbana: University of Illinois Press, 1997). Like Clarissa Sharpe, many planters' wives saw one or more of their children die at an early age. Their efforts to find peace in the face of tragedy are described in *Motherhood in the Old South: Pregnancy, Childbirth, and Infant Rearing* (Baton Rouge: Louisiana State University Press, 1997) by Sally G. McMillen. Suzanne Lebsock's path-breaking *The Free Women of Petersburg: Status and Culture in a Southern Town, 1784–1860* (New York: Norton, 1984), illuminates the full range of legal disabilities suffered by married women.

Wyatt-Brown's *Southern Honor* is a valuable source on planter family life, as are Jane Turner Censer, *North Carolina Planters and Their Children, 1800–1860* (Baton Rouge: Louisiana State University Press, 1990) and Steven M. Stowe, *Intimacy and Power in the Old South: Ritual in the Lives of the Planters* (Baltimore: Johns Hopkins Press, 1990). Victoria E. Bynum, *Unruly Women: The Politics of Social and Sexual Control in the Old South* (Chapel Hill: University of North Carolina Press, 1992), is an imaginative and important examination of women who challenged patriarchal authority. Susan Conner would be one example, although Bynum concentrates on women below the planter class. Arguably the most unruly of southern women, those who took black lovers, are examined in Martha Hodes's entertaining and provocative *White Women, Black Men: Illicit Sex in the Nineteenth-Century South* (New Haven: Yale University Press, 1997).

In 1959 Stanley M. Elkins published his controversial *Slavery: A Problem in American Institutional and Intellectual Life* (Chicago: University of Chicago Press, 1976), which claimed that the horrors of the trans-Atlantic slave trade and life within the "closed" confines of plantation slavery wiped out all remnants of African culture and turned slaves into "Sambos" who identified completely with the interests of their masters. Much of the literature on slavery written during the 1970s and 1980s was dedicated to disproving Elkins' thesis. John W. Blassingame, *The Slave Community: Plantation Life in the Antebellum South* (New York: Oxford University Press, 1979), first published in 1972, was an especially influential work. Blassingame demonstrated that Sambo was a stereotype, not a reality, and that slaves actively took steps to shape the conditions under which they lived, preserving a sense of their own self-worth. Leslie Howard Owens explored similar themes in *This Species of Property: Slave Life and Culture in the Old South* (New York: Oxford University Press, 1977). Thomas L. Webber, *Deep Like the Rivers: Education in the Slave Quarter Community, 1831–1865* (New York: Norton, 1981), examines how knowledge was transferred from one generation of blacks to the next, while *From Sundown to Sunup: The Making of the Black Community* (Westport, Conn.: Greenwood, 1973), by George P. Rawick, was the first study of slave life to rely heavily on the slave narratives. Paul D. Escott's *Slavery Remembered: A Record of Twentieth Century Slave Narratives* (Chapel Hill: University of North Carolina Press, 1979) also looked at the W.P.A. interviews, subjecting them to close quantitative analysis. Sterling Stuckey's *Slave Culture: Nationalist Theory and the Foundations of Black America* (New York: Oxford University Press, 1988) is ambitious, provocative, and forcefully argued. However, those skeptical of Afrocentric interpretations of the black American experience will undoubtedly have reservations about some of his larger claims.

Charles Joyner, *Down by the Riverside: A South Carolina Slave Community* (Urbana: University of Illinois Press, 1986), demonstrates perhaps the greatest strength and most conspicuous weakness of the studies of slave culture produced in response to Elkins. The book offers abundant evidence of the steps slaves took to build a strong, autonomous community life. At the same time, Joyner scarcely mentions the coercive authority of the slave-owners. As a result, it becomes easy for readers to lose sight of the fact that slavery left many blacks with deep psychological wounds. A book that pays close attention to the interaction between slaveowner and slave is *Singing the Master: The Emergence of African-American Culture in the Plantation South* (New York: Viking Penguin, 1994) by Roger D. Abrahams, a study of the corn-shucking ritual.

A seminal work on the development of black songs and folktales is Lawrence W. Levine's *Black Culture and Black Consciousness: Afro-American Folk Thought from Slavery to Freedom* (New York: Oxford University Press, 1978). It should be supplemented by Dena J. Epstein's informative *Sinful Tunes and Spirituals: Black Folk Music to the Civil War* (Urbana: University of Illinois Press, 1981). Eileen Southern, *The Music of Black Americans: A History* (New York: Norton, 1997) is a well-respected survey. Two works by John Michael Vlach illustrate the growing interest shown by historians in material culture: *Back of the Big House: The Architecture of Plantation Slavery* (Chapel Hill: University of North Carolina Press, 1992) and *The Afro-American Tradition in Decorative Arts* (Athens: University of Georgia Press, 1990).

Although the events this book seeks to explain took place during the antebellum years, it is worthwhile drawing attention to three works dealing with slave culture in the colonial period (in addition to the books already cited by Ira Berlin and Philip Morgan): Allan Kulikoff, *Tobacco and Slaves: The Development of Southern Cultures in the Chesapeake, 1680–1800* (Chapel Hill: University of North Carolina Press, 1986); Mechal Sobel, *The World They Made Together: Black and White Values in Eighteenth-Century Virginia* (Princeton: Princeton University Press, 1988); and Gwendolyn Midlo Hall, *Africans in Colonial Louisiana: The Development of Afro-Creole Culture in the Eighteenth Century* (Baton Rouge: Louisiana State University Press, 1995).

I have already outlined the basic contours of the debate over the slave family. In 1965, drawing on the findings of the eminent sociologist E. Franklin Frazier, Daniel Patrick Moynihan authored a report for the Labor Department entitled *The Negro Family: The Case for National Action* in which he traced what he characterized as the pathology of family life in black neighborhoods to the crippling effects of slavery. A decade later, Herbert G. Gutman published a devastating rejoinder. *The Black Family in Slavery and Freedom, 1750–1925* (New York: Random, 1977) maintained that, whatever the situation in post–World War II urban ghettos, slave families had been remarkably strong and resilient. Other historians have to some extent modified Gutman's findings since then, raising questions in particular about his claims for the predominance of two-parent nuclear families. But to a significant degree they have reinforced his fundamental conclusion that the slave family functioned in a supportive, caring way. To sample the best of the current literature, see Ann Patton Malone, *Sweet Chariot: Slave Family and Household Structure in Nineteenth-Century Louisiana* (Chapel Hill: University of North Carolina Press, 1996), and Brenda E. Stevenson, *Life in Black and White: Family and Community in the Slave South* (New York: Oxford University Press, 1997). Like Stevenson, Orville Vernon Burton in *In My Father's House Are Many Mansions: Family and Community in Edgefield, South Carolina* (Chapel Hill: University of North Carolina Press, 1987) examines both white and black families. Larry E. Hudson, *To Have and to Hold: Slave Work and Family Life in Antebellum South Carolina* (Athens: University of Georgia Press, 1997), and Betty Wood, *Women's Work, Men's Work: The Informal Slave Economies of Low Country Georgia* (Athens: University of Georgia Press, 1995), investigate the intersection of work and family. I might add that not everyone is persuaded Moynihan got it wrong. In *Rituals of Blood: Consequences of Slavery in Two American Centuries* (Washington: Civitas/Counterpoint, 1999), Orlando Patterson suggests that slave families were nothing more than reproductive units patched together to serve the interests of plantation owners.

I quoted both Jacqueline Jones and Deborah Gray White on the experiences of black women. Jones's *Labor of Love, Labor of Sorrow: Black Women, Work, and the Family from Slavery to the Present* (New York: Vintage Books, 1986) is a fine survey. *Ar'n't I A Woman?: Female Slaves in the Plantation South* (New York: Norton, 1999) by White is the best account we have for the antebellum period. Ironically, there is no comparable volume on slave men, although some of my students complain that Blassingame's *The Slave Community* might as well be called *Men in the Slave Community* since the only stereotypes he examines are "Sambo," "Nat," and "Jack." One well-recognized gap in our understanding has now been addressed by Wilma King in *Stolen Childhood: Slave Youth in Nineteenth-Century America* (Bloomington: University of Indiana Press, 1998).

Herbert Aptheker published his path-breaking *American Negro Slave Revolts* (New York: International Publishers, 1993) more than fifty years ago, in 1943. While many historians have taken him to task for exaggerating the extent of slave rebelliousness, Aptheker convincingly shattered the long perpetuated myth that blacks were either too well treated, too docile, or too slow-witted to mount serious resistance against white authority. Since then, we have a number of fine studies of documented slave revolts, from Peter Wood's *Black Majority*, which examines the largest uprising in the colonial period, to Stephen B. Oates' *The Fires of Jubilee: Nat Turner's Fierce Rebellion* (New York: HarperCollins, 1990). Two engrossing but very different interpretations of an abortive rebellion spawned by the ideological ferment of the Revolutionary War are Douglas R. Egerton, *Gabriel's Rebellion: The Virginia Slave Conspiracies of 1800 and 1802* (Chapel Hill: University of North Carolina Press, 1993), and James Sidbury, *Ploughshares into Swords: Race, Rebellion, and Identity in Gabriel's Virginia, 1730–1810* (New York: Cambridge University Press, 1997). Another aborted rebellion that inspired terror in whites, this one led by a free black, is the subject of *Denmark Vesey: The Buried History of America's Largest Slave Rebellion and the Man Who Led It* (New York: Knopf, 1999) by David Robertson. You have already heard my reservations about Winthrop Jordan's *Tumult and Silence at Second Creek: An Inquiry into a Civil War Slave Conspiracy* (Baton Rouge: Louisiana State University Press, 1996). Two works that attempt to put developments in the South into comparative perspective are Eugene D. Genovese, *From Rebellion to Revolution: Afro-American Slave Revolts in the Making of the Modern World* (Baton Rouge: Louisiana State University Press, 1992) and Michael Mullin, *Africa in America: Slave Acculturation and Resistance in the American South and the British Caribbean, 1736–1831* (Urbana: University of Illinois Press, 1994).

Violent uprisings capture the popular imagination, but slaves overwhelmingly chose less dangerous ways to challenge the authority of their masters. John Hope Franklin and Loren Schweninger have recently produced a major study of one common form of resistance: *Runaway Slaves: Rebels on the Plantation* (New York: Oxford University Press, 1999). An older work touching on the same subject is Gerald W. Mullin, *Flight and Rebellion: Slave Resistance in Eighteenth-Century Virginia* (New York: Oxford University Press, 1974). Sylvia R. Frey's *Water from the Rock: Black Resistance in a Revolutionary Age* (Princeton: Princeton University Press, 1991) examines the efforts of blacks to turn the turmoil of the American Revolution to their own advantage.

Unless we make the probably unwarranted assumption that Reverend Joseph Stratton was responding to a personal request from Henderson, Reuben, and Anderson when he came to pray with them a few days before their execution, we have little basis for speculating about the religious attitudes of the slaves on Cedar Grove. Yet Eugene Genovese, Sylvia Frey, and many other scholars argue that Christianity was central to a spirit of resistance in the quarters. The most authoritative account on the religious experiences of blacks remains Albert J. Raboteau's *Slave Religion: The "Invisible Institution" in the Antebellum South* (New York: Oxford University Press, 1990). Other valuable works are Mechal Sobel, *Trabelin' On: The Slave Journey to an Afro-Baptist Faith* (Princeton: Princeton, University Press, 1988); Margaret Washington Creel, *"A Peculiar People": Slave Religion and Community-Culture among the Gullah* (New York: New York University Press, 1988); and Sylvia R. Frey and Betty Wood, *Come Shouting to Zion: African*

American Protestantism in the American South and British Caribbean to 1830 (Chapel Hill: University of North Carolina Press, 1998). Some years ago when I was going through a collection of private papers at Howard University, I came across a couple of letters from a man ridiculing religious devotion. Granted, he was a free black living in the North. But we have no study of those slaves who may have been skeptics or would have agreed with Karl Marx that religion is an "opiate" distracting oppressed peoples from the true cause of revolution.

A number of the works I've already cited include interpretations of the defense of slavery—*Slavery and Freedom* by James Oakes, for example, and *The White Image in the Black Mind*, by George Fredrickson. For a summary of the principal arguments raised in defense of slavery by white southerners see the introduction to Drew Gilpin Faust (ed.), *The Ideology of Slavery: Proslavery Thought in the Antebellum South, 1830–1860* (Baton Rouge: Louisiana State University Press, 1981). The same book also includes a number of representative selections by apologists for the institution. Eugene D. Genovese, *The World the Slaveholders Made: Two Essays in Interpretation* (Middletown, Conn.: Wesleyan University Press, 1988) offers a penetrating analysis of the thought of George Fitzhugh. To sample Fitzhugh's writings, have a look at *Cannibals All! Or Slaves Without Masters* (Cambridge, Mass.: Harvard University Press, 1990), edited by C. Vann Woodward. Larry E. Tise, *Proslavery: A History of the Defense of Slavery in America, 1701–1840* (Athens: University of Georgia Press, 1990), argues that proslavery thought had northern as well as southern origins.

In the end, the great majority of southern whites seem to have convinced themselves that blacks simply lacked both the intellectual capacity and moral sensibilities necessary to function in a free society. They managed to do this despite the fact that there were more than a quarter of a million free blacks in the slave states on the eve of the Civil War. The best survey of the history of the free black population is Ira Berlin's *Slaves Without Masters: The Free Negro in the Antebellum South* (New York: The New Press, 1992). For a fascinating look at those free blacks who acquired slaves of their own, see Michael P. Johnson and James L. Roark, *Black Masters: A Free Family of Color in the Old South* (New York: Norton, 1986). Many readers find the evidence Johnson and Roark present of blacks buying and selling other blacks deeply disturbing. Loren Schweninger also concentrates on members of the elite in *Black Property Owners in the South, 1790–1915* (Urbana: University of Illinois Press, 1990). Tommy L. Bogger, *Free Blacks in Norfolk, 1790–1860: The Darker Side of Freedom* (Charlottesville, Va.: University of Virginia Press, 1997), is a useful case study. An older work that still commands attention is John Hope Franklin, *The Free Negro in North Carolina, 1790–1860* (Chapel Hill: University of North Carolina Press, 1995). T. H. Breen and Stephen Innes, in *"Myne Owne Ground": Race and Freedom on Virginia's Eastern*

Shore, 1640–1676 (New York: Oxford University Press, 1994), show that, during the early colonial period, free blacks enjoyed equality with whites before the law, something that always comes as a great surprise to my students. It helps me make the point that there was, and is, no reason to assume that the history of race relations follows some inevitable course.

Few southerners openly challenged the proslavery consensus in the South during the antebellum years. One notable exception was Hinton Rowan Helper, whose polemical assault on slavery is still in print: *The Impending Crisis of the South: How to Meet It* (North Stratford, N.H.: Ayer Co. Publishers, 1977). Although in discussing the murder of Duncan Skinner I have not looked at the intellectual origins of antislavery thought in Western civilization, I should at least mention the works of David Brion Davis, whose writings are a model of erudition: *The Problem of Slavery in Western Culture* (New York: Oxford University Press, 1988); *The Problem of Slavery in the Age of Revolution, 1770–1823* (New York: Oxford University Press, 1999); and *Slavery and Human Progress* (New York: Oxford University Press, 1986).

As I've already explained, it was northern opposition to the expansion of slavery, not to its continued existence in the South, that led to a profound restructuring of political parties in the 1850s, leaving John McCallin a Democrat and Alexander Farrar a leading figure in the American Party. The story of that restructuring has been told numerous times by an impressive array of historians, and I can do little more here than draw attention to a handful of notable works. If you were to read a single study, I would suggest *The Impending Crisis, 1848–1861* (New York: HarperCollins, 1977), by David M. Potter (completed after his death by his friend Don E. Fehrenbacher). Though a generation old, *The Impending Crisis* is beautifully written and filled with insight into the many ironies that marked the sectional breakdown. A much more recent interpretation by another scholar with impressive literary talents is William W. Freehling's *The Road to Disunion: Secessionists at Bay, 1776–1854* (New York: Oxford University Press, 1991). This is the first of a scheduled two-volume study. Michael F. Holt, in *The Rise and Fall of the American Whig Party: Jacksonian Politics and the Onset of the Civil War* (New York: Oxford University Press, 1999), presents a history of antebellum politics through examination of the party most clearly committed to sectional compromise. *Slavery and the American West; The Eclipse of Manifest Destiny and the Coming of the Civil War* (Chapel Hill: University of North Carolina Press, 1997), by Michael A. Morrison, examines the issues underlying the territorial controversy. Other books worth looking at for anyone particularly interested in the southern side of the sectional debate are: William J. Cooper, Jr., *The South and the Politics of Slavery, 1828–1856* (Baton Rouge: Louisiana State University Press, 1980); *The Development of Southern Sectionalism, 1819–1848* (Baton Rouge: Louisiana State University Press, 1948) by Charles S. Sydnor; and Kenneth S. Greenberg, *Masters and Statesmen: The Political Culture of American Slavery* (Baltimore: Johns Hopkins Press, 1988). *John A. Quitman: Old South Crusader* (Baton Rouge: Louisiana State University Press, 1995), by Robert E. May, examines the life of the Natchez planter who was the most powerful Democrat in Mississippi. I have uncovered no evidence of Quitman's thoughts on the charges leveled against John McCallin.

If voters in the North were something less than passionate about the need to destroy slavery, it was in large part because they shared with their southern counterparts a commitment to white supremacy. The best overview of the prejudice faced by northern blacks is Leon F. Litwack's *North of Slavery: The Negro in the Free States, 1790–1860* (Chicago: University of Chicago Press, 1965). A number of more recent works document how blacks in the North responded to pervasive discrimination: Graham Russell Hodges, *Root and Branch: African Americans in New York and East Jersey, 1613–1863* (Chapel Hill: University of North Carolina Press, 1999); Gary B. Nash, *Forging Freedom: The Formation of Philadelphia's Black Community, 1720–1840* (Cambridge, Mass.: Harvard University Press, 1991); James Oliver Horton, *Free People of Color: Inside the African American Community* (Washington: Smithsonian, 1993); James Oliver Horton and Lois E. Horton, *In Hope of Liberty: Culture, Community, and Protest among Northern Free Blacks, 1700–1860* (New York: Oxford University Press, 1998).

It's difficult to think of a slave society as "democratic." Confine your attention to white males, however, and the term has a certain validity for the Old South, although how much is open to debate. For a quick overview of the advancement of democracy during the first half of the nineteenth century, you could hardly do better than read *American Revolutionaries in the Making: Political Practices in Washington's Virginia* (New York: Free Press, 1965), by Charles S. Sydnor, followed by the relevant chapters in his *The Development of Southern Sectionalism*. Rhys L. Isaac documents the rise of egalitarian sentiments during the Revolutionary era in *The Transformation of Virginia, 1740–1790* (New York: Norton, 1988), his Pulitzer Prize–winning study.

More than fifty years ago, Frank L. Owsley radically altered perceptions of the Old South by disproving the widely held view that the vast majority of whites were either rich or poor. Relying on statistical studies of individual states provided by his graduate students (who got their data from the manuscript census—and, keep in mind, this was before computers, so the work was mind-numbingly tedious), Owsley argued that most southern whites were neither rich nor poor but middle-class farmers—yeomen, to use the term favored by historians. Herbert Weaver produced the relevant volume on Mississippi: *Mississippi Farmers, 1850–1860* (Gloucester, Mass.: Peter Smith, 1990). Owsley summarized his findings in *Plain Folk of the*

Old South (Baton Rouge: Louisiana State University Press, 1990), originally published in 1949.

Two highly regarded and influential books that stress the egalitarianism of southern yeomen are J. Mills Thornton III, *Politics and Power in a Slave Society: Alabama, 1800–1860* (Baton Rouge: Louisiana State University Press, 1978) and Lacy K. Ford, *Origins of Southern Radicalism: The South Carolina Upcountry, 1800–1860* (New York: Oxford University Press, 1991). Stephanie McCurry, in her influential *Masters of Small Worlds: Yeomen Households, Gender Relations, and the Political Culture of the Antebellum South Carolina Low Country* (New York: Oxford University Press, 1997), contends it was not equality yeomen sought but a democratic republicanism that acknowledged distinctions in class while confirming the right of each white man to exercise patriarchal authority over members of his own household, slave and free. J. William Harris explores the complicated pas-de-deux between planters and farmers in *Plain Folk and Gentry in a Slave Society: White Liberty and Black Slavery in Augusta's Hinterlands* (Baton Rouge: Louisiana State University Press, 1998). The situation of the yeomen outside the plantation belt is dealt with in Steven Hahn, *The Roots of Southern Populism: Yeoman Farmers and the Transformation of the Georgia Upcountry, 1850–1890* (New York: Oxford University Press, 1985) and John C. Inscoe, *Mountain Masters: Slavery and the Sectional Crisis in Western North Carolina* (Knoxville: University of Tennessee Press, 1996). Important information on who held political office during the antebellum period can be found in Ralph A. Wooster, *The People in Power: Courthouse and State-house in the Lower South, 1850–1860*, now out of print.

The experiences of Irish immigrants such as John McCallin are captured by Kerby A. Miller in *Emigrants and Exiles: Ireland and the Irish Exodus to North America* (New York: Oxford University Press, 1988). As I've already noted, it was quite late in my research when I discovered that John McCallin was Catholic. That suddenly made the question of how Irish Catholic immigrants won social acceptance relevant to my study. The simple, flippant answer is, they became white. The more serious answer—involving how ideas about whiteness evolved over the course of the nineteenth century—is addressed in a number of recent works on the formation of racial identity. David R. Roediger's *The Wages of Whiteness: Race and the Making of the American Working Class* (New York: Verso, 1998) is an invaluable piece of scholarship. Also noteworthy are Noel Ignatiev's *How the Irish Became White* (New York: Routledge, 1996) and a two-volume study by Theodore W. Allen, *The Invention of the White Race: Racial Oppression and Social Control* (New York: Verso, 1994) and *The Invention of the White Race: The Origin of Racial Oppression in Anglo-America* (New York: Verso, 1997). Roediger, Ignatiev, and Allen concern themselves principally with Irish Catholics, but it's worth mentioning that there is an increasing body of work dealing with other immigrant groups. See, for example, *Whiteness of a Different Color: European Immigrants and the Alchemy of Race* (Cambridge, Mass.: Harvard University Press, 1998), by Matthew Frye Jacobson.

⁂

Finally, this book is dedicated to the memory of J. H. Hexter, as well as to my students, because he—and they—have forced me to think hard about the nature of historical inquiry. Two of Jack Hexter's books are particularly valuable if you want to gain some insight into what might be called the tricks of the trade: *Doing History* and *The History Primer*. You'll have to go to a library or used bookstore to find them, however. Both are out of print.

Acknowledgments

To produce a work of history, it is generally necessary to spend months (or years) ploughing through boxes of documents or gazing at reels of microfilm, often in libraries or archives some distance from home. That is normally followed by many more months (or years) organizing the evidence and struggling to find the words and narrative form best suited to tell the story you have pieced together. To an outsider it must seem like a very solitary exercise. However, no historian reaches the end of a project without having accumulated substantial intellectual debts along the way. The following paragraphs represent an exceedingly inadequate way of beginning to repay my own such debts.

Let me begin with my editor, Susan Ferber. In addition to shepherding me through the occasionally inscrutable publishing process, Susan provided me with valuable advice about how to make my presentation more useful and generally accessible. (As did her predecessor at Oxford, Thomas LeBien). She also—and for this I'm especially grateful—allowed me to tell the story of the murder in my own, admittedly unconventional, way.

It is routine for historians, as for other writers, to ask friends and colleagues to comment on drafts of their work. I am very grateful to Larry Powell, Marc Kruman, Mimi Miller, Jennifer Richards, and Marc Egnal (as well as the unidentified scholars who refereed the manuscript for Oxford) for offering me the benefit of their thoughtful criticism. Not only did they save me from a number of embarrassing factual errors, but they also, in challenging particular arguments I made, helped me identify aspects of my interpretation that needed refinement (or abandonment). I also owe thanks to Joey Slinger for the many evenings we walked our dogs together, griping and joking about the problems of writing (among a multitude of other subjects). I benefitted immensely from those exchanges, if in ways I find it difficult to put into words. Joey also provided the moral support I needed to produce the single footnote (deleted in revisions).

In the course of my research I ran into a problem many historians have faced. After returning home from an extended trip to Mississippi and Louisiana, I realized that the documents I'd photocopied raised new questions requiring further research in the libraries, archives, and courthouses I'd just left. Another trip south was not immediately possible. And so I turned to Larry Powell, who lives in New Orleans, for assistance. He put me in touch with Peter Caron, who did an invaluable job of acquiring copies for me of all the court records in Catahoula parish relating to the estate of Absalom Sharpe and collecting evidence on the legal rights of widows in Louisiana. I got additional information on antebellum law from Archie Campbell, Christine Lambert, Michael Hoffheimer, and Michelle Hudson.

Michelle also secured me the services of Vera Richardson, an extraordinarily resourceful genealogist. It was Vera who turned up the evidence of John McCallin's common-law marriage to Frances Robertson as well as the baptismal records of their three children. She also directed me to the naturalization papers that McCallin filed in Philadelphia, the source for my description of his life before he arrived in Mississippi.

Carol Hubert introduced herself to me at a conference in Natchez. Her husband is a distant relative of Jesse Skinner and she was doing research on the Skinner family. Was I interested in her findings?, she politely asked. That gracious offer led to most of what I was able to tell you about the background of Duncan Skinner.

The wonderful maps and illustrations were produced by my good friend Phil Richards. At various points I have emphasized how much imagination is involved in re-creating the past, leaving the immodest impression, I suppose, that I see myself as a very creative individual. But without question the finest acts of imagination in this book are the dramatic painting on the cover depicting the discovery of Duncan Skinner's body and the three portraits. For his drawing of Alexander Farrar, Phil was working from a very blurry reproduction of a daguerreotype, for his drawing of Clarissa Sharpe from a photograph of a likeness of her on a cologne bottle. (And here I must thank Dorothy Sojourner for generously making the bottle available to me.) But his most remarkable achievement is the portrait of John McCallin. To the best of my knowledge, no picture of McCallin has survived. (The letter from Alexander Farrar to Henry Drake mentions a daguerreotype, so I live in hope.) However, Phil came up with a visual interpretation based on a photograph of his grandson, John McAllen, acquired for me by Vera Richardson.

Finally, there are my debts of a more personal nature. To my children Maia, Beatrice, and Seth, for years of humoring me, driving me to distraction, filling the house with noise and laughter (both at opportune and inopportune times), giving me their advice (sometimes when I asked for it), and, above all else, sharing their love with me and allowing me to share my love with them.

And to the most important person in my life, my wife, Sandra. For joining me on my many flights of imagination, while doing her best to ensure that I occasionally remember to touch down into something that might be regarded as reality.

Note to Readers

To share your own views on the death of Duncan Skinner and to examine any additional evidence that may become available over time, consult the web site www.deathofanoverseer.com.

Index

abolitionists, 81, 118, 121, 132

Abrahams, Roger, 107

Adams County, Mississippi, 5, 10, 21, 36, 117, 163, 165, 182
  assessment rolls, 164
  Board of Police, 35–36, 162, 167
  circuit court, records of, 40–41, 51–52, 179–180
  courthouse, 30–32
  probate court, 104, 126–127, 129–130

Adams County Light Guard, 37

Africans, English perceptions of, 135–138, 142, 151

Alexander, James W., 168

American Party ("Know Nothings"), 25–26, 31–32, 117, 165
  origins of, 122–123
  in Natchez district, 123–124

American Revolution, 86, 143–144

Anderson, 27, 31, 39, 78, 91, 131 (*see also* execution of Henderson, Reuben, and Anderson; trial of Henderson, Reuben, and Anderson)
  and alleged feelings of remorse, 17, 68
  appraised value of, 35, 127
  apprehended, 14
  hidden by slaves on Magnolia, 14, 17, 95, 98
  as husband and father, 104–106
  implicated by Reuben, 12–13, 62–63

  role in murder of, 18, 63–66
  as runaway, 28, 76
  and stolen money, 18, 94

Archy (son of Jane), 104

Arcola plantation, 126

Aventine plantation, 96

Ayers, Edward, 170, 185

Baird, John W., 64, 162

Baker, E. B., 168

Baton Rouge, Louisiana, 193

Baynard, George, 127

Beck, John, 94–95

Bengal plantation, 166

Benjamin (son of Anderson), 104

Berkeley plantation, 125

Best, George, 136–137

Betty (wife of Anderson), 104–105

Bingaman, Adam, 70

Birney, James, 118

Black Boy (Wright), 105–106

Blassingame, John, 103, 152

Bombay plantation, 166

Bonne Ridge plantation, 82, 92, 97, 125–129, 162

Botto, John, 29, 33, 114

Bowman, Robert, 24, 27, 166, 182

Boyd, Alex, 26, 124

Brown, William Wells, 110

Burn Place plantation, 166

Burrell (husband of Jane), 13, 34, 81, 104

Calhoun, John, 145, 147
Cannibals All! (Fitzhugh), 147
Carlisle plantation, 81
Cass, Lewis, 121
Cartwright, Samuel A., 99
Catahoula Parish, Louisiana, 82, 92, 125, 127
  district court, 127
Celia, A Slave (McLaurin), 171
census records, 90, 154, 167, 179–184
Cedar Grove plantation. *See also* investigation
  description of, 9, 16
  in Clarissa Sharpe's will, 24, 88
  in financial settlement between Alexander Farrar and Clarissa Sharpe, 128–130
  as part of Absalom Sharpe's estate, 125–126
  recovered by Clarissa Sharpe from her husband's heirs, 126–128
  Sharpe residence at, 19–20, 22, 193
Charleston, South Carolina, 98–99, 155
Chaucer, Geoffrey, 135
Chesnut, Mary, 70
Christy, David, 145, 147
Clarissa (daughter of Anderson), 104
Clark, Robert, 169
Clem (slave on Fonsylvania), 89–90, 99–101
Cold Mountain (Frazier), 185
Commencement plantation, 27, 95, 115, 160
Compromise of 1850, 120
Conner, Susan, 125–126
Conner, William C., 169
Cotton is King (Christy), 145
coroner's jury
  Skinner's death ruled accidental by, 9, 76, 160, 172
  testimony at trial by, 34, 64, 173–174
County Derry, Ireland, 19
Cuba, 114, 123
Cyrus (son of Jane), 104

Darlington County, South Carolina, 90–91
Davenport, Charley, 96
Davis, Amasa, 169
Davis, David Brion, 138
Davis, Thomas F., 163
Democratic Party, 31, 123–124
  in Adams County, 123
  in national politics, 120–122, 158

democracy
  commitment of whites to, 117, 160
  expansion of, 157–160
  planters' suspicion of, 178
Dorcas
  as alleged messenger for John McCallin, 74
  and cover-up of murder, 97–98
  and the Jezebel image, 154
  as John McCallin's alleged lover, 14, 17–18, 27, 67–71, 75, 77, 183
  John McCallin's involvement in murder denied by, 72–73
  relationship to other slaves, 97, 102
  and stolen money, 13–14, 75
  testimony at trial by, 34, 64, 173
  testimony before grand jury by, 31, 64
Douglas, Stephen, 120–121
Douglass, Frederick, 107
Drake, Benjamin M., 166
Drake, Henry W.
  biographical information on, 166
  letter to Alexander Farrar from, 24–26, 41, 117
  as member of committee in Waterproof, 24, 27, 182
drapetomania, 99
Dred Scott decision, 118
Du Bois, W. E. B., 177
Dun, R.G. & Co. Agency, 32–33, 129–130, 164
Dunbar, Robert, 162–163
Duncan, Stephen, 81

Eden, Richard, 136–137
Elizabeth Female Academy, 115
Elkins, Stanley, 103, 150
Elliott, E. N., 84
Ellison, William, 154–155
Ennis (slave belonging to Dempsey Jackson), 99
European laborers, 82–83
execution of Henderson, Reuben, and Anderson, 35–37, 111, 175

Farrar, Alexander K., 13–14, 32, 37, 81–82, 88–89, 94–95, 104, 108, 114, 125, 147, 174, 182 (*see also* investigating party)
  as administrator of Absalom Sharpe's estate, 126–130

on alleged motives of John McCallin,
19, 66–67, 113
and the American Party, 117, 123–124
biographical information on, 10, 21,
115, 129, 143
on character of John McCallin, 17,
67–68
and financial dealings with Clarissa
Sharpe, 127–131
on interrogation of Dorcas, 72
on John McCallin's alleged role in
murder, 66–67
on John McCallin's return to Cedar
Grove after murder, 67, 75–76
letter to Henry Drake from, 26–27, 39,
42–50, 71–75, 77, 91, 124, 130,
173
letter to William Foules from, 35–36,
111, 175
and management of investigation,
160–163, 178
and meeting at Kingston, 163–164
Papers of, 39–41, 68, 73, 82, 126–127
portrait of, 11
and relationship with Jesse Skinner,
160
reputation of, 129–131
testimony of Clarissa Sharpe taken by,
28, 77
and Waterproof committee, 166, 182
Farrar, Ann, 108
Farrar, Caleb, 64, 162
Farrar, Daniel (father of Alexander
Farrar), 129
Farrar, George Daniel (son of Alexander
Farrar), 88, 116
Faulkner, William, 4, 39
Fayette Female Academy, 115
filibustering, 114, 123
First Presbyterian Church of Natchez,
36, 108, 116
Fitzhugh, George, 147–149, 151
Fonsylvania plantation, 89–91, 99–101
Ford, Fountain W., 162, 167–168, 173
Forrest, Edwin, 29
Foster, James, 115
Foules, William B.
as employer of Y. W. McBride, 17, 64–
65, 95
as member of Adams County Board of
Police, 35–36, 167–168

testimony of Clarissa Sharpe taken by,
28, 77
Foulk, Esau, 169
Fox-Genovese, Elizabeth, 154
Franklin, John Hope, 5
Frazier, Charles, 185
Fredrickson, George, 133
free blacks, 31, 70, 143, 154–156, 178
Friendly Moralist Society, 155
fugitive slaves, 70, 95–96, 101, 105

Gabriel's Rebellion, 144
Galtney, Thomas, 167–168
Genovese, Eugene, 83–85, 110, 149
Gillespie, William J., 164
Gone with the Wind, 114, 153
Gordon (son of Anderson), 104
Gordon, James, 166
Gordon, William, 166
grand jury, 31, 34, 167, 172
indictment handed down by, 41, 51–
52, 63–64, 175, 178
Green, Charles, 169
Griffin, William, 162
Groves, Dr. G. G., 82
Gutman, Herbert, 104

Haiti, 83, 144
Ham, Noah's curse on, 136–138
Hammond, James, 149–150, 152
Harris, Joel Chandler, 106
Harvard University, 34, 88, 116
Hayden, D. M., 164
Helper, Hinton Rowan, 176–177
Henderson, 27–28, 31, 36, 68, 76–78, 111
(see also execution of Henderson,
Reuben, and Anderson; trial of
Henderson, Reuben, and
Anderson)
assessed value of, 35, 127
and division of stolen money, 94
implicated by Reuben, 12–13, 66
interrogated by investigating party, 13–
14, 17–18
possible conspiring with Dorcas by,
97–98
role in murder of, 12, 62–66
testimony against John McCallin by,
14, 17, 66–67, 72–75, 91, 131
Hermitage plantation, 115
Hexter, J. H., 3–4

Hibernian Society of Natchez, 19, 159
Hillyer, Giles, 37, 59, 63–64 (*see also*
        Natchez *Courier*)
    biographical information on, 31–32
    commentary on trial in *Courier* by, 33,
        160, 169–170, 175
    and opposition to retrial for Reuben
        (slave on Mandamus), 171–172,
        176
Historic Natchez Foundation, 41, 51
history, practice of, 3–5, 39, 40, 61–62,
        65, 102–103, 179–182, 185–186
Hoggatt Jr., Nathaniel, 164
Homochitto River, 160
honor, code of, 130, 163

Ignatiev, Noel, 184
The Impending Crisis of the South
        (Helper), 176–177
industrialization in the North, 86–87
Ingraham, Joseph Holt, 93, 113, 116, 149–
        151, 159
interracial sex, 70–71
investigation
    and interrogation of slaves on Cedar
        Grove, 10, 12–14, 17, 68, 91
    and interrogation of slaves on
        Magnolia, 17–18, 68
    and interrogation of slaves on
        Mandamus, 18
    physical coercion of slaves during, 13–
        14, 72, 75
investigating party, 5, 26, 34, 69, 71, 154,
        176, 180
    accused of class prejudice, 113–114,
        117
    accused of framing John McCallin,
        111, 113, 131–133
    accused of political persecution, 117,
        123–124
    composition of, 161–162
    composition of group supporting
        findings of, 162–163
    endorsed by Kingston meeting, 164–
        165
    notice published in newspapers by, 18,
        21, 23, 40–41, 161
    and predisposition to implicate
        someone white, 152, 156, 178
    slenderness of evidence collected by,
        78

as source of evidence for prosecutor,
        160
    statement of support for, 18–19, 26,
        162, 180
    verdict reached by, 18, 66–67, 97, 174–
        175
Irish Catholics, 19, 117, 122, 132, 184

Jackson, Mississippi, 34, 132
Jackson, Andrew, 158
Jackson, Dempsey P., 30, 70, 99, 150
    as chairman of meeting in Kingston,
        21, 23, 25, 71, 117, 164
Jackson, James, 30
James, D. Clayton, 116–117
Jamestown, 135, 138–139
Jane
    alleged implicating of John McCallin
        by, 26, 75
    interrogation of, 12
    and position as cook, 91–92, 97–98
    and cover-up of murder, 12, 62, 97
    and stolen money, 13, 81
    testimony at trial by, 34, 66, 173
    testimony before grand jury by, 31, 64
    as wife and mother, 104–105
Jefferson, Thomas
    racial beliefs of, 140–144, 151
Jefferson College, 89, 93, 115
Jefferson County, Mississippi, 182–183
Jenkins, John Carmichael, 88
John (slave on Fonsylvania), 89–90, 99–
        101
John (slave on Mandamus), 171
John (son of Jane), 104
Johnson, Michael, 154–155
Johnson, William, 31, 154–155, 158
Jones, Jacqueline, 72
Jordan, Winthrop, 102, 139, 142
Journal of American History, 179

Kansas-Nebraska Act, 121–122
King, Caleb, 21
Kingston, Mississippi
    devastated by tornado, 21, 29
    location of, 9, 15
    history of, 21
    as stronghold of Whig support, 123
Kingston, meeting at, 21, 132, 180
    notice in newspapers about, 40, 66–
        67, 192

questions raised at Waterproof about, 24–26, 117, 165

resolutions passed at, 23, 41, 124, 167

as undemocratic gathering, 163–166

Lebsock, Suzanne, 124

legal system
and property rights of married women, 124–125
treatment of slaves accused of crimes within, 167, 169–172
testimony by blacks against whites prohibited by, 18, 78, 80
unwritten authority of planters within, 159–161 (*see also* plantation law)

Lem (brother of Henderson), 13–14, 34, 68, 72

Levine, Lawrence, 110

Liberty Party, 118

Lincoln, Abraham, 96, 119–120, 123, 144, 151

Lind, Jenny, 29

Locke, John, 140

Lok, John, 135

Londonderry, Ireland, 180

Louis (slave belonging to Dempsey Jackson), 99

Louisiana Purchase, 119–121

Louisiana State University, 30, 40

Lucas, James, 90

Lydia (daughter of Anderson), 104

Lyell, Sir Charles, 109

Magnolia plantation
as hiding place for Anderson, 14, 95
interrogation of slaves on, 17–18, 65, 68
knowledge of murder kept secret by slaves on, 98
testimony at trial by slaves from, 34, 64, 173

Magruder, Eliza, 92, 98

Mahala (daughter of Anderson), 104

Mandamus plantation, 28
interrogation of slaves on, 17
knowledge of Skinner murder kept secret by slaves on, 98

manifest destiny, 118–119

Marshall, George M., 167–168

Martin, William T., 123, 154
biographical information on, 33, 169
closing statement at trial by, 34, 160, 178
and prosecution of Henderson, Reuben, and Anderson, 34, 169, 174–175

Mason, Richard, 168

McBride, Y. W.
Dorcas's knowledge of, 95
indictment against slaves accused of murdering, 64–65
murder of, 17, 23, 35, 164
retrial ordered for Reuben in murder of, 171, 176
trial of slaves charged with murdering, 169, 171

McAllen, Ada, 184

McAllen, Frances, 182–184

McAllen, Frank, 183–184, 186

McAllen, John, 184

McAllen, Margaret, 182–184

McAllen, Udoxie (daughter of Frank McAllen), 184

McAllen, Udoxie (daughter of John McCallin), 182–184

McCafferty, Frank, 167, 180

McCaleb, James, 168

McCallin, John, 34, 39–40, 59, 80, 102, 107, 123, 132, 159, 175, 177, 185–186, 193 (*see also* Dorcas; Farrar, Alexander; Sharpe, Clarissa)
accused by Henderson of instigating murder, 17, 66, 91, 160
accused of warning slaves, 17, 23, 67
allegations against Alexander Farrar by, 19, 25–27, 126, 130
and allegations of a frame-up, 111, 113, 131
attitude of Absalom Sharpe toward, 71
biographical information on, 19–21, 113–114, 167
blamed for murder of Duncan Skinner, 18–19, 66–67, 111, 161–162, 178
case presented by Alexander Farrar against, 26–27, 69
census entries on, 180–182
as characterized by Alexander Farrar, 27, 67
as characterized by Dempsey Jackson, 21, 71

McCallin, John (*continued*)
  charges of political persecution by, 26,
    117, 124, 165
  children of, 182–184
  class prejudice against, 114, 117, 149,
    165
  and Democratic Party, 117, 165
  and Frances McAllen (wife), 182–184
  as Irish Catholic, 117, 122–123, 132,
    156, 184
  and knowledge of Y. W. McBride, 95,
    102
  and meeting at Kingston, 21, 23, 164–
    165
  and meeting at Waterproof, 24–28,
    165–167, 181–182
  notice published in newspapers by, 19,
    21, 23–24, 26, 40–41, 163
  portrait of, 20
  and reappearance at Cedar Grove
    following murder, 28, 67, 75–77,
    131
  and relationship with Duncan
    Skinner, 19, 73
  stolen money hidden in trunk of, 12–14
  weaknesses in case against, 72–78, 91
McCullough, Hamilton, 27, 165, 166
McDaniel, Hattie, 153
McDonald, James, 124, 171–172
McLaurin, Melton, 171
McNeill, William H., 5
Mercer, William Newton, 81
Metcalfe, Oren, 35–37, 160, 169
Metcalfe, Orrick, 164
Minor, William, 89
Mississippi Free Trader, 40, 179
  criticism of the planting elite by, 159
  report on execution of Henderson,
    Reuben, and Anderson in, 36
  as organ of the Democratic Party, 32,
    124
  supports retrial for Reuben (slave on
    Mandamus), 171–172
Mississippi High Court of Errors and
    Appeals, 158, 172–174
Missouri Compromise, 119, 120–121
Montgomery, Eli, 167
Moynihan, Daniel Patrick, 104
Murphy, Patrick, 184
Murray, Charles, 99
Myrdal, Gunnar, 5

Natchez, Mississippi, 9, 18, 20, 24, 27–28,
    32–33, 36–37, 67, 76–77, 84, 90–
    92, 114–115, 127, 180, 182, 185, 193
  class antagonism in, 30, 159
  cosmopolitan character of, 19, 123
  development of, 28–30
  free blacks in, 31, 154–155
  residence of planters in, 30, 70, 81, 83,
    88–89
  social structure in, 30, 70, 116, 159
  slaves in, 30–31, 93, 108
  yellow fever epidemic in, 21
Natchez *Courier*, 40, 61
  articles on murder in, 41–42, 63, 76
  as organ of the American Party, 31–32,
    117
  report on execution of Henderson,
    Reuben, and Anderson in, 37
  report on sentencing of Henderson,
    Reuben, and Anderson in, 35
  report on trial of Henderson, Reuben,
    and Anderson in, 34, 52–58, 63–
    66, 98, 169–170, 174–175
  on retrial for Reuben (slave on
    Mandamus), 171–172, 176
Natchez district, 39, 113, 143
  location of, 28–29
  planters of, 70, 116, 123
  political allegiances in, 123
  slave prices in, 128
  slave rebelliousness in, 98–99
The Natchez Institute, 114–115
Natchez-under-the-hill, 28–30, 70
nationalism, 117–120
nativism, 122–123
Neely, John, 193
New Orleans, 28–29, 70, 99, 114, 120, 181
Newton (slave belonging to Dempsey
    Jackson), 99
nonslaveholders, 164, 177–178
  attitude toward planters among, 30,
    158–159, 163
  and support for slavery, 176–178
northern laborers, 82, 86–87, 149, 156
northern manufacturers, 87, 148–149, 156
Notes on the State of Virginia (Jefferson),
    141–142
Nott, Josiah, 146–147

Oakes, James, 86
Olmsted, Frederick, 29, 91–93, 99, 116, 159

Order of the Star-Spangled Banner, 122
Osborne (son of Anderson), 104, 106
O'Sullivan, John L., 118
overseers, 9–10, 88–91, 98, 126

party politics, 117, 120–124, 165
paternalism, 83–85, 95
Patterson, Orlando, 150
The Peculiar Institution (Stampp), 155
Petersburg, Virginia, 124
Philadelphia, Pennsylvania, 19, 122, 180
Phillips, Richard W., 168
Phillips, Ulrich, 82, 84
Phipps, Routh H., 163, 168
Pickett, George, 21
Pierce, Franklin, 120–121
Pipes, Charles, 164
Pipes, Lewis, 163–164
Pipes, Robert, 163–164
plantation law, 80–88, 159–160, 170–171
planters
    class consciousness among, 21, 30,
        70, 113–117, 158–159, 165,
        178
    education of children by, 114–115
    marriage patterns of, 70, 116–117
    and relations with overseers, 88–91
    and sense of obligation to slaves, 81–
        90, 100, 108–109, 152
    in the West Indies, 83, 87
Planters' College, 84
plough driver, 73–77
    and cover-up of murder, 75
    implicates John McCallin, 17, 27–28,
        67, 73–77
Polk, James, 118–119
polygenesis, 147
popular sovereignty, 121
Port Gibson, Mississippi, 84
Posey, Judge Stanhope, 173, 175
    biographical information on, 33, 168–
        169
    orders retrial for Reuben (slave on
        Mandamus), 171
    and sentencing of Henderson,
        Reuben, and Anderson, 35, 178
Preston, Zenas, 24, 27, 165–166
Princeton University, 34, 36, 115
probate records, 92, 97
proslavery argument, 143–152, 155, 175–
    176, 178, 182

Quakers, 140
Quegles, John B., 169
Quitman, John, 31, 114, 123

racial ideology. *See also* Africans, English
    views of
    in the antebellum South, 146–147,
        149–156
    during the Revolutionary era, 140–144
    in the free states, 117–118
    and Jezebel image, 154
    and Mammy image, 153–154
    and Nat image, 152–154
    and Sambo image, 150–151, 153
racism, definition of 142–143
Randolph, Mary, 182–184
Rawlings, A. D., 168
Reidy, Joe, 185
Republican Party, 122, 123
Reuben (slave on Cedar Grove) 17–18,
        27, 31, 39, 78, 91, 131 (*see also*
        execution of Henderson, Reuben,
        and Anderson; trial of
        Henderson, Reuben, and
        Anderson)
    and alleged feelings of remorse, 68
    appraised value of, 35, 127–128
    confession by, 12, 62–63, 65–66
    and grand jury indictment, 64–65
    and position as carpenter, 92, 97
    role in murder of, 12–13, 62–64, 98
    and stolen money, 13, 94
Reuben (slave on Mandamus), 64–65,
        171–172, 176
Richmond, Virginia, 98–99, 144
Richmond *Enquirer*, 147
The Ridges plantation, 98
River Place plantation, 88
Roark, James, 154–155
Robertson, Frances. *See* McAllen,
        Frances
Robertson, Udoxie. *See* McAllen,
        Udoxie (daughter of John
        McCallin)
Rodney, Mississipi, 182–185
Roediger, David, 177
Rogillio (overseer on Fonsylvania), 89–
        91, 100–101
Rose Hill plantation, 36
Rowan, James, 168
The Ruling Race (Oakes), 86

St. Joseph, Louisiana, 67, 113, 181
Saint-Domingue, 144
Second Creek, Mississippi, 102, 132
Samuel, Richard, 36
Scott, Israel, 164
Scott, J. S., 168
Sharpe, Absalom, 24, 92, 97, 143, 193
   estate of, 125–130
   and John McCallin 20, 69, 71, 165
Sharpe, Clarissa, 33, 36, 40, 82, 97, 162,
   167–168
   biographical information on, 24, 179,
     193
   compensation for executed slaves
     received by, 35
   and estate of Absalom Sharpe, 104,
     125–27
   and financial dealings with Alexander
     Farrar, 19, 24, 27, 127–130
   and investigating party, 13, 77
   portrait of, 25
   and relationship with Duncan
     Skinner, 10, 14, 24, 73, 89,
     91, 174
   and relationship with John McCallin,
     14, 17–18, 21, 67–69, 71, 76, 114,
     117, 130–131
   testimony against John McCallin by,
     26, 28, 124
   will of, 24, 88
Sharpe, Edward, 24
Sharpe, Levy, 24
Sharpe, Thomas Morgan, 24
Shields, Gabriel, 96
Shields, Joseph D., 33–34, 150
   biographical information on, 33–34,
     169
   and defense at trial, 34, 172–176
Shields, William Bayard, 33–34
Skinner, Benjamin, 9–10, 162
   Skinner, Duncan 9, 39–40, 104, 110,
     126, 179–180 (*see also* McCallin,
     John; Sharpe, Clarissa)
   presumed attitude of slaves toward,
     97–98, 101
   biographical information on, 9, 90–91
   money stolen from cabin of, 12–13, 18,
     81, 94
   tombstone of, 193–194
   treatment of slaves by, 17, 91, 92, 101

Skinner, Duncan, death of, 65–66
   considered as insurrection, 101–102
   described in grand jury indictment,
     64–65
   described by Reuben, 12–13
   explained by defense attorneys, 34
   explained by investigating party, 18,
     62, 66–67
   recounted in Natchez *Courier*, 63–64
Skinner, Jesse, 9–10, 67, 74, 76, 160, 162
   and relationship with Alexander
     Farrar, 160
   verdict of coroner's jury questioned
     by, 10
Skinner, Lemuel, 91
Skinner, Mary Eliza, 160
Skinner, Nicy, 91
The Slave Community (Blassingame), 103
slave narratives, 96, 101, 180
slavery, laws regarding (*see also* legal
     system)
   and compensation for owners of
     executed slaves, 35
   marriage of slaves prohibited by, 104
   and question of "fairness" for slaves,
     170–171
   and responsibilities of masters to
     slaves, 79–80
   and slaves charged with capital
     crimes, 167
*Slavery: A Problem in American
     Institutional and Intellectual Life*
     (Elkins), 103
Slaves
   buying and selling of, 87–88
   family life of, 95, 103–106
   folk culture of, 103–107
   in Natchez, 30–31
   punishment of, 72, 75, 91
   and relations with masters, 80–92, 94–
     95, 100, 104, 107–108 (*see also*
     plantation law)
   religion of, 35–36, 103, 107–111, 140
   resistance by, 98–102, 110–111, 132–
     133, 152–153
   sense of community among, 93–96
   status distinctions among, 91–98, 105
   in the West Indies, 83, 99
Smith, Richard, 184
Smithland plantation, 10

Society for the Propogation of the
    Gospel, 139–140
Sociology for the South (Fitzhugh), 147
Sojourner, Absalom, 162, 173
Sojourner, William, 162, 168, 173
Song of the South, 106
Southampton County, Virginia, 98
Stampp, Kenneth, 155–156
Stateburg, South Carolina, 154–155
Stietenroth, Charles, 169
Stratton, Reverend Joseph, 36, 108
Stringfellow, Thornton, 146–147
Styron, William, 78, 98
Surget, Jacob, 128–129
Susan (slave presumably owned by
    Duncan Skinner), 91
Swayze, Alfred, 28, 50, 77, 124, 167
Swayze, Henry Clay, 168
Sydnor, Charles S., 157–158

Taney, Roger, 118
Tensas Parish, Louisiana, 20, 27, 165–
    166, 169, 180–182
    assessment rolls, 113, 180–181
Tensas River, 128
Thomas, John, 184
Thomas, Joseph, 24
Thorn, John, 164
de Tocqueville, Alexis, 118
Tom (slave on Mandamus), 171
tornado of 1840, 21, 29
Treaty of Guadalupe Hidalgo, 119–120
trial of Henderson, Reuben, and
    Anderson, 31–34, 168–169, 180
    court records for, 40–41
    defense presented at, 172–176
    as described in the Natchez *Courier*,
        52–58
    jury at, 33–34, 169–170, 179
    as "morality play," 175–176, 178
    witnesses at, 64
Tumult and Silence at Second Creek
    (Jordan), 102
Turner, Nat, 98, 111

University of Virginia, 33, 115

Van Eaton, Henry S., 33, 158, 169
Vesey, Denmark, 98–99
Vicksburg, Mississippi, 89
Vidalia, Louisiana, 28, 76

Wade, W. C., 169
Wailes, Benjamin L. C., 88–89, 100,
    123
Walworth, Douglas
    biographical information on, 33–34,
        169
    and defense at trial, 34, 172–176
Walworth, John P., 33
Warrenton, Mississippi, 89
Washington, Mississippi, 115
Washington, George, 140, 143
Washington County, Mississippi, 125,
    127–128, 130
Waterproof, Louisiana, 24, 67
    as home of John McCallin, 20, 76, 113,
        167, 181–182
Waterproof, meeting at, 39, 72, 77, 132,
    180
    findings of, 27–28, 166–167
    notice in newspapers about, 40
    reasons for, 24–26, 165
    resolutions passed at, 181–182
    as undemocratic gathering, 166
Webster, Noah, 157
West, Benjamin, 29
Whig Party, 120–123
White, Deborah Gray, 105
White Over Black (Jordan), 139
Whitney, Eli, 143
Wilkinson County, Mississippi, 33, 169
Williams, David P. 10, 19, 160–165
Wilson, Alexander L., 169
"Woman's Law," 125
Woodville, Mississippi, 33, 35, 159
Woodward, C. Vann, 185
Wright, Richard, 105–106
Wyatt-Brown, Bertram, 130–131, 169

Yale University, 3, 115
yellow fever epidemic of 1853, 20–21,
    67